8 KEYS TO RECOVERY FROM AN EATING DISORDER WORKBOOK

8 Keys to Mental Health Series

The 8 Keys series of books provides consumers with brief, inexpensive, and high-quality self-help books on a variety of topics in mental health. Each volume is written by an expert in the field, someone who is capable of presenting evidence-based information in a concise and clear way. These books stand out by offering consumers cutting-edge, relevant theory in easily digestible portions, written in an accessible style. The tone is respectful of the reader and the messages are immediately applicable. Filled with exercises and practical strategies, these books empower readers to help themselves.

8 KEYS TO RECOVERY FROM AN EATING DISORDER WORKBOOK

CAROLYN COSTIN
GWEN SCHUBERT GRABB

W.W. Norton & Company

Independent Publishers Since 1923

New York / London

Important Note: *8 Keys to Recovery from an Eating Disorder Workbook* is intended to provide general information on the subject of health and well-being; it is not a substitute for medical or psychological treatment and may not be relied upon for purposes of diagnosing or treating any illness. Please seek out the care of a professional healthcare provider if you are pregnant, nursing, or experiencing symptoms of any potentially serious condition.

Copyright © 2017 by Carolyn Costin and Gwen Schubert Grabb

All rights reserved
Printed in the United States of America
First Edition

For information about permission to reproduce selections from this book, write to
Permissions, W. W. Norton & Company, Inc., 500 Fifth Avenue, New York, NY 10110

For information about special discounts for bulk purchases, please contact W. W. Norton
Special Sales at specialsales@wwnorton.com or 800-233-4830

Manufacturing by Sheridan Books
Production manager Christine Critelli

Library of Congress Cataloging-in-Publication Data

Costin, Carolyn, author. | Grabb, Gwen Schubert
8 keys to recovery from an eating disorder workbook / Carolyn Costin and Gwen Schubert Grabb.
Eight keys to recovery from an eating disorder workbook
First edition. | New York : W.W. Norton & Company, [2017] |
8 keys to mental health series | Includes bibliographical references and index.
LCCN 2016029075 | ISBN 9780393711288 (pbk.)
LCSH: Eating disorders--Treatment--Popular works. | Mind and body--Popular works.
LCC RC552.E18 C6663 2017 | DDC 616.85/26--dc23 LC record available at https://lccn.loc.gov/2016029075

ISBN: 978-0-393-71128-8 (pbk.)

W. W. Norton & Company, Inc., 500 Fifth Avenue, New York, N.Y. 10110
    www.wwnorton.com
W. W. Norton & Company Ltd., 15 Carlisle Street, London W1D 3BS

7 8 9 0

To all beings who struggle with:
accepting what is,
loving themselves completely
seeking happiness through internal vs. external means
or recognizing their true soul self . . .
This book is from all my teachers, through me, to you
With love from yourself
Carolyn Costin

For these mothers in my life—my mother, Lynn, who always
loved me unconditionally and taught me the power of words
and writing in the delicate fusion between emotion and reality;
and to Carolyn, who taught me the power of authenticity
and saved my soul then, and again.
With gratitude and love, Gwen

Contents

Acknowledgments ix
Introduction xi

KEY 1: Motivation, Patience, and Hope 5

KEY 2: Your Healthy Self Will Heal Your Eating Disorder Self 31

KEY 3: It's Not About the Food 61

KEY 4: Feel Your Feelings, Challenge Your Thoughts 83

KEY 5: It IS About the Food 123

KEY 6: Changing Your Behaviors 159

KEY 7: Reach Out to People Rather than Your Eating Disorder 187

KEY 8: Finding Meaning and Purpose 209

References and Resources 255
Index 261
About the Authors 269

Acknowledgments

We would like to thank our families, friends, clients, and colleagues for supporting and encouraging us to write this companion workbook to accompany our original 8 Keys book. Thank you to everyone at Norton (especially Deborah Malmud) for giving us this opportunity again. To Abby Gold and Diana Burge, we are in debt for excellent feedback and advice on the manuscript at critical times. We are always full of gratitude for our clients, who have taught us so much and especially want to thank those who allowed us to share their personal writing and/or part of their journey on these pages, though some written material was shortened or edited and a few cases were combined due to space and confidentiality.

Introduction

The feedback on our book, 8 *Keys To Recovery From An Eating Disorder*, has been phenomenal. Eating disorder sufferers and their families from around the world have thanked us for the book, and especially for the inspiring message of hope that they or their loved one can be fully recovered.

We hear from readers going through the book alone as well as those who use the book with their therapists, in therapy groups, at treatment centers, and even with family members who offer support. Therapists, dietitians, and other professionals write us too, saying they love the book because in addition to the useful information and assignments, it provides them with a comprehensive and structured way to guide clients through the complex and difficult process of recovery. We are grateful for all the feedback and for the opportunity to expand the 8 *Keys* book by providing a second edition with new material and a workbook format.

The Workbook

Last year Norton asked us if we would write a companion workbook to go along with the original manuscript, reviewing the 8 Keys while giving additional information, exercises, and assignments with space to write directly in the workbook itself. The result is a balance between the original book and new material, such that this workbook can serve as a companion to the original book or can be used on its own. The original book has more detailed information about each Key and different assignments, quotes, and personal reflections, so if you do not have it you might consider getting it, but it's not necessary.

You don't need to have a formal eating disorder diagnosis to benefit from this workbook. If you restrict, binge, purge, excessively diet, are a scale addict, or engage in any self-defeating or destructive food- or weight-related behaviors, this workbook can help you. As you read through these pages, you will be looking at your situation with food and your body in a new way. The assignments will guide you in exploring your thoughts, feelings, and coping strategies and help you change your behaviors and heal.

HOW TO BEST USE THIS WORKBOOK

No matter how you came to this workbook, it will help you develop insight and awareness into yourself, your relationship with food, and your relationship to people and life. Simply opening it up suggests at least some small part of you wants something to be different in your life, and that is enough to get started.

Everyone's journey of healing and recovery is unique. Likewise, there are many ways to approach this workbook. This is your workbook. You can choose the pace at which you go through this material, deciding what assignments to do and how long you spend on them. The workbook format makes it easy to do the assignments and share them with a professional or any other support person of your choosing. The more you feel in control of this process, the more beneficial it will be for you. That does not mean you wouldn't benefit from a nudge or boost from time to time.

In an effort to simulate, even a tiny bit, what it is like to be in therapy with us, the tone is of us talking directly to *you* and providing you with the information, exercises, Goal Sheets, and Food Journals we give our clients. We share things from and about other clients and ourselves. And occasionally we offer a tip or idea to help you with a particular assignment.

From the feedback we received on the original 8 Keys, we believe this workbook will facilitate your journey to recovery, whether you are just starting out on the path or find yourself stuck somewhere along the way.

SELF-HELP VS. PROFESSIONAL HELP

Although the 8 *Keys* books are considered *self-help* books, we know from our personal and professional experience that recovery is hard and doing it alone much harder—and can be too hard for some. A book cannot replace therapeutic, medical, or psychiatric care. If you have an eating disorder, we recommend you get professional help from a treatment team experienced in treating eating disorders. The team may consist of a therapist, doctor, dietitian, and psychiatrist. At the same time, we know there are many reasons (financial, geographical, practical) that make it difficult for many people to get adequate professional help. You might also feel you are not ready for that kind of help, or don't need it. The workbook might help you clarify what you can do.

Hopefully you already have professional help or support of some kind, and if not, as you read though the book, we hope you find the resources or motivation to seek out whatever help is appropriate for you. If you have a therapist whom you feel comfortable with, but who isn't trained in treating eating disorders, using this book can be a helpful guide for both of you.

GETTING PERSONAL

Throughout the workbook you will read personal accounts from others, including us. Everyone who contributed to this workbook has suffered from an eating disorder and is either recovered or working on that goal. We know from our own recovery, our years of experience treating others, and from research, how helpful and important it is to hear from and connect to others who have recovered. Clients consistently tell us that knowing we were recovered was one of the most helpful aspects of their treatment. Our own personal reflections are shared exactly as they occurred, but some quotes from clients have a few details changed to ensure confidentiality. In the original 8 *Keys* book, both of us share aspects of our personal stories from our illness to being recovered, giving readers a glimpse into the process of treatment from both sides of the couch. Twenty years ago, Gwen was a client at Monte Nido Treatment Center when it first opened in 1996. Carolyn, who is the Founder of Monte Nido, was also a therapist and the clinical director at that time. If you have resistance or fears about going into a treatment facility, or have been discouraged or afraid to seek professional help, reading our personal reflections in the original 8 *Keys* book and the information we include here might help you feel differently. In this workbook, we continue to share our own reflections and how we personally apply the concepts we teach. In the past few years since the original book was published, both of us experienced significant losses and life events that were challenging. Thankfully, being recovered, we know how to deal with the painful and difficult aspects of life in a healthy way. We continue to work at balancing our lives, accepting who we are, and keeping our traits working for us instead of against us, all of which this workbook is meant to help you do as well.

THE ASSIGNMENTS

As you read through each key, we prompt you to do assignments. Many people struggle over doing the assignments and ask us if they are really necessary. As strange and time-consuming as the assignments might seem, there is no doubt in our minds that the people who take the time to do them will be able to absorb and utilize the material much better than those who just read the book. When, or in what order, you do them is not important, nor is doing them right away. You might be ready and dive into the assignments, complete every exercise, and share your progress with a trusted friend or therapist. On the other hand, you might read through the workbook before you decide to complete a single exercise. Either approach—or any approach in between—is fine. We usually have clients do the assignments during the week and bring them in to sessions to discuss. If you want support, and to connect with other readers, we created a Facebook page called "8 Keys to Recovery From an Eating Disorder Group" so our readers can post their experiences, ask questions, and share ideas.

WHAT YOU WILL NEED

Even though this is a workbook, we recommend having a journal to write in as well. Although there is space for you to write your answers, there are many assignments for which you will need or want more space than the workbook provides. Sometimes we ask you to make a list and then, due to space limitations, select only an item or two from the list to work on further. In many cases it is valuable for you to work through most or all of the items on your list, so having your own journal is important.

The only other thing you need is time, in order to read, think about, and work on the assignments. Some are quick and easy to do in a few minutes, but others take more time and effort to complete. Some of the assignments are aimed at getting information and gaining the insight needed to do the next assignment, so keep that in mind when deciding which ones to do. If you come across an assignment you don't have time to do, you can wait until later and can add it to your weekly Goal Sheet.

THE IMPORTANCE OF WEEKLY GOALS

Recovery entails doing a lot of new things in many arenas and can be overwhelming. It helps to break recovery goals down into specific, manageable steps you can commit to each week. At the end of this Introduction, we have included a blank weekly Goals Sheet and one that has been filled out with *several* examples of the kinds of goals you can make. We suggest making copies of the Goals Sheets and using one each week. Setting reasonable weekly goals is something we do with our clients and something we strongly suggest and encourage you to do throughout the workbook. It really does help.

If you are working with one or more professionals the weekly Goals Sheet is a useful tool for everyone. The sheets make it easy for all parties to specify goals, have written records to refer to, and keep track of progress.

The Goals Sheet covers areas related to each Key so you can choose small and manageable goals from one, a few, or every Key each week. Some weeks you will do more in one area, while during other weeks, a different Key will seem more important.

Some of the assignments are designed to help you gain insight, and some are more behavioral. You might chose to do some assignments just in the workbook and not even mention them on your Goals Sheet, but others will clearly be more appropriate to put on your Goals Sheet, particularly ones that you will be working on throughout the week or longer. Experiment and see what feels right to you.

SUGGESTIONS FOR SETTING GOALS

It's helpful to be as specific as possible about the goals you set. Making sure your goals are observable and measurable helps you know if you accomplished them, and helps others who are trying to help you know, too. Instead of writing, "I will take more walks," write how many walks you want to take, for about how long, and even when and where.

The next suggestion we have is to write your goals in terms of a range instead of absolute numbers. People with eating disorders often have a complicated relationship with numbers (weight, calories, miles, etc.) so keeping your goals in terms of a range can help with any tendencies toward perfectionism or rigidity. It's good practice to allow some leeway for things that sometimes

Introduction

get in the way of the plan. The goal has to be specific, but with some flexibility so you have a greater chance at being successful. So, "I will take walks" turns into "I will take 3 or 4, 20- to 30-minute walks this week, in the morning before work."

Lastly, it's important to respect where you are in the recovery process. For example, if you are bingeing and purging every day it probably isn't realistic to set a goal of not doing it ever again. It would make more sense at this stage of recovery to set a goal to delay bingeing for 15 minutes and journal, or to reach out to 3 friends before you binge or purge. Setting realistic goals is important for many reasons. If you set your goals too low you won't progress much, and if you set them too high you might get frustrated and lose motivation to keep going. Finally, the sample Goals Sheet contains several goals for each category so you can see various ideas, but we suggest starting with only one or two in each area, or possibly even setting goals in only a few areas.

It might seem like we are telling you not to push yourself, but making changes is difficult, and losing motivation and giving up is much more problematic than going slow and steady. Staying motivated is challenging for a number of reasons. For one thing, recovery takes longer than many people realize. Also initially you will feel more like you are losing something rather than gaining your life back, making you feel worse before you feel better. We believe the biggest reason you won't get well is if you give up and stop trying, so we do what we can to lessen frustration and feelings of defeat and increase the chances you will hang in there and succeed.

GETTING STARTED

Even though we thought long and hard over the order of the 8 Keys, don't get too concerned with the order in which you read them. Each Key addresses a separate aspect of recovery, and although they are all connected, they are also separate and if one sparks your interest, start there. The first two Keys are about motivation and learning the concept of the Eating Disorder Self and the Healthy Self. We put them first because we believe they will help you with all the other Keys, so it's where we recommend starting, but wherever you start is fine.

Changing your behaviors and embarking on recovery can be a stressful and scary endeavor. You may have tried to get better and failed many times, or maybe this is your first try, but either way—regardless of how many times you may have tried and failed and regardless of how unmotivated or afraid you are right now—you really can do this. We did it ourselves, even though we had many setbacks and at times believed we couldn't. We have also treated countless others, many who felt discouraged or even hopeless, transform themselves and go on to lead wonderful and full lives without the soul-crushing, heartbreaking oppression of an eating disorder. You might tell yourself you can't recover because you are different, or your eating disorder is different, but we hear that all the time and it is just not true. We get it, though, because most people with an eating disorder think that way, at least at some point.

Whoever you are and whatever your story, you can get better. It might take you longer than others, it might be hard, and you might wonder if it's worth it. Those who are recovered today will tell you they thought the same things you are thinking now. No matter what, you are either going to stay sick for the rest of your life or get better, and in the end *you* are the one who determines that. Let this workbook help you get started being the person you want to be.

—Carolyn Costin and Gwen Schubert Grabb

8 KEYS TO RECOVERY FROM AN EATING DISORDER WORKBOOK

WEEKLY GOALS   DATE _____

What I accomplished last week: *I was able to increase my carbs and I reached out to my mom instead of restricting when I was mad.*

What my setbacks were: *I binged and purged after the party and lied.*

What I learned: *I must figure out how to reach out for help.*

GOALS FOR THIS WEEK

Motivation Goals: *Write at least five pros and cons of getting rid of my eating disorder. Make at least three calls to find a group to join where I could be around others working on getting better.*

Challenging my Eating Disorder Self /Strengthening my Healthy Self Goals: *Write out one dialogue between my eating disorder self and healthy self. Write back to my eating disorder self before engaging in a behavior, make a list of ten Healthy self statements.*

Underlying Issues Goals: *Figure out the assets of my traits that I see as liabilities. Work on the Real Issues assignment in Key 3.*

Food Behavior Goals: *Have a bagel 2-3 times this week and after each time I can go to the gym for 40 to 60 minutes. No skipping breakfast, do not buy binge foods. Try one new food.*

Other Behavior Goals (Recovery Sabotaging): *(e.g., weight, exercise, body checking, etc.) Stop weighing myself, give someone my scale or throw it away, get rid of at least one item of clothing that is too small but I have been saving to "fit into" again. Go to the gym (If I eat a bagel see above). Go for 20 to 30 min Walk at least once this week.*

Relationship Goals: *Tell my brother about my eating disorder, make a list of why I don't reach out and write counterarguments, (Key 7). Reach out to a friend, at least once when I want to binge, purge, or restrict, ask my sister not to talk about weight.*

Spirituality/Soul Goals: *Make a gratitude list, call about joining the church choir, buy a book on meditation, make a list of soul moments, find a yoga class that incorporates mindfulness.*

Self-Care Goals: *Call and make an appointment with a therapist. Wear comfortable shoes to work, say no to dinner with my friend who has an eating disorder.*

WEEKLY GOALS   DATE _____

What I accomplished last week: _____

What my setbacks were: _____

What I learned: _____

GOALS FOR THIS WEEK

Motivation Goals: _____

Challenging my Eating Disorder Self /Strengthening my Healthy Self: _____

Underlying Issues Goals: _____

Food Behavior Goals: _____

Other Behavior Goals (Recovery Sabotaging): *(e.g., weight, exercise, body checking.)* ____

Relationship Goals: _____

Spirituality/Soul Goals: _____

Self-Care Goals: _____

EXAMPLE OF A FOOD JOURNAL

DATE_____

Time	Food and Amount	Hunger (Fullness)	Feelings	Urges/Purge
8:00	1 cup yogurt, an orange, ½ c granola	3-7	Feeling hungrier in the a.m.	N/N
10:30	Luna bar, coffee latte	3-5	Needed something, stressed	N/N
12:30	Turkey sandwich	3-6	Not quite satisfied, feeling anxious	N/N
4:00	Small bag of trail mix, apple	2-7	Lunch wasn't enough, got too hungry	Y/N
7:00	Bean and cheese burrito, chips (about 25) then lost count, salsa, guacamole ¼ c	3-8.5	Out with friends, too many chips, feeling guilty and frustrated with myself	Y/Y

KEY 1 MOTIVATION, PATIENCE, AND HOPE

"Try not to think of the process of recovery as giving up your eating disorder, but rather as getting yourself back, or maybe even finding your real self for the first time."

Recovery from an eating disorder is one of the hardest things you will ever do. There are three crucial ingredients that will help you get started and stick with it. The first of our 8 Keys is about those three ingredients—motivation, patience, and hope. You will undoubtedly experience varying degrees of motivation, patience, and hope throughout the recovery process. There will be times when you lose motivation, run out of patience, or can't find any hope. Like happiness, these feelings don't just come and stick around of their own accord, but there are things you can do to help establish and hang onto them during this process. Key 1 is designed to explore and work on ways to do just that.

Motivation = Forces Determining Your Behavior, Incentive, Reason

We have rarely met clients who are initially totally ready and willing to stop their eating disorder behaviors. All our clients, probably like you, have some ambivalence, and this ambivalence affects motivation. Thankfully, lack of motivation doesn't mean you can't get well, but it does present a challenge to be dealt with and hurdles to overcome. Dealing with your ambivalence is part of the recovery process. Lack of motivation is not a weakness; we understand it and consider it a big part of our work as eating disorder therapists. It is our job to help motivate you and deal with the ambivalence we know is there. We also know it might be hard or confusing for you and your loved ones to understand your lack of motivation and ambivalence to recover. There aren't many life-threatening illnesses where the person suffering is afraid to get well. It's hard to make sense of it sometimes, and for others to understand that, as bad as it seems, there are parts that feel safe, familiar, and even good to you. Hopefully, as you explore and work through the book, you will begin to understand your own ambivalence better and as a result, you will be able to help the people you care about understand it better as well.

ASSIGNMENT: LOOKING AT MY MOTIVATION

What motivated me to pick up, purchase, or read this book?

_____
_____
_____

What motivates me to want to get better?

_____
_____
_____

Sometimes, when you write down and look over the reasons you want to get better, it helps to clarify your motivation. But, since there is most likely ambivalence or fear arising in you as well, it can also make it hard to understand why, if you have all these reasons to get well, you haven't done so. Why do you seem to get in your own way? There are of course a myriad of reasons that bring about ambivalence and affect your motivation. One of the analogies we use to help people understand this dynamic is the syndrome that traps people in an abusive relationship.

ASSIGNMENT: ABUSIVE RELATIONSHIP SYNDROME

List all the reasons you can think of why someone would be afraid to leave an abusive relationship. For example, "She is afraid to be without him."

_____
_____

If we now change the question to:
Why are you afraid to leave your eating disorder? Use the list above and see if the same reasons apply.

For example:
I am afraid to leave my eating disorder because: _____
_____
_____

Choose 2 others from list: _____
_____

What similarities do you see in the two lists? Journal your thoughts about the difficulty in leaving an abusive relationship and your difficulty "leaving" your eating disorder. Write about how this analogy might be helpful for you to keep in mind.
_____
_____

ASSIGNMENT: I WANT GET BETTER, BUT . . .

Like most of our clients, you can probably think of reasons why you want to get better, yet there are a number of statements floating around in your head along the lines of, "I want to get better, but . . ." You may have written some of these in the previous assignment, but there are probably more that don't directly relate to leaving an abusive relationship. Take some time to complete as many "I want to get better, but . . ." sentences as you can. Writing these down will help you become more concrete and specific about your ambivalence, or what gets in the way of you getting better. Use your journal to do more than 3.

I want to get better, but _____
_____

I want to get better, but _____
_____

I want to get better, but _____
_____

KEY 1: MOTIVATION, PATIENCE, AND HOPE

Go over your list and look closely at each statement. Some statements might be thoughts or feelings generated internally in your mind like, "I've had it too long," or "I am afraid I'll get fat." Put an "I" for "Internal Obstacles" next to those. Some statements might reflect external situations or practicalities that actually get in the way, such as, "I don't have the money to pay for a therapist," or "I live with someone who also has an eating disorder." Put an "E" next to those to represent "External Obstacles."

Look over your statements categorized as internal or external. If you take a closer look at the statements you labeled "E" for external, practical reasons that interfere with you getting better, you can probably find beliefs or fears hiding underneath. For example, not having money to pay for therapy or living with someone who has an eating disorder are both very real external situations that can make things more difficult for you. You might need to make some changes in your living situation, create boundaries, or let go of some unhealthy relationships in your life.

Financial limitations create obstacles, but they don't mean you can't get well. Free support groups, online mentoring programs, and self-help books like this one are available. There are also organizations such as Project Heal and the Manna Fund that offer scholarships. Even if you can't find the resources or have no access to professional help, we don't want you to think you can't get well. Many people (including Carolyn) have recovered without the use of a treatment program or therapist. That being said, even though it can be done, we recommend getting whatever help is available because it is much harder to do this alone.

External obstacles will present difficulties you might need to work around, but the beliefs or fears that these obstacles mean you can't recover are just that—beliefs and fears. In truth, there are very few, if any, actual reasons you can't recover. The only real obstacles in the way of you getting well are your own thoughts and feelings. This is actually good news, because In Key 4 you will be learning to identify and respond to your thoughts and feelings in new and healthier ways.

ASSIGNMENT: WHY I CAN'T GET BETTER

So, now that you have learned and hopefully absorbed the information in the above assignment, we will ask you again. Can you think of any real reasons why you cannot get better? If you can, write it here. _____ . The space is tiny because there are no reasons why you can't get better. We have not found one in our collective five decades of seeing clients.

Motivation, Readiness, and Change

Behavior change is not an event. It is a process of events that happens in stages and occurs over time. Research has shown us that the stages people go through in order to change a habitual behavior are very predictable. Your readiness and motivation are related to these stages. Think of someone you know who has (or had) a habit, like smoking, that he or she wanted to break. Chances are, for a long time this person didn't even consider changing (quitting) or think this behavior was a problem. Even once a problem is acknowledged, it is hard to change. Eventually, he or she might contemplate making a change for a long time without actually doing anything, or might get motivated and try to change, but then get discouraged for some reason and quit trying.

It is helpful to know where you are in relationship to the stages of change. You may have heard some version of these stages, due to the fact that clinicians have used different variations of the stages of change for several years. In our 8 Keys book we discuss five stages of change adapted from different resources. Here we describe it a bit differently, with six stages of change taken directly from the The Transtheoretical Model, which is an integrative, biopsychosocial model based on principles developed from more than 35 years of scientific research, intervention development, and empirical studies. Understanding these stages is important because knowing what stage you are in can assist you, and others wanting to help you, to approach change in a way that is easy to understand and more likely to lead to success rather than frustration.

According to the research informing this model of change, fewer than 20% of people with high-risk behaviors are ready to take action at any given time. This means that treatment protocols or suggestions geared to individuals ready to take action will be ineffective for those not at that stage. You may have already experienced eager friends or professionals who were trying to be helpful, and even though you knew what they were saying made sense, you couldn't take in any of the advice or do anything suggested. If this dynamic persists, your motivation will surely suffer, and feelings of hopelessness can take over. For these reasons, understanding where you are in terms of motivation and readiness for change is instrumental for meeting you where you are, and determining which questions, assignments, and interventions will be most helpful in increasing your motivation, reducing resistance, and getting you ready to move forward. You might progress through these stages in a linear fashion or you might find yourself in one stage and then regress back to an earlier one, but it is good to know that this is common and expected.

STAGES OF CHANGE

1. **Pre-Contemplation:** In this stage you are not ready to take action. It might be that you are not sure you have a problem that needs changing. You might not know the potential consequences of your behaviors, or you might not care. In this stage, you are likely to avoid talking or thinking about changing your behaviors. People may describe you as being "in denial," unmotivated, or apathetic and you may agree, or you might feel you just aren't ready yet. The fact is, even if you are in pre-contemplation, there are very helpful ways to intervene and generate new insights or a different perspective, which can gently move you toward the contemplation stage. Some examples of pre-contemplation interventions would be asking if you would be willing to read this workbook without doing any of the assignments, inquiring whether or not you are open to talking about all the reasons you aren't ready or don't want to change, and frequently reinforcing the fact that nobody can make you change if you don't want to, so every decision is completely up to you.

2. **Contemplation:** In this stage you are getting ready to take some action, but you are weighing the pros and cons. Continually going through a cost-benefit analysis of whether or not to make a change can keep you stuck at this stage in the form of *chronic procrastination*; you are thinking about it, but not yet motivated enough to take any real or immediate action. You can, however, take some small steps to help you find the motivation needed at this point for you to just try something. Reading books from and talking to people who have recovered are

just a couple of examples and can be very helpful. There are several small step assignments in this workbook.

3. **Preparation:** If you are in this stage, you are ready for action and may have already taken some action in the past. In this stage, you might still be exploring options, but you are also preparing for change by doing things like contacting a therapist or looking into a treatment center, or (hint) doing the assignments in this workbook. Moving to the next level requires choosing something and taking action. Remember, if you choose something and it isn't helping, don't let that destroy your motivation. People often need to try a few different things before finding what motivates them to continue moving toward recovery.

4. **Action:** In this stage you are currently taking action, making changes, getting feedback, and making adjustments. You are actively in the process of making changes in your eating disorder behaviors and working toward recovery. You may get disheartened and your motivation will wax and wane because changing these behaviors is hard. Recovery feels worse before it feels better, which can be tiring and make you feel like you are *going up the down escalator* for a long time. This is all very normal and gets easier with time.

5. **Maintenance:** You are in this stage if you have already made changes and are now responding to old triggers and new stressors in different ways. Rather than working on changing behaviors, your actions and goals are now aimed at maintaining your new behaviors to prevent you from slipping back or relapsing. Evidence suggests this stage can last from 6 months to 5 years. It is important to remember your recovery work will continue long after the acute behaviors are gone. For example, many people will leave treatment (for various reasons), after their behaviors are under control, but cessation in behavior is just the tip of the iceberg. The 1990 Surgeon General's report revealed that after 12 months of continuous abstinence, 43% of individuals returned to regular smoking. It was only after 5 years of continuous abstinence that the risk for relapse dropped to 7%. You may fully recover long before these statistics suggest, but it is wise to consider that permanent change usually requires some vigilance for longer than you might think. We don't share this to depress or scare you, but to point out that you will need to protect your recovery for

a while. During the maintenance stage you might find yourself lacking the motivation needed to continue certain behaviors that have been helpful, such as journaling, following a meal plan, or going to therapy. If this occurs, you may need some help, or some trial and error, to help figure out what's okay to stop and what would be wise to continue for a while longer.

6. Termination: This is the stage we call "being recovered." At this point you are no longer tempted to use your eating disorder behaviors. According to this model of change, you have reached 100% self-efficacy. You now have the ability to be effective on your own. Your healthy self has become strong enough to keep you on track and managing your life without your eating disorder, regardless of what stressors or difficulties come your way. Your eating disorder is a thing of the past.

In order to recover, you will go through these stages of change at your own pace. If you have reached a plateau, and don't seem to moving toward the next stage, the next assignment is for you. Answering the questions will help you with evaluating your current situation as well as providing new and valuable insights, both of which can help you find some motivation to continue.

If you continue to be stuck, it might be time to seek a different level of help, such as seeing a therapist or finding a new one, joining a group, seeing a dietitian, or considering a treatment program.

ASSIGNMENT: MY CURRENT STAGE OF CHANGE AND MOTIVATION

Choose the stage of change that best fits where you think you are right now. For each stage, we list where you might get stuck and the questions to answer. If you are confused about which stage you are in, or you think you are between two stages, answer the questions for both. You might find it useful to answer the questions in every section. If you find yourself repeating things you have already written about in an earlier assignment, don't worry—repetition helps solidify information. You might also come up with new thoughts that arise as we ask similar questions in different ways.

1. **Pre-Contemplation Stage (not ready to take action).**
   If you don't think you have a problem or just don't want help, consider these questions.

   - *Why don't you think you have a problem?* _____
   _____
   _____

   - *Are you open to the possibility that you might have a problem?* _____
   _____
   _____

   - *Why are you reading this book?* _____
   _____
   _____

   - *Do the people closest to you think you have a problem?* _____
   _____

   - *List all the reasons why you don't want to change.* _____
   _____
   _____
   _____

   - *Do you want to want to change?* _____
   _____
   _____

2. **Contemplation Stage (getting ready to take some action, weighing the pros and cons)**
   If you feel stuck or keep procrastinating, these questions might be helpful.

   - *What are the pros and cons of staying the same vs. changing?* _____
   _____
   _____

   - *What will your future likely be like if you do change and what will it be like if you don't?* _____
   _____

- *How does continuing in your eating disorder help or hurt your health and happiness?* _____
  _____
  _____

- *What are the risks to your relationships if you stay the same and what are the risks to your relationships if you recover?* _____
  _____

- *What are your fears or other feelings about giving up your eating disorder?*
  _____
  _____

- *Who can you talk to who might help you go over your pro and con list and help you decide?* _____
  _____

- *What is a small step you could take that is not too risky for you?* _____
  _____

3. **Preparation Stage (ready for action but still preparing)**
   If you know you want to change, but can't get yourself started or don't know what to do, consider these questions.

   - *What will you lose and what will you gain by giving up your eating disorder?*
     _____
     _____

   - *What are the obstacles you can see that keep you from trying? Or moving forward?* _____
     _____
     _____

   - *What would help you overcome these obstacles?* _____
     _____
     _____

- *Who could support you in this process?* _____
_____
_____

- *How could they help you?* _____
_____
_____

- *What small step toward change could you take at this time? (Even the slightest movement is helpful.)* _____
_____
_____

4. **Action Stage (taking action, getting feedback, and making adjustments)**
   If you feel stuck, defeated, and your motivation is waning, these questions may help.

   - *What progress have you made so far, no matter how minimal you think it is?*
   _____
   _____

   - *What progress have others noticed?* _____
   _____
   _____

   - *When you didn't feel stuck or defeated, what was happening or who was helping you?* _____
   _____
   _____

   - *What do you want your relationship with food to be like? What needs to happen to get there?* _____
   _____
   _____

   - *What are you willing to give up for your eating disorder? What are you not willing to give up?* _____
   _____
   _____

KEY 1: MOTIVATION, PATIENCE, AND HOPE

- *Is there a small step or decision you could make right now that would help you?* _____
  _____

- *Where can you find someone to talk with who has recovered?* _____
  _____
  _____

- *Where can you get some additional help? What is stopping you?* _____
  _____
  _____

- *What rewards or consequences can you come up with to help motivate you? (See Key 6)* _____
  _____
  _____

5. **Maintenance Stage (you have made and continue to make changes)**
   If you are struggling to figure out how you can continue to make changes or maintain the changes you've already made, or you are not sure what's okay to stop doing and still maintain recovery, consider these questions.

   - *What situations or feelings make you most vulnerable to slipping or relapsing?*
     _____
     _____

   - *Do you notice any familiar patterns when you find yourself struggling to maintain recovery?* _____
     _____

   - *What skills need to be developed to maintain the progress you have made?*
     _____
     _____

   - *What or who can help you develop more skills or strengthen the ones you have?*_____
     _____

- *What type of structure do you think would best support your continued recovery?* _____
  _____
  _____

- *What would be the first behavior or feeling state that would signal you are slipping?* _____
  _____
  _____

- *What or who can help you with accountability to prevent slips or relapse?*
  _____
  _____

- *Who can you contact when you are overwhelmed and need help?* _____
  _____
  _____

- *How can you help yourself reach out to a support person?* _____
  _____
  _____

6. **Termination Stage:** *This is the stage we call* **"being recovered."** *At this point you are no longer even tempted to use your eating disorder behaviors. You don't need motivation to keep going because* **you have arrived**.

Patience = Capacity for Waiting, Endurance, Staying Power

"Have patience, all things are difficult before they become easy."

—SAADI

"Patience is not the ability to wait but how you act while you are waiting."

—JOYCE MEY

Whoever said patience is a virtue was right. Today, in this world of instant gratification, waiting for things that take time is increasingly difficult. Patience is not a quality that you have or you don't—it is a skill that you can learn. Think about it: Have you ever seen a patient baby or toddler? Patience is not passive, nor easy; it is active and purposeful. You'll need to practice patience to get better at it, and the sooner the better because you will need patience to work on changing entrenched habits and patterns, and many other things necessary for recovery, as well as the long haul of life.

We say in the 8 Keys that the people who don't get better from an eating disorder are the ones who stop trying. Continuing to try requires patience. Your eating disorder most likely developed slowly and got worse over time. Recovery happens in a similar way. Chances are if you have had your eating disorder for years, it is going to take some years to fully recover. This can be hard for you to hear and for loved ones to accept, but if everyone understands this and accepts it, it will be less frustrating for all and you will be less likely to lose hope and give up. Hopefully, it will also help others to have patience with you.

To have patience you have to keep going sometimes even if you don't yet see the end result. This is why being exposed to people who have recovered is so helpful. You might not be able to see the end result for yourself but seeing it in others (who at one point also could not see it for themselves) can help you realize your perspective is just limited right now and that having patience will pay off.

It is hard to be patient if you look too far ahead at all the things you'll need to do to recover or you compare yourself to others and get frustrated about where you are in the process. Everyone's journey is different in terms of progress in recovery. You can only go as far and as fast as is right for you. You will undoubtedly have days, weeks, or perhaps longer where you think you can't do it and you lose patience. Try not to judge yourself or get anxious or upset if it's going slowly or you have setbacks. That is a part of the process. It can help to think about how patient you might be with someone else in your shoes. Expect and accept the ups and downs of recovery, and give yourself the grace you would give anyone else in the same position.

If you believe it has been too long, you're too old, too entrenched, or you have tried everything already, you might lose patience altogether and give up assuming you can't recover. We have seen people recover who had their eating disorder for over 30 years, or who had been hospitalized more than 20 times. It might take a long time, but the bottom line is, don't give up, you can recover.

Hearing from others who have been through the recovery process can provide helpful insights about patience.

> *"Patience has been crucial for my recovery, in a few ways. In early recovery, I needed to be patient with treatment, and stop creating artificial timelines for getting back to my 'real life.' The more I tried to rush the process, the quicker I found myself slipping backwards. I hated this saying, but it was true: Recovery was my full-time job. If that meant doing work far below my qualifications so that I could focus on eating my food and staying healthy, so be it. That's what I needed to do. My life has grown exponentially since then, and since I took the time to find true health, I am able to actually thrive in it."*
>
> —G. R.

> *"I've had to be patient in terms of my growth. It's easy to look at how far I still have to go and be frustrated that I'm not further along in the process, but when I shift my focus and think about how far I've come, things seem a lot different. My eating disorder and the mindset that surrounds it took years and years to develop—I can't expect it to all go away at once. Patience isn't about making excuses for a lack of progress; it's about allowing myself a little grace in the process. As long as I'm doing my best in the moment, I don't have to beat myself up for not yet being there."*
>
> —P. K.

ASSIGNMENT: EXPLORING PATIENCE

How is patience or lack of patience affecting you at this point? _____
_____
_____

What tends to make you impatient and what makes it easier for you to have patience? _____
_____
_____

Who is someone you know who is very patient? What helps him or her with patience? _____
_____
_____

Are there other people affecting your patience? How can you get help dealing with them? _____
_____
_____

Have you tried anything to help you slow down and develop more patience (meditation or mindfulness practices)? _____
_____
_____

What do you think might help you improve your patience? _____
_____
_____

Hope = Want, Expectation, Desire

> *"Hope never abandons you, you abandon it."* —GEORGE WEINBERG

> *"The best way to not feel hopeless is to get up and do something. Don't wait for good things to happen to you. If you go out and make some good things happen, you will fill the world with hope, you will fill yourself with hope."*
>
> —BARACK OBAMA

ASSIGNMENT: HOW HOPEFUL ARE YOU?

Rating yourself on a scale from 0% to 100%, how likely do you think it is that you will become fully recovered? You might believe you have a 50% chance of being recovered and 50% that you won't, you might feel you have an 80% chance of full recovery and 20% chance of not making it there.

I believe I have a _____ % chance of being fully recovered and _____ % chance of not ever getting there.

If you didn't write 100%, why not? What is in the way of you believing 100% that you can recover? _____
_____

Who gives, or has given, you hope that you can recover? _____
_____

There is Hope. You Can Be Recovered

"Hope is like a road in the country; there was never a road, but when many people walk on it, the road comes into existence." —LIN YUTANG

An important part of our philosophy, which also sends a huge message of hope to our clients, is our belief that **you can be recovered**. This means you can get over your eating disorder fully, not be in remission or managing it, but to a place where it is gone, out of your life forever. We know this is the truth. Not only have we experienced it ourselves, we have seen and helped many others get there too. It is important for you to know what to expect when you get there, so below we describe what being recovered looks like:

"Being recovered is when you can accept your natural body size and shape and no longer have a self-destructive relationship with food or exercise. When you are recovered, food and weight take a proper perspective in your life, and what you weigh is not more important than who you are; in fact, actual numbers are of little or no importance at all. When recovered, you will not compromise your health or betray your soul to look a certain way, wear a certain size, or reach a certain number on the scale. When you are recovered, you do not use eating disorder behaviors to deal with, distract from, or cope with other problems." (Costin & Grabb, 2012)

Our belief that people with eating disorders can be fully recovered is now shared by many therapists and others who treat eating disorders. It is a belief that Carolyn has been espousing for over 30 years, and one that has given hope back to many people who had lost it long ago.

"I had no hope for getting better. In fact I was told I would have to learn to manage my illness because full recovery was not possible for people with eating disorders. I thought that if I had to deal with this for the rest of my life that it was not worth it to ever try to get better. Then I met Carolyn and saw the light in her eyes when she said she was fully recovered for over 30 years and if she could do it so could I."

After the *8 Keys* book was published we received a lot of correspondence telling us how much hope people gained from reading that being recovered is possible. Many people erroneously believed that they would always be "in recovery" or "recovering" from their eating disorder.

> *"The first time I ever heard the idea that I could be fully recovered was in your 8 Keys book. Thank you from the bottom of my heart. It gave me so much hope that I am not a lost cause and got me to try treatment again."*
>
> —WOMAN FROM AUSTRALIA

> *"I had no idea people recovered from eating disorders. Your stories and hearing from other people who recovered renewed my motivation to get better. Now I need to find someone to help me, but the biggest thing holding me back was myself. I had given up hope."*

Getting to "Recovered" is Not a Linear Process

As we have already stated, recovery does not progress in a linear fashion, and you may find yourself taking two steps forward and then one step back and then one step forward and three back. You might make some progress, but then find yourself reverting back to old behaviors when life presents you with a new or stressful situation you haven't learned to manage. Slips and relapses can be very discouraging, but they can also be informative because they show you where you are vulnerable and what areas need more attention. As difficult as these setbacks can be, they do not mean that you are back where you started, but rather that you had an experience you were unable to cope with *at that point in time*. You can learn from your setbacks and get stronger and better at handling things, so remember, no matter how bad it gets there are plenty of reasons to hold on to hope. We are not saying this to make you feel better; we are saying it because it is true.

PHASES OF RECOVERY

There are several phases that people go through on their way to becoming recovered from an eating disorder. Familiarizing yourself with the phases of recovery and what to expect will help you understand where you are in the process, and what to look for. Below is a summary of the phases taken from Key 1 in the *8 Keys* book.

Ten Phases of Eating Disorder Recovery

1. I don't think I have a problem.
2. I might have a problem but it's not that bad.
3. I have a problem but I don't care.
4. I want to change but I don't know how and I'm scared.
5. I tried to change but I couldn't.
6. I can stop some of the behaviors but not all of them.
7. I can stop the behaviors, but not my thoughts.
8. I am often free from behaviors and thoughts, but not all the time.
9. I am free from behaviors and thoughts.
10. I am recovered.

You might be unclear about exactly which phase you are in. You might feel like one of the above fits you right where you are at this point in your life or you might feel like you are in between two, or even experiencing a few different phases at once. You might have gone through a phase and moved on only to slip back into it again.

ASSIGNMENT: WHAT PHASE OF RECOVERY AM I IN?

Look carefully at the phases of recovery and do your best to write about where you think you are right now, and why.

_____
_____
_____
_____

BEEN THERE, DONE THAT

Finding a connection with someone who has recovered and who is willing and able to help you in your journey is extremely beneficial. It doesn't matter if this person is a professional, friend, teacher, mentor, or otherwise. People who have recovered have undoubtedly made it through periods where they lost patience and motivation, slipped back, thought they would not make it, or perhaps even lost hope. Learning how others who have gone before you got through difficult times can help you stay motivated, hopeful, and patient with yourself and it can be inspiring to hear stories of success and how different and great life can be on the other side.

Sometimes role models can come in ways we don't expect. For example, meeting others who haven't recovered can also be a motivator. One client explains it this way :

"I just couldn't stay motivated to stick to any plan. People said they were scared for me and asked me if I was scared of dying. Sometimes I would lie and say I was, but in all honesty I wasn't. I was much more afraid of eating normally or going back to how I used to be. Once I had a medical complication and it scared me for a few days, but that wore off. I agreed to join your group, but I doubted it would help. I was hoping that there might be people in this group who were further along in recovery than I was and would inspire me to keep going. However, it turns out that the most helpful person in the group was an older woman who had been struggling for 30 years. Being in the group with her was the first time I felt more afraid of not getting well than recovering. I knew that if I didn't work harder to get well, I would end up like her, still sick 30 years from now, if I lived that long. She never got married, had children or traveled. Her life was very small and she was anxious, sad and alone. The group and seeing that woman were a turning point for me. I realized I really needed to try if I wanted to change the course of my life. I also realized no matter what, for better or worse, we are all role models in some way. We usually think that having a positive role model is better, but in my situation, a negative one helped motivate me to get serious about recovery and fight for it."

ASSIGNMENT: INTERVIEW SOMEONE WHO IS RECOVERED

Find at least one person who has recovered from an eating disorder to interview, even if it is over the phone. Use the questions below as a guide and add any others you have. Write about the experience and what you learned

What surprised you most about the process of recovery? _____
_____
_____

What general advice would you give me to help me in this process? _____

_____

_____

What do you wish someone had told you about the recovery process? _____

_____

_____

What do you wish you had done sooner? _____

_____

_____

Were there specific turning points you can remember? _____

_____

_____

Do you have any tips for dealing with body image? _____

_____

_____

What helped you to stay motivated, or get motivation back if you lost it? _____

_____

_____

How did you stay patient or deal with losing your patience during the process?

_____

_____

How did you use others to help during your recovery? _____

_____

_____

How long did it take for you to feel fully recovered? _____

_____

_____

Is there anything you can share with me that will give me hope? _____

_____

_____

Other _____
_____
_____

Other _____
_____
_____

Other _____
_____
_____

Summary of what I learned: _____
_____
_____
_____
_____
_____
_____

Quotes From Clients Who Have Recovered

"Nelson Mandela said, 'It always seems impossible until it's done.' Eating disorder recovery is like that. Having patience was so important. I needed to have patience with the recovery process and myself. There were days where everything was going great and things were looking up. Then other days I just wanted to give up and give in to the voice inside that said it would never get easier and I should stop trying. It is so important to not give in to that voice. If you have the patience and courage to hold on to the small healthy voice inside, the bigger that voice will get and the eating disorder voice will get smaller. One day when you look back, you will realize you won't even hear the voice that tells you it is impossible. You will already have proved that it is."

"Before I came to treatment and even while I was there, I thought I would never be able to stop binging and purging. I thought it was impossible. I thought other people could recover, but not me. Now it's been almost 9 years *or so since I have had any eating disorder behaviors. There are days when I think back about what I used to do and I think I wouldn't want to do that to myself. The other days I just don't think of it at all. It's amazing and I am so thankful."*

"Don't let anyone tell you that it can't be done. I had my eating disorder for 25 years and spent years going to 12-step groups and therapy. What changed was when I stopped making the eating disorder my enemy and learned what it was doing for me so I could learn to do it for myself. I now give back as an eating disorder mentor and I tell everyone not to give up. Being recovered is available to anyone, though it might take some longer than others to get there."

Getting There—Being Recovered

Just as there is not a day you can point to and say, "That is when I officially got an eating disorder," there is no specific day when you will be recovered. You will have glimpses of being recovered along the way and then you will notice you feel free from it for increasingly longer periods of time until eventually you realize that you are living life without the thoughts, feelings, or behaviors of an eating disorder. Only you can determine when you are there. Being recovered doesn't mean never having a bad feeling about your body, or never wishing it were different, or never feeling bad about what you ate. These are feelings that normal people have sometimes. Our culture is so obsessed with thinness, dieting, and losing weight that it is nearly impossible not to ever have any negative thoughts or feelings about food or your body. One way to differentiate normal feelings and those influenced by an eating disorder is to look at the duration, intensity, and degree of distress caused by these feelings, and whether or not these thoughts and feelings led to, or were precipitated by, eating disorder behaviors. Understanding the difference between what is normal or disordered in relationship to body image, food, and weight can be confusing in the beginning of recovery, but it will get easier as you progress.

ASSIGNMENT: A DAY IN MY LIFE WHEN I AM RECOVERED

In the *8 Keys to Recovery* book we have an assignment called, *A Day In My Life When I Am Recovered*. We ask readers to imagine a day in the future when they no longer have an eating disorder and to write about it in great detail. If you have not done this assignment, now would be a good opportunity to do it, and even if you have done it, doing it again will just reinforce your vision of a recovered life.

_____
_____
_____
_____
_____
_____
_____
_____
_____

A Client's Reflection:

How Teaching Swimming Lessons Helped with my Own Recovery

I stand on the edge of the pool next to a shivering little child. Stepping forward, we dip our toes into the cool, blue water and the child begins to scream. I soothingly coo, "It's okay. You're okay," over and over. The child quiets a bit to consider my words. Silence follows. Then I say again, "It's okay, just give it a try." The child's wide eyes question me, but I point out that our feet are in fact already in the water and nothing bad has happened yet. "We're wet, you see? We're wet and in the water and nothing bad is happening," I gently say. Then I ask the child to sit down and put her legs into the water. More protests. More yelling and crying. I was asking for a change and that was obviously very scary, but still whimpering and holding my hand tightly, the child follows my lead, lowering herself onto the ledge. "You're okay. Just try."

For the whole day and the entirety of the next, we sat on that edge and practiced and learned how to kick. Then for another couple of days we learned and practiced how to use our arms. At first the child moaned, "I can't". "Okay, okay, I hear you. I understand. Just keep trying." "But I am *trying*," the child whined. Tears well up in her eyes as frustration and hopelessness overtake her. I sense the child's despair; she is thinking it feels wrong, bad, but the truth is she was trying *something new, something totally novel, and that's why she was making mistakes and why it felt so odd. My words were met immediately with a teary-eyed fit of fear and resistance. "No, no, noooooo! I can't swim. I don't know how."*

Each day I would present my offer, and each day the child would become too gripped with catastrophizing fear and refuse, until one day I sat the little girl down and instead of negotiating I gave a command. I finally realized you cannot bargain with a psyche ruled totally by fear. "I know you're afraid and you think that you can't, but you have to just give it a try. Remember how you didn't want to get into the water at first, but you trusted me and we gave it a try and it wasn't bad at all?" Grasping my hands tightly, the child allows me to lower her into the water "It's okay, look you're okay," I tell her. "Nothing bad has happened," I whisper. After a few moments the child calms down enough to open her eyes and see that I was in fact right, and she begins to trust that maybe I was telling the truth.

This whole story relates to my recovery and the recovery process in general, because learning to swim and journeying toward recovery are actually quite similar. They both require a huge leap of faith and one giant and important decision: to try. Then you must spend time practicing the skills, and doing the work: talking, feeling, eating, and so on. You continue to push off from the wall and give it a try.

So give it a try and see what happens, because you cannot have a life worth living if you don't start by giving recovery a try!

—K. S.

Final Thoughts

Nobody can make you get better, but we hope this workbook will help you see that getting better is something you want to do, and can do. Even if you are not completely ready to give up your eating disorder, some part of you wants to get better, and is interested, or at least willing to explore the possibility of having a better life. This *part of you* we are talking about is the part of you that picked up this workbook and the part we refer to as your "Healthy Self." Key 2 will give you information and assignments that will help to strengthen your Healthy Self so it can get back in control.

KEY 2 YOUR HEALTHY SELF WILL HEAL YOUR EATING DISORDER SELF

Personal Reflection: CAROLYN

If you came to me with an eating disorder and I could teach you only one thing, it would be that the battle you have to fight to get better is not between me and you, or your parents and you, or anyone else and you. It is between you and you, your Eating Disorder Self and your Healthy Self. You were born with a healthy core self that has been taken over by another part of you that over time has gained a life of its own—your Eating Disorder Self. My first realization of these two selves was during my own eating disorder. I was on my way to a Christmas party in college and I had the thought, "When you get to the party you are not going to eat anything. Nothing. Not one bite." Then, I heard another voice respond, "It is easy for you to pass up food. Go to the party and see if you can eat a cookie." What I learned to call my "Eating Disorder Self" spoke up again, "You are just trying to give yourself an excuse to eat cookies, and if you do you will lose all the willpower and self-discipline I have given you." And then the other part of me, my healthy core self, responded again, "It doesn't take any willpower for you to pass up food, that is easy for you, you do it all the time. What is harder for you is to eat a cookie. If you really want to demonstrate willpower, eat a cookie." This was my first realization that my eating disorder had become a split-off part of myself and that I still had a healthy core. I started having more dialogues like this and writing them down in my journal. Recognizing I had a Healthy Self that could challenge what my eating disorder was telling me was an important and significant aspect of my recovery. Rather than focusing on getting rid of the eating disorder, which had not worked, I learned what my Eating Disorder Self was trying to tell me, and what it provided for me that my Healthy Self did not. So I focused on strengthening my Healthy Self so it could take over the job. The interesting and important thing is that I did not get rid of my Eating Disorder Self; I got rid of the eating disorder behaviors. Rather than remaining a split-off part, my Eating Disorder Self integrated back into my core, and I became whole again. Today what used to be my Eating Disorder Self is more like a part of my core self that serves as an alarm system, letting me know when I need to pay attention and attend to something.

Recognizing Your Eating Disorder Self and Healthy Self

The exercises and assignments in this Key were designed to help you recognize and understand your two selves. Our goal is to help you strengthen the part of you that is healthy, and learn from as well as challenge the incessant and critical Eating Disorder Self that is currently in charge.

Your Eating Disorder Self developed over time. As you engaged in eating disorder behaviors, your thoughts and actions began to take on a life of their own. Eventually, a whole smattering of thoughts, feelings, and behaviors, different from your "Healthy Self" coalesced into a separate identity: the "Eating Disorder Self." This separate self tells you that you are fat and lazy and to restrict what you eat, or purge your food, whereas the other part of you knows better than to starve yourself or vomit what you eat. This "you" would never tell others to do what your eating disorder tells you. It is your Healthy Self and it knows better. Some people use the term "healthy *voice*" and "eating disorder *voice*" instead of "*self*" when describing this dynamic. You will see both terms used in this book. You can use whatever term feels right for you, but it is important to understand that the eating disorder is not the same thing as the Eating Disorder Self. Remember, we seek to get rid of the eating disorder, but the Eating Disorder Self, minus the behaviors, gets reintegrated back into being a part of your healthy core.

RESISTANCE TO THE EATING DISORDER SELF VS. HEALTHY SELF CONCEPT

If your eating disorder has been ruling your life for a long time, you might have lost connection to your Healthy Self. You might think your Eating Disorder Self is "who you are." If you have anorexia, you may initially resist this concept because you think your thoughts and feelings are being disregarded. This is a legitimate feeling if people discount your thoughts or feelings by saying things like, "That's just your eating disorder talking," as if what you are saying isn't valid or does not need to be discussed. It is unfortunate when this happens. We believe both your Eating Disorder Self and your Healthy Self deserve to be heard, understood, and attended to.

ASSIGNMENT: DO YOU RELATE TO ANY OF THESE THOUGHTS?

Noticing your ambivalent thoughts and how differently you would advise or treat others than you treat yourself may help you recognize your two parts of self. Look over the statements below and put "Y" for Yes, or "N" for No in front of each one.

_____ *Part of me wants to get better and part of me doesn't.*
_____ *I would never restrict my (kids' or friends') food like I restrict mine.*
_____ *My clothing size indicates I'm thin, but I don't see or feel it.*
_____ *Part of me wants nothing more than to stop bingeing, but then later I binge.*
_____ *I agree to do something different with food, which will help me move toward recovery, but when the time comes to do it, another part of me takes over and talks me out of it.*

If you put a "Yes" in front of *any* of these statements, hopefully you can see there are two forces at work inside of you. It is really this simple: One is your Eating Disorder Self and the other is the Healthy Self you were born with, which is still in there waiting to be freed up and put back in charge.

Below is a client's point of view as she shares a dialogue she wrote between her Eating Disorder Self (EDS) and Healthy Self (HS):

EDS: Oh my God. A chicken sandwich? No. Not acceptable, I can't believe I'm thinking of eating that. It will make me fatter than I already am. Don't eat it, no . . . STOP. You can stop this. If you don't eat it, maybe you can be thin again, right? Be good! Get a salad.

HS: Wait, wait, wait. You don't want to go back there. You have been down this road so many times, and we both know where it ends. I don't think this is just about the sandwich. People can eat sandwiches and not get fat. You too. *You have just trained yourself to not eat stuff like that, but you can change that. I think you're upset about something else. There are so many things right now you are not talking about—college, mom, Kirby . . .*

EDS: Oh, shut up. I'm having a fat day . . . every day is a fat day. Chicken sandwiches don't make fat go away . . . they make it worse. And I want to be thin. I should get a salad.

HS: *It's not that you can't eat salads but you need to know that you're not going to gain weight with either choice. You have been eating lots of salads and then you don't feel satisfied. If you do not eat enough you will end up bingeing. Neither of us want that.*

EDS: But if I binge I can always purge.

HS: *Yes you could, but then there we go again, back to the same old cycle we are trying to end . . . get hungry, don't eat enough, binge, purge, feel miserable, then say once again that it's the last time. We can actually eat food we like and be okay. And we have to start somewhere, even if it's really hard. You're upset about something. If you don't restrict, binge, or purge, we might figure out what it is. We might begin to heal.*

EDS: I'm not like other people who have problems, I just want to be skinny, not fat like you are going to make our body. When I was in total control, we were beautiful. We wore tiny clothes, and everyone thought we were special. Then you started wanting to get better and eat more and that got us fat.

HS: *Well, it might feel to you like fat but we are still underweight by every standard there is. What we were and still are is "messed-up." We were not "special," we were sick with anorexia and out of control and sad. It's because of you that we couldn't focus and had to drop out of school. And since I know we are smart, it must be you. It's because of you that we lost our boyfriend and our parents don't trust us. When you were in control, we were so sick we couldn't dance at the prom. Our blood work scared the doctors. No one thought we looked good, they thought we looked awful and had a problem. You have confused thinness for control and people's worry with admiration. It feels comforting to have people worry about us. This is important and something worth talking about. So let's eat the sandwich and deal with it and talk about the things that are really important to talk about.*

Note: We try to keep everyone's dialogue as they wrote it so in this Key you will notice that different clients use the term "I" or "You" or "We" when communicating with their different selves. This is a personal choice. Some clients use all the pronouns, for example, "I'm trying to have a life and you seem to only care about us losing weight." Experiment with them all and use what feels and works best for you.

YOUR HEALTHY SELF WILL HEAL YOUR EATING DISORDER SELF

If people try to step in and force you to get rid of your eating disorder, it typically goes into hiding or fights back, often becoming stronger. If you just hold the eating disorder at bay, or control the symptoms by white-knuckling it every day, recovery will be temporary, which is why so may people relapse. You have to be in on it. You have to be the one talking back to your Eating Disorder Self if you want to be fully recovered. No one else can get rid of your eating disorder for you, but we can help you get to a point where your Healthy Self can.

To strengthen your Healthy Self, you need to acknowledge, listen to, and learn how to effectively talk back to your Eating Disorder Self. You will need to start learning to respond to your Eating Disorder Self as you would to someone else saying these things to you. Your Healthy Self will increasingly get stronger as you understand what you need and learn new coping skills to take care of yourself rather than letting the eating disorder be in control.

INTEGRATING YOUR EATING DISORDER SELF AND HEALTHY SELF

Over time, as you practice challenging your Eating Disorder Self, your sense of powerlessness over your eating disorder will subside. You will have fewer eating disorder thoughts and feel less compelled to use your current behaviors. At some point, you will realize the automatic nature of your eating disorder thoughts and behaviors isn't there anymore. Your Eating Disorder Self has become part of your core Healthy Self, and you no longer experience two separate parts of yourself anymore. We have listed the 10 basic stages you go through to get to this place we call being *integrated* and *fully recovered*. There is no way to tell how long each stage will take, and it is not always a linear process. It's common to find yourself in one stage and then slip backwards to another, so don't mistake this for failure or a sign you can't get better. And you don't have to do anything special for integration to happen; it happens automatically as your Eating Disorder Self is no longer necessary and that split off part of you rejoins the whole.

STAGES OF INTEGRATION

These were initially published in the *8 Keys* book and have been updated here.

1. You engage in eating disorder behaviors with no real understanding of a separate Eating Disorder Self. You feel like your behaviors are you. Even if you want to get better, the idea that you have an Eating Disorder Self and a Healthy Self might never have crossed your mind or may seem stupid, frustrating, or belittling.

2. You begin to notice that there are eating disorder thoughts that are different from other healthy thoughts you have, but you believe your Eating Disorder Self is the main you or the way you are. You experience ambivalence about getting better or engaging in eating disorder behaviors, but don't fully recognize this as your Eating Disorder Self and Healthy Self or know what to do about it. Others might point out that you seem like two different people at times. Your awareness of these two conflicting aspects of yourself increases during this phase, but you don't think it's possible to get your Healthy Self back in control.

3. In this stage, you see there is a Healthy Self inside you who knows what to say to other people, but not to yourself. You begin to see this healthy part of you has been repressed or overshadowed, and you would like to reinstate its control over your life. You may make attempts to challenge your eating disorder, but then still engage in the behaviors. You may need someone to help you in determining which part of you is your Healthy Self and which part is your Eating Disorder Self. You may doubt this philosophy or "technique" will work for you and need a lot of encouragement in order to keep trying.

4. At this stage, you have experienced your Healthy Self talking back to your Eating Disorder Self and are beginning to understand that the real fight is inside of you. You are better at recognizing when it's your Eating Disorder Self talking and better at challenging and responding to this voice from your Healthy Self. You realize that you need to not only challenge the Eating Disorder Self, but also learn from it and discover what it is doing for you.

5. During this stage, there is a lot of battling going on between your Eating Disorder Self and your Healthy Self. Your Healthy Self is getting stronger and beginning to take charge more often, but it is not stronger than the Eating Disorder Self yet. This stage takes some time, as your Healthy Self continues to learn the most effective ways to talk and respond to your Eating Disorder Self.

6. In this stage, your Healthy Self continues getting stronger until it catches up and then surpasses the strength of your Eating Disorder Self. At first your Eating Disorder Self and Healthy Self might seem to be equally in control, both winning about 50 percent of the time. As your Healthy Self increasingly wins out over your Eating Disorder Self, it gets reinforced, making it more likely to happen again. Even though there may long periods of no progress or even setbacks, over time you will notice your Healthy Self in control more and more of the time.

7. Your Healthy Self is now in control of your eating disorder symptoms most of the time. Your Eating Disorder Self still sneaks in and takes over during times of stress or great difficulty. You feel like you need to be constantly vigilant to keep the eating disorder symptoms at bay. Sometimes you might even experience a bout of eating disorder behavior, but then you get back on track with your Healthy Self in charge again.

8. Your Healthy Self is in charge, but remnants of your Eating Disorder Self are still around. You are not using overt eating disorder behaviors, but you still have eating disorder thoughts. You may also be doing other behaviors that are not technically eating disordered, but could easily be a slippery slope backwards, like weighing yourself, trying to lose "a little" weight, body checking, or exercising too much. In this stage, you are able to make decisions from your Healthy Self, but your Eating Disorder Self is still lurking around, just not being acted upon. People often mistake this stage and the next stage as "recovered," which can be discouraging because it feels like you will have to remain on high alert for the rest of your life in order to protect yourself from acting on eating disorder thoughts or tendencies. But this is not the end, there is more. It gets better.

9. In this stage, it feels like your Eating Disorder Self is no longer in charge and not even around, so your eating disorder might really be gone, but you are careful and worried it might come back. You can still remember

what it was like, you still occasionally think about it or what it might be like to engage in a behavior, but you don't really want to. You definitely feel like you are "in recovery," but are not yet sure or confident enough to say it is gone and you are "recovered." Again, this is not the end, but you will be here for a while to solidify things. It is hard to know when you will move from recovering to being recovered. You won't wake up one day and it's gone, but over time you will realize you think about it less and less until one day you realize it's gone for good. Then you will be in the last and final stage.

10. This is not even a stage . . . you are whole again. You are not thinking in terms of Healthy Self or Eating Disorder Self anymore. You have no interest in or urge toward eating disorder behaviors, and no thoughts or pulls in that direction. You are not vigilant or on guard in case your Eating Disorder Self speaks up or comes back. You turn to other people to get your needs met, or handle things on your own. You are not thinking this is your Healthy Self in control, but rather this is who *you* are—a person without an eating disorder. Your Eating Disorder Self and Healthy Self are integrated. You are recovered.

ASSIGNMENT: WHAT STAGE AM I IN?

In the space below, explain the stage of integration you are in right now.

_____
_____
_____
_____

LEARNING FROM AND TAKING RESPONSIBILITY FOR YOUR EATING DISORDER SELF

Be careful how you relate to and talk with your Eating Disorder Self. Treating your Eating Disorder Self like it is separate from you, or the enemy, can easily get in the way of recovery. Thinking of your eating disorder as "all bad," or the enemy may cause shame and a desire to hide your thoughts, feelings, and behaviors. The problem with seeing your eating disorder as the enemy and keeping it hidden is that you will miss the valuable information your symptoms are trying to express. On some level, you feel like your eating disorder is helping you, or necessary to some degree, otherwise you wouldn't find letting go of it so difficult.

Viewing your eating disorder as a separate entity instead of a part of you can also lead to abdication of responsibility for your behaviors and your recovery. Thoughts like, "My eating disorder made me do it!" are common, but not helpful or even accurate. Your eating disorder is not an entity outside of you, as much as you might like it to be, nor is it the "real" you, or stronger than you, even though sometimes it might feel that way. It's a part of you, or the expression of a part of you, that is trying to protect or help you, and in many ways it probably feels like it does.

Your Eating Disorder Self is the part of *you* that made you do the behavior, not some entity outside yourself. This is an extremely important difference, because if you perceive your Eating Disorder Self as a separate entity, you can be fooled into thinking it is stronger than you. However, your Eating Disorder Self cannot be more powerful if it *is a part of you*. It gets all its power from you. Taking responsibility for your eating disorder means paying attention and understanding what your Eating Disorder Self is doing for you and then working to heal those wounds or get those needs met in healthier ways.

WRITING ASSIGNMENT: WHAT MY EATING DISORDER DOES FOR ME

Write down three things you think your eating disorder does for you, such as keeping you thin, helping you release or deal with your anger, or making you feel unique or special. Writing these down helps to clarify the issues for your Healthy Self to work on. For example, if you think your eating disorder helps you express and deal with anger, it indicates the need to find healthy ways to deal with anger. That example might sound obvious, but it can actually be very challenging to understand the cryptic messages underneath your thoughts and behaviors. (Tip: The next few assignments have you working on three things your eating disorder does for you. There are undoubtedly many more than three, so we suggest working through them in your journal or adding it to your weekly goals.)

1. *What my eating disorder does for me:*

   _____

   _____

   _____

   This indicates I feel _____ *and need* _____

2. *What my eating disorder does for me:*

   _____
   _____
   _____

   This indicates I feel _____ *and need* _____

3. *What my eating disorder does for me:*

   _____
   _____
   _____

   This indicates I feel _____ *and need* _____

IS IT REALLY TRUE?

Whatever you think your eating disorder is doing for you, use your Healthy Self to explore what evidence you have that shows it is really true. For example, if you write, "It makes me feel more confident," the evidence could be that you go out more and have more fun with people, or you feel less insecure in social situations. However, you might discover that even if you think your eating disorder makes you feel more confident, you can't support it with any evidence or maybe you will find it used to help you feel more confident, but not anymore.

If you are thinking, "My eating disorder helps me be in control," and your evidence is that you can skip desserts easily or you never miss a workout, you might want to think again. Just because it is easy doesn't mean you are in control. It is likely that your Eating Disorder Self obligates you to skip desserts, or never miss a workout, and to disobey that rule feels impossible or very difficult. When your Eating Disorder Self has taken choice out of the equation and you can no longer choose to have dessert or not, or skip a day of working out, you are not in control anymore. You have actually lost control of your control. As you can see, exploring the evidence, or the truth, can point out your own blind spots and help you target what to work on.

COST VS. BENEFIT

There will be things that you believe the eating disorder does for you—for instance, "It helps me numb out," or "It keeps me thin"—that you *can* support with evidence. However, if you look at the cost of this behavior in your life—or the price you have to pay—you might find that is costing you too much. There are strings attached to anything the eating disorder "does for you," and to get better, your Healthy Self will need to find another way to accomplish the same thing.

WRITING ASSIGNMENT: EVIDENCE AND COST/BENEFIT ANALYSIS

Go back to the assignment where you listed three things your Eating Disorder Self does for you. Rewrite those statements here and then answer the evidence, cost, and benefit questions.

1. *What my eating disorder does for me:* _____
   _____
   _____

   Evidence to support or not support this: _____
   _____
   _____

   Benefit versus the price I pay: _____
   _____
   _____

2. *What my eating disorder does for me:* _____
   _____
   _____

   Evidence to support or not support this: _____
   _____
   _____

   Benefit versus the price I pay: _____
   _____
   _____

3. *What my eating disorder does for me:* _____
_____
_____

Evidence to support or not support this: _____
_____
_____

Benefit versus the price I pay: _____
_____
_____

Sometimes it takes writing all these things out to see that you are acting on faulty beliefs rather than facts. It can be hard to admit that what you thought would make you happy, secure, or loved really isn't panning out, especially if you have already sacrificed a lot. Remember, even if you have gone a long way down the wrong path, turning around is still the best and right thing to do. By doing this assignment and many others, your Healthy Self is gathering the information and insight it needs to more effectively challenge your Eating Disorder Self. We call this "being on to yourself."

If your eating disorder wasn't doing something for you, you wouldn't still have it around and it wouldn't be so hard to recover. We can both remember feeling this way and how difficult it was to let go of our behaviors and learn new and healthier alternatives. Although the cost or price we were paying for our behaviors eluded us in the beginning, we can easily see now that whatever benefits we were getting from the eating disorder were not worth the costs. In the end, it took away much more than it ever gave. Understanding what your eating disorder is doing for you, as well as the cost or what it is taking from you, does not mean you will then be ready to give it up. However, this information can provide you with valuable insight into the ongoing battle in your head, which will help you challenge your Eating Disorder Self more effectively.

If you have a hard time coming up with answers when doing the assignments, think about how you used to handle things, how you see others dealing with the same situation, or how you would advise someone else.

WRITING ASSIGNMENT: FINDING YOUR HEALTHY SELF

Once again, using the same examples from the previous assignments, and adding any new ones, write again what your eating disorder does for you. This time, try to respond to the statement from your Healthy Self. For example, if you write that your eating disorder makes you feel special, your Healthy Self can respond by pointing out why that isn't actually true, not really working, or providing other ways you can, or want to, be special.

Example:

My eating disorder: Takes my mind off of other worse problems

Healthy response/alternative: Distraction only works temporarily because the problems are still there and thinking about them comes back, and then I feel bad about my behaviors and my problems. It is true that distraction can sometimes be a helpful coping strategy, but there are other, healthier distractions like yoga, playing an instrument, meditation, poetry, or any hobby that I can throw myself into for awhile. Even if none of those work as quickly or as well as the eating disorder, they don't have the consequences or side effects.

1. My eating disorder: _____
   _____
   _____

   Healthy response/alternative: _____
   _____
   _____

2. My eating disorder: _____
   _____
   _____

   Healthy response/alternative: _____
   _____
   _____

3. My eating disorder: _____
   _____
   _____

Healthy response/alternative: _____
_____
_____

STRENGTHENING YOUR HEALTHY SELF

Hopefully, the previous assignments have given you an idea of what thoughts or feelings are being managed by your eating disorder and have provided you with some experience in responding from your Healthy Self. It will take awhile to figure out the most effective Healthy Self statements, and don't worry if you aren't sure you really believe the ones you have come up with so far. Chances are you have countless eating disorder thoughts and feelings every day, so you will have many opportunities to improve and develop a repertoire of Healthy Self responses that are helpful, true and unique to you.

Here are some examples from clients:

1. I am more than my body. I don't love people because of their bodies.
2. Any self-esteem I think I'm getting from this is being cancelled out by the feeling of self-betrayal I have because of what I am doing to get it.
3. Even if I don't like the way my body looks, it's not okay to hurt or abuse it.
4. I know I can't trust what I see in the mirror. I have distorted body image.
5. Bingeing and purging will never help me feel good about myself.
6. I'm not really expressing anything by doing this. I need to use my voice.
7. If purging is the problem, it can't be the solution. I want to find real solutions.
8. Isolating from everyone to do my behaviors doesn't make me feel less lonely.
9. I don't have to react. Try to do three other things first before engaging a behavior.
10. Unless my body needs food, eating is not going to fill up my emptiness.

It is helpful to look at examples of Healthy Self statements from other clients, but it is important to come up with your own. Having statements from your Healthy Self that are unique and meaningful to you and your situation will make it easier for you to effectively respond in the moment.

ASSIGNMENT: CREATING HEALTHY SELF STATEMENTS

Write out a few statements your Healthy Self can say back to eating disorder thoughts or urges. Even if just a small part of you thinks they are true, write them down anyway. You can always change them.

1. _____
2. _____
3. _____
4. _____
5. _____
6. _____
7. _____
8. _____
9. _____
10. _____

These are a few to get you started. Now, take some time and write in your journal as many of these statements as you can. Keep your list handy so you can add to it as you become more aware. Remember, these are recovery-minded, helpful statements that at least a part of you believes and would tell others.

PRACTICE TALKING BACK TO YOUR EATING DISORDER THOUGHTS

This assignment goes a step further by asking you to write down some recent Eating Disorder Self (EDS) thoughts, followed by a Healthy Self (HS) response. If you get stuck, refer to the examples in the previous assignment or seek help from someone. You can also look at all the examples provided in the 8 Keys book.

EDS thought: _____

_____

HS response: _____

_____

EDS thought: _____

_____

HS response: _____

_____

EDS thought: _____

_____

HS response: _____

_____

EDS thought: _____

_____

HS response: _____

_____

You can practice responding to your eating disorder thoughts many times a day, anywhere, at anytime. You don't always have to write them out, but it is good to do so in the beginning because it will help you figure out what responses really work for you.

COMMENTS FROM OTHERS

Aside from having to deal with your own eating disorder thoughts, most of our clients need to learn how to respond to unhealthy, unhelpful, or "triggering" comments they hear from family, friends, and others.

More often than not, the people in your life are well-meaning and try to be helpful or at the very least, not make things harder for you. Talking about food, weight, and dieting is very common in our culture, making it almost impossible to avoid hearing these kinds of conversations. Being prepared can help you protect yourself and your recovery. With some preparation, you are less likely to react in ways that will not be helpful for anyone.

ASSIGNMENT: HOW DO YOU RESPOND?

Think for a moment and then write how you usually respond when someone says something unhelpful or triggering to you about food or weight.

_____

_____

_____

Some people are well-meaning and try to help even though it often doesn't feel that way, and sometimes others are just talking about dieting, or food, because it is a cultural obsession and has nothing to do with you, even though it often feels like it does. Taking time now to explore these likely occurrences, being prepared with helpful and healthy responses, and also knowing whether it's best to respond out loud or just inside your head, can all make a huge difference in the outcome. Being able to respond from your Healthy Self and do what is right for you is one of the most protective and important skills you can develop. Knowing when and what to say out loud often feels the most difficult because there are many relationship variables to consider. Taking into consideration the strength and nature of your relationship, past history, frequency of interaction, and other personal factors is a lot to think about, but will all help you determine if you should respond inside your head or say something out loud. You may even need to limit your time around certain people for awhile in order to protect your recovery, which can be very hard to navigate.

Here are some examples of each:

1. Your friend says,

    "I don't want to go for ice cream anymore. It's too fattening."

    Healthy Self Response: (out loud)

    "No certain food is really fattening, overeating or eating habits can be, but not any one food."

    Healthy Self Response: (to yourself)

    "This is not someone who will be helpful with me around food. I think I will ask someone else to go with me from now on."

2. A fitness trainer says:

    "You should weigh yourself daily to keep fit."

    Healthy Self Response: (out loud)

    "I tried that and I didn't find that useful for me, or healthy. I want to

be fit, but weighing makes me focus on the number rather than the real goal, which is health."

Healthy Self Response: (to yourself)

"Others may be able to do this and it doesn't hurt them, but I know for me it is not a good idea. He doesn't know me, or about my ED history, he says that to everyone so he isn't telling me that for any particular reason. If he says it again, I will ask him to stop suggesting it, or maybe I will just try a different trainer."

ASSIGNMENT: PRACTICE RESPONDING TO POSSIBLE COMMENTS

Look at the following statements from other people. They will likely provoke a response from you. Practice writing a Healthy Self response to say out loud and one to say to yourself. Be careful not to argue or judge others. (Tip: if you have trouble, ask for help from a friend or professional.)

1. "We should go on a diet together."

    Healthy Self Response: (out loud) _____

    _____

    Healthy Self Response: (to myself) _____

    _____

2. "You look so much healthier now. You look better with a little meat on your bones."

    Healthy Self Response: (out loud) _____

    _____

    Healthy Self Response: (to myself) _____

    _____

3. "They say sugar is what's making everyone fat. You should not eat any food with sugar in it."

    Healthy Self Response: (out loud) _____

    _____

Healthy Self Response: (to myself) _____

_____

4. "You don't look like you have an eating disorder. You look great."

   Healthy Self Response: (out loud) _____

   _____

   Healthy Self Response: (to myself) _____

   _____

5. "You are so thin, I don't know what you are so worried about. I wish I could have an eating disorder for awhile."

   Healthy Self Response: (out loud) _____

   _____

   Healthy Self Response: (to myself) _____

   _____

ASSIGNMENT: RESPONDING TO ACTUAL COMMENTS

Make a list of actual upsetting behaviors or comments you've heard from others. For example, someone comments on your body or someone else's, tells you they aren't eating carbs, or talks about needing to lose weight. Write a Healthy Self response to say out loud and one you say to yourself.

Comment/Behavior: _____

Healthy Self Response: (out loud) _____

_____

Healthy Self Response: (to myself) _____

_____

Comment/Behavior: _____

Healthy Self Response: (out loud) _____

_____

Healthy Self Response: (to myself) _____

_____

Comment/Behavior: _____

Healthy Self Response: (out loud) _____

_____

Healthy Self Response: (to myself) _____

_____

JOURNALING BEFORE ENGAGING IN AN EATING DISORDER BEHAVIOR

Journaling *before* engaging in any eating disorder behaviors can help you gain access to your Eating Disorder Self and bring your Healthy Self forward. Your Eating Disorder Self does not want to do this assignment (or any of them) so if you are doing it this means your Healthy Self has stepped up, even though you will be writing out the thoughts and feelings of your Eating Disorder Self.

Notice we did not say to journal *instead of* doing the behavior, but rather *before* you do the behavior. If we ask clients to journal instead of acting on the behavior, many won't try it at all because they really want to engage in the behavior and don't want to be stopped. So, let us be clear, we know you might engage in the behavior anyway and that is okay. This is a first step, so although journaling might stop you from going through with the behavior, it's not the primary purpose. The purpose of doing this journaling is to help you gain access or insight into the part of you that wants to do the behavior, what it needs or wants, and what it fears might happen if you don't. We ask you to journal before because once you engage in the behaviors your feelings are masked and much harder to get to, which is why this assignment can bring valuable insights.

You will eventually be asked to write from the part of you that wants to do the behavior and the part of you that wants to get well. These exercises are called Healthy Self vs. Eating Disorder Self dialogues, and they are most helpful in interrupting behaviors.

Often in the beginning of treatment when clients try journaling, we hear statements like, "I didn't know what I was feeling or thinking so I couldn't write anything." Try not to get discouraged from attempting to journal even if you aren't sure what you are feeling. Instead of trying to think about how you feel and what to write, start by simply writing about what you are thinking about in that very moment. For example, if you are delaying bingeing and purging and having writer's block, just write about that. It might look something like, *"I have no idea why I am even trying this. I have no idea what I am thinking or feeling except for being annoyed that I am doing this and thinking it's a waste of time. Obviously I wish it could work and just writing that makes me realize how afraid I am to try."* Journaling about what is going on inside your head at that moment is great and once you get started, you might find it easier to find the feelings and words that eluded you at the beginning.

One Client's Example:
"I want to eat what I want and I don't want anyone stopping me. I don't care about trying to even stop myself because I feel like if I don't do this I'm going to come unglued. I want to eat the entire chocolate cake my mom has in the fridge and then I want to follow that with the rocky road ice cream. I might want to get rid of that food, get it out of my body, before I eat more. I feel bad even saying it now but I don't want to think about that. My head is screaming at me to get started, hurry before someone comes home. After the ice cream I want a few bowls of cereal. And if I still feel like more I will because I want to eat whatever I want. This is one place where I get to do what I want. I don't like sticking my fingers down my throat to get all the food out, but that is the price I pay for getting to eat what I want. Screw everyone trying to stop me, this will make me feel better right now."

Personal Reflection: CAROLYN
Journaling before an eating disorder behavior is critical to getting better, even if you end up going through with the behavior. You will gain access to both parts of yourself and learn things you might never realize otherwise. For instance, in the example above, the client and I discussed if there was anywhere else in her life she gets to do what she wants because that seemed like a theme. I also reminded her that she came to me saying *she* wanted to stop bingeing and purging and yet, in her writing, she talks about not wanting others to stop her. I reassured her that I am okay with her life choices and she is

the one who needs to decide if she wants to keep bingeing and purging or not. I told her I would not judge her or tell her she can't see me anymore if she chose to keep her eating disorder, though our goals would be different. Clients often have to be reminded that the true battle is the one inside between the part of them that wants to stop and the part that doesn't.

Even if at first you have no idea what to write, get mixed up, or feel awkward, over time you will get better at writing whatever is going on, identifying your feelings (then or later), and keeping the Eating Disorder Self at bay, even if only temporarily. Eventually you will get your Healthy Self back in the driver's seat.

ASSIGNMENT: NOTICING MY THOUGHTS BEFORE ENGAGING IN BEHAVIORS

The next couple of times you have the urge to engage in an eating disorder behavior, write down exactly what you want to do and why you want to do it, and any other thoughts or feelings.

(Tip: Write exactly what you want to do with food. For example, if you want to binge and purge, stay away from using those words, as they are shortcuts and don't really describe what you actually want to do or what you are thinking or feeling.)

I have the urge to: _____
Because: _____
_____

I have the urge to: _____
Because: _____
_____

ASSIGNMENT: DIALOGUE WITH YOUR EATING DISORDER SELF AND HEALTHY SELF

Now you are ready to try a full dialogue. When you feel an urge to engage in a behavior, listen to and then write what your Eating Disorder Self is telling you, including what behavior it wants to engage in, and try to include why, even if it is as simple as, "I want to skip dinner because I don't want to get fat." Then, respond from your Healthy Self. Your Eating Disorder Self will undoubtedly have something else to say, so write that and then let your Healthy Self respond again. Keep going until you have said all you want to say, but don't let the Eating Disorder Self have the last word.

Eating Disorder Self (EDS): The behavior I want to engage in and why: _____
_____
_____

Healthy Self (HS): _____
_____
_____

EDS: _____
_____
_____

HS: _____
_____
_____

EDS: _____
_____
_____

HS: _____
_____
_____

The following is an example of one client's dialogue:

ED: What have I eaten today/how many calories have I had?
HS: Stop it. It's not about the calories.
ED: I need to know so I'm not anxious. I just need to know.
HS: Wait, why do I need to know?
ED: Because I don't know how much I've eaten and I feel like I'm always eating but I'm still not sure if it's enough because I'm still thinking about

food, but then I wonder if I'm eating too much. I just want to know that I am okay.

HS: *How will thinking about how many calories I've consumed help me know I am okay?*

ED: *Because then I can make sure I have the right amount.*

HS: *What does that mean? How does that help me?*

ED: *I'm not sure.*

HS: *Knowing how many calories I've already eaten is not a good way for me to deal with my food. There was a time when people did not even know what a calorie was and they knew what to eat. Calorie counting will only trigger me to compare myself to my past or to others, and it then impacts my sense of how hungry or full I am when it really shouldn't.*

ED: *But it's helped in the past.*

HS: *It only made me less anxious in the moment, but counting calories actually caused more anxiety, taught me to rely on external things not internal bodily cues, and made me not trust myself. Even though I thought it would keep me in control, the truth is I ended up out of control of my life because I lost so much weight. It limited my food choices, impacted the amount I ate, and I have used a meaningless number to determine my worth, peace of mind, and happiness.*

ED: *Yeah, but I still want to feel better right now!*

HS: *If I want to feel better and I'm afraid of not being okay, I can find other ways to calm down. First, am I safe? Is there anything actually happening that is hurting me right now? Am I breathing? Am I hungry? Am I lonely? Take a deep breath, check in with my five senses, make a cup of tea, do a few simple yoga poses, call a friend, or write a blog post. If I still feel anxious after any or all of these, what could that really be about? It's okay to be afraid right now. This is a transition period.*

ED: *That just seems way too hard when all I need to do is count calories and stay in a range.*

HS: *But that has not worked now for a few years. I have to stop believing it will. This will be hard, these feelings are normal, but once I listen to and regain trust in my body and soul, things will be much easier. People do it all the time, I believe I can do it, and I know that doing it will help me live the life I want and not one dictated by an eating disorder.*

We can't overemphasize the importance of doing these dialogues. You can write them out or actually role-play dialogues with someone else. You will discover where your Healthy Self gets stuck, becomes a bully, or is mean. You will realize where the Eating Disorder Self has stronger arguments and the Healthy Self is weak and needs work. All of this will retrain your Healthy Self, bringing back its power and ability to respond.

Personal Reflection: GWEN

As Carolyn and I went back and forth, probably overthinking as we tend to do, trying to decide which assignments to include in each Key, I would sometimes wonder whether or not you, our readers, would actually take the time to do them. I have been there and know there are many reasons for this—not having enough time, not knowing the answer, not wanting to see it on paper, and many more. I'm sure you will notice how many times we suggest "putting it on your Weekly Goals Sheet," also challenging, which is why we are always saying, if possible "take it to a therapist or a support person."

Even though this is a self-help book, recovery is very hard, and sometimes too hard for many people, including myself, to do it alone. During my treatment, both the writing and sharing part of these assignments and listening to others, helped me gain the insight and perspective I needed to understand myself, choose recovery and get there, but this was after suffering with all types of eating disorders for over 15 years.

In 1980 there weren't many books, and no self-help books for eating disorders, but had I been asked to write down the benefits vs. emotional toll I was paying by having my eating disorder, and had enough insight to know the answers, my list would have included: feeling like a fake and therefore very disconnected from people, incapable of intimacy, superficial relationships, self-betrayal, shame, low-self esteem, low energy, no interest in sex, no enjoyment in life or much desire to do the things I used to enjoy (like read or watch movies), isolation/loneliness, hopelessness, anxiety, irritability, hypersensitivity, fear of the future, and a mental state that vacillated between self-absorption and self-criticism—a toxic combo. In this soul-sucking cycle, I would perseverate obsessively about how bad I was, and what extreme action must be done to correct it. Of course, I could never do whatever was good enough, which would inevitably trigger harsher self-reproach and criticism, and so on and so on. Although everyone will have different emotional costs and consequences, I'm sure you will agree that I was not a healthy person.

So, if I would have done that assignment and seen how much my eating disorder was taking from me, and if I was brave enough to be honest, the only benefits on the list would have been: *Less* fear of being or getting fat (*lessening* my fears of rejection and abandonment) and feeling "in control of myself" and therefore, hopeful about feeling good about myself and happier in the future.

When I look at that, it just doesn't seem worth it. Right?

At that time, I doubt I would have realized how easy those so-called benefits are to poke holes into. The truth is, I was much more afraid of gaining weight than I had ever been (even when I was actually overweight), and a part of me was even vaguely aware that my plan for a happier future was weak and undeveloped. I didn't know to call it my ED Voice yet, but it wasn't totally lost on me that having the belief and hope that all of this misery could somehow result in happiness was a little crazy, and would more likely result in an early death, like Karen Carpenter, who was my only reference. I really thought strength, control, or hope was driving my behaviors, but really it was all fear and my life was getting smaller and smaller to keep it out.

So, the bottom line of this personal reflection is this: If I would have seen on paper the costs and benefits of my eating disorder and all that it was taking away from me, would it have made a difference? I can't say for sure, but I honestly think it could have. I know they are hard to do on your own. I realize being in treatment helped me to do these assignments, but they are the same, or similar to those here, only better as they have been fine-tuned and tested over time. I have seen them working for many years as a patient and then as a therapist, and am quite certain they will help you better understand the battle in your mind, body, and soul and give you the ammunition you need to override and quiet the ED Voice in your head. So, if you haven't done any of the assignments yet, it is not too late to start.

SAYING GOODBYE TO YOUR EATING DISORDER SELF

At the end of Key 2 in the *8 Keys* book, there is an assignment to write a goodbye letter to your Eating Disorder Self. Here is an example of one client's letter.

Dear Eating Disorder Self,

It feels really weird to actually sit down and write with the intention of saying good-bye to you. You're like an old friend, someone who has been with me for a long time, someone who knows me in ways that most others don't. And to put an end to our relationship for good makes me really sad, but I know now it is right.

I am finally strong enough to say goodbye to you. I know there will be times when my strength wavers. There will be times when life does not go my way and that's when I will miss you the most. I will want to turn to you. Who else can make me forget my problems and feel like everything is okay? Can I endure the pain without you? If things don't go my way, not only can I not turn to you for comfort and protection, but I also won't be able to blame you. I will have no more excuses, nowhere to hide.

But it's time to grow up and accept responsibility for myself and my actions. It's time to take care of myself and to truly believe that I deserve the care. I have to face my fears, face my future, and risk failure but have the strength to get back on my feet without you. I am scared knowing that this good-bye is real and permanent, but there is something I feel even stronger than that fear. I feel it throughout my body and it's calm and it's warm and it's this feeling that I will be okay in spite of the struggle. And I can be thankful for you because you allowed me to get the help I needed to find my strength, to search my soul, to examine my life and my being. For a while there may be times that I will regret saying goodbye, but I know this is the right thing and I know I will get over those feelings as my Healthy Self gets even stronger. Actually you will always be here with me. I don't need the behaviors anymore so this is a full good-bye to them but you will be my reminder to pay attention, to speak up, to get my needs met, to find a healthy way to deal with the various issues life presents. I will never forget you and the lessons I learned because of you. And I will remember to respect you because I know how powerful you can be. Good-bye, J

ASSIGNMENT: WRITE YOUR GOODBYE LETTER TO YOUR EATING DISORDER SELF

Saying good-bye. This is important even if you do not yet feel ready to let the eating disorder go. You can tell your Eating Disorder Self what it has done for you, but also the price you have had to pay and that you will no longer follow its directives. When writing your own letter, articulate why you don't need the eating disorder behaviors anymore. (This will bring out whatever resistance there still is to giving it up.)

ASSIGNMENT: WRITE BACK FROM YOUR EATING DISORDER SELF

Let your Eating Disorder Self respond to your good-bye letter. You don't have to respond right away, but it is best to do so within a few days. Let it write back and give you reasons why you shouldn't say good-bye. It might threaten you or scare you, make several arguments about why you won't be okay without it, and try to convince you it is still necessary. It might take awhile to learn how best to challenge your Eating Disorder Self, so doing this assignment at various times during recovery will help illuminate the reasons your Eating Disorder Self still thinks you need it around.

ASSIGNMENT: HEALTHY SELF COME BACK

You never want your Eating Disorder Self to have the last word if you can help it, so do the best you can to combat whatever the Eating Disorder Self said about your good-bye letter.

(Tip: Remember, try not to become hostile or abusive toward your Eating Disorder Self. Talk to your EDS like you would a friend whom you are trying to help.)

FINAL THOUGHTS

We have never met a client who did not have a Healthy Self. Some are weaker or more buried than others, but even if you doubt it, you have one. Doing these assignments might feel strange or silly, but they will help you realize the strength and power you actually have—the same strength and power you have to help others, but haven't been able to find for yourself. It took awhile for your Eating Disorder Self to take over, so be patient. It will take awhile for your Healthy Self to get back in control. Continuing to try, doing the assignments, and asking for help are monumental steps in the process. The next section of the workbook, Key 3, provides you with exercises and assignments to take you further by helping you understand and work with the various factors that helped cause or contribute to your eating disorder.

KEY 3
IT'S NOT ABOUT THE FOOD

Even though your relationship with food has taken over your life, and normalizing your eating is essential for recovery, simply creating a meal plan or gaining weight won't cure an eating disorder. . . . Consistent monitoring and control of your behaviors can help you gain weight or stop the binge-and-purge cycle, and that is an important piece of recovery, but for most this is not enough to guarantee lasting results

— 8 KEYS TO RECOVERY FROM AN EATING DISORDER

If you have an eating disorder, there are many factors that have come together to make this happen. In order to increase your awareness and understanding of what may have caused or contributed to your eating disorder, this Key explores your psychological issues, biological vulnerabilities, relationships, and life experiences, which can help you address any issues you have in these areas.

ASSIGNMENT: WHAT CONTRIBUTED TO YOUR EATING DISORDER?

Even if you are not sure, write a summary of what you think contributed to the development of your eating disorder. After finishing this workbook, you might want to come back and add anything new that you learned.

_____
_____
_____
_____
_____

EATING DISORDERS ARE "NOT ABOUT THE FOOD"

There are four main reasons eating disorders are more than a problem with food:

1. An eating disorder is not caused by any particular food and is not a simple addiction to food.
2. An eating disorder is not caused by, but is fueled by, a cultural obsession with appearance and particularly weight.
3. Although many people diet, underlying risk factors make certain people more susceptible to developing an eating disorder.
4. It's the biological makeup of you, not the biological make up of the food you eat that contributes to the development of an eating disorder.

1. AN EATING DISORDER IS NOT CAUSED BY ANY PARTICULAR FOOD AND IS NOT A SIMPLE ADDICTION TO FOOD

Although it's a controversial subject, there is no proof that an eating disorder is an addiction. However, there are similarities to an addiction, such as engaging in the behavior despite aversive consequences, being secretive, the need to increase the behaviors, and even feeling withdrawal when trying to stop the behaviors, which are important to address. The various Keys do help with those issues; for example, Key 1 helps you look honestly at the adverse consequences and Key 7 teaches you how to reach out to others rather than remain secretive. Research on binge eating indicates that for certain people, bingeing on highly palatable foods can cause a dopamine brain response similar to what happens with cocaine, and can be thought of as causing an *addiction* to bingeing. However, it is bingeing on these foods rather than eating a normal amount of the food, like having a dessert at night or a candy bar at the movies, that triggers this response. All that being said, if you feel like an addiction model would be helpful for you, our experience has shown that thinking of your eating disorder as a behavior addiction (bingeing) rather than a substance addiction (sugar and white flour) will help you have more success. Although there is disagreement in the field, we believe that an eating disorder is not something you will have for the rest of your life. Once you're recovered, there will not be foods you must abstain from to prevent you from relapsing, but there will be behaviors you have to change.

2. AN EATING DISORDER IS NOT CAUSED BY, BUT FUELED BY A CULTURAL OBSESSION WITH APPEARANCE AND PARTICULARLY WEIGHT.

There are many studies and indicators that body dissatisfaction plays a role, even if not the only role, in the development of an eating disorder. In one study of adolescent girls, body dissatisfaction emerged as the most potent predictor of who will develop an eating disorder. (Behav Res Ther. 2011 Jun 28.) Messages about the importance of appearance over substance and the emphasis on being thin affect most of us in some way, but those who develop eating disorders seem to be especially vulnerable. Exploring and dealing with how the cultural obsession with appearance and thinness affects your perception and attitude toward your body is important.

You might think you are not all that affected by living in this culture. Even asking you to think about it is like asking fish how are they affected by living in water. When you have nothing to compare to, it is hard to know how you would feel about your body if you had grown up in a culture where appearance and thinness were not so highly valued. Although we don't think the culture *causes* eating disorders, it promotes dieting, and the more people who diet, the more cases of eating disorders will occur. The following assignment asks you to explore the culture's effect on you.

ASSIGNMENT: HOW HAS THE CULTURAL FOCUS ON THINNESS AFFECTED YOU?

Answer the following questions about how the culture has affected your feelings and behaviors toward your body.

What messages did you get earlier in life that influenced your feelings about your body?

_____
_____
_____

What messages do you get now that influence how you feel about your body?

_____
_____
_____

What is the last popular magazine you bought, and how did it make you feel about your body or affect your behavior?

_____
_____
_____

What have you seen in movies or on television that affects how you feel about your body and your eating behavior?

_____
_____
_____

How do friends or co-workers who diet, complain about, and compare bodies influence you?

_____
_____
_____

What is your history of dieting, and how has it worked for you or against you?

_____
_____
_____

Write any other comments you'd like to about the how the culture has affected you.

_____
_____
_____

There are a variety of ideas provided in this Key to help you learn how to protect yourself from cultural influences and improve your relationship with your body. Looked at individually, they may seem small and insignificant compared to the enormity of cultural influences, but doing them will add up and can actually make you feel better and hopefully even give you a new perspective.

ASSIGNMENT: LIMITING CULTURAL INFLUENCES TO IMPROVE BODY IMAGE

Look over the following exercises and activities. We suggest adding one of these to your Goal Sheet every week and writing about your experience in your journal.

1. Stop buying and reading fashion and popular culture magazines. They have been shown to make people feel worse about themselves.
2. Do something physical like nature walks, yoga, or tai chi where you connect with your body in a healthy and thoughtful way that is not focused on calorie burning, weight loss, or looking better.
3. Don't talk about your own body or other people's appearance negatively. Research by Eric Stice and others indicates that a mere three to five minutes of "fat talk" significantly increases body dissatisfaction, which is a key risk factor for the development of eating disorders.
4. Journal about your body in terms of appreciating its function vs. appearance. Detail some of the things it does for you or allows you to do. Deliberately slow down and pay special attention to appreciate your body and how it allows you to do things like walk, hug, dance, see.
5. Be a good role model for younger people who are learning from you by nurturing your body. For example, get a massage, take a bath to relax, rest when tired.
6. For females: Research or find examples of respected, powerful women for whom their power had or has nothing to do with weight or beauty. Make a list of women who are known for what they have contributed rather than how they looked.
7. For females: Spend time focusing on what it means to be a woman, in a more internal and spiritual sense. Read books about the sacred feminine. Learn about ancient female traditions and rituals. Share your knowledge with others.
8. For males: Speak out or write a letter to gym owners, fitness trainers, or advertisers about how men's bodies are increasingly being portrayed in a way that is impossible to achieve for most humans without taking steroids or developing an exercise obsession, and how this is damaging.
9. For males: Read books like *The Adonis Complex* by Harrison G. Pope, Jr. and Katharine Phillips or *Making Weight* by Arnold Andersen, Leigh

Cohn, and Tom Holbrook, to better understand the issues of men and body image in this culture.

10. *Go shopping with a friend who can help you try on clothes without looking at sizes, and then have him or her cut the tags out of the clothes you buy.*
11. *Try removing any large mirrors in your house, or covering them. Use only small ones in the bathroom for putting on makeup or putting in contacts, etc.*
12. *Buy and wear loose, comfortable clothes, or at least clothes that aren't tight.*
13. *Avoid television shows or commercials where there are overt discussions about dieting or triggering dialogue or images.*
14. *Write a letter or an email to the network or producers of a particularly offensive commercial, show, or magazine, letting them know how the material they presented made you feel. Tell them you will no longer be supporting their show, periodical, or product. Be specific and clear and demand they stop what is damaging and offensive. This kind of activity can be empowering and rewarding. Some of our clients have received neutral responses, but others have actually brought about significant changes, such as getting companies to remove offensive weight loss ads.*

Doing any of the above exercises will help you take a stand against the current cultural influences. Like many women suffragettes who fought for the right to vote, you may not see the changes you seek in the culture in your own lifetime, but you can work on protecting yourself from it now and begin planting seeds for change in the future.

SIGNS OF HOPE

There are some hopeful signs showing that our society is becoming aware of the consequences of our obsession with and relentless pursuit of thinness and doing something about it. For example, in 2015 the French Parliament passed a law requiring working models to be above a certain body mass index (BMI) to prohibit modeling agencies from hiring dangerously thin models. The law also requires altered photographs of models to be clearly labeled. Under the law, models need a doctor's certificate to certify they are fit to work, and employers could be jailed or fined 75,000 euros (about $85,000), if the rules are breached. In early 2016, a British clothing brand decided to require its models to eat a meal in the presence of company employees to ensure they were eating. Abercrombie & Fitch changed their clothing ads in response to a campaign started by one brave young girl with an eating disorder who decided to challenge the company's use of skinny models in highly sexualized ads. Though not enormous changes amongst the current tide, these are encouraging steps showing that we can make a difference if we stand up, speak out, and make enough noise about something rather than remain complacent. We are beginning to see people in power waking up and paying attention to what is going on and making some much needed changes.

BODY IMAGE

Most people with body image issues complain about them, try to get in shape or diet, but don't resort to physically and mentally destructive behaviors. A number on a scale doesn't make most people feel so worthless or desperate that they become self-destructive. Most people have limits about what they are willing to do to themselves to change their body, no matter how bad they feel about it. If you have an eating disorder, those limits are stretched way too far or maybe are not even there. An important part of getting and being well is developing limits you are unwilling to cross to "fix" or change your body.

PERCEPTION, ATTITUDE, AND BEHAVIOR

To better understand and deal with your body image issues, it is helpful to break it down into three specific aspects:

Perception

What you see when you look directly at yourself or in a mirror.

Perception is more than just "seeing" because it is affected by context and circumstance, such as where you are, the people you are with, and to whom you are comparing yourself. For example, most people are more likely to perceive themselves as fat when comparing themselves to ballerinas than to people coming and going at an airport. Our human habit of comparing ourselves becomes exaggerated, and therefore even more problematic, in those with eating disorders.

Think About It

Do you compare yourself to all the people in the theater watching the movie, or the stars on the screen?

Do you compare yourself to all the other people taking an exercise class, or to the instructor?

Do you compare yourself to all the other people you know, or to the models you see in ads?

Comparing yourself to unrealistic standards or to digitally altered images of people who don't really exist is fruitless and fraught with endless disappointment and problems.

Something interesting about perception, and this might be hard to believe, but body image dissatisfaction and body size are *not* correlated the way you might think they would be. If they were correlated, people with eating disorders who are underweight would have fewer body image problems, but they often have more. Usually, the *thinner* they become, the more afraid and convinced they are that they are fat or getting fat.

Attitude

The meaning you attach to your perception of your body.

It is one thing to see your thighs as big or bigger than someone else's, but quite another thing is what you make of what you see. A healthy person might think, "My thighs are bigger, hmm. I don't really like that. Oh well." Or (a personal favorite) "My thighs look bigger. I think this is a bad mirror." But someone with an eating disorder is more likely to think, "My thighs are so big, they are unacceptable, and nobody will love me," or "My thighs are so big, I literally can't live with them this way." These statements reflect the high degree to which your self-worth is attached to your body's appearance, particularly weight. This way of thinking becomes very ingrained and difficult to change, but is worth the work. **It is not your body itself, or even what you see, but rather the meaning and attitude toward yourself and your body, which cause you to feel and then act in certain ways.** Being dissatisfied with your perception of your body (body image dissatisfaction) is a better predictor of eating attitudes, behaviors, and dieting pathology than all other risk factors such as self-esteem, depression, and social anxiety combined.

Behavior

Your perception *and* attitude fuel your behaviors.

Behaviors like restricting, purging, or burning off calories can achieve weight loss, initially alleviating body image distress. However, when these seemingly helpful behaviors develop into an eating disorder, you end up with more problems than you temporarily solved.

Changing your behavior is critical, but it is also important to deal with your perception and attitude, or you will likely return to old behaviors. There are many things you can do, such as: actively working to stop comparing yourself, learning to accept your natural, healthy size and shape, and having realistic expectations. When you truly accept that hurting your body to make it look a certain way will not make you happy or get you what you really want, eating disorder behaviors are no longer as alluring. You know deep down that they aren't working. . .

3. ALTHOUGH MANY PEOPLE DIET, UNDERLYING RISK FACTORS MAKE CERTAIN PEOPLE MORE SUSCEPTIBLE TO DEVELOPING AN EATING DISORDER

Learning about the variety of *risk factors* that increase one's vulnerability to developing an eating disorder can help you assess which factors apply to you.

ASSIGNMENT: YOUR PERSONAL RISK FACTORS

Look over the following list and check all the risk factors that apply to you.

- _____ *being overweight as a child*
- _____ *dieting as a child*
- _____ *body image dissatisfaction*
- _____ *having a mother who diets or has an eating disorder*
- _____ *having a relative with an eating disorder*
- _____ *anxious temperament*
- _____ *early menstruation*
- _____ *being bullied or teased*
- _____ *engaging in sports that focus on weight, such as ballet, cheerleading, wrestling, and gymnastics*
- _____ *certain careers like modeling or acting (image focused)*
- _____ *a history of childhood abuse*

You probably had no idea that when you started trying to "fix" or improve your body, you would end up with a mental illness and a bigger problem to fix. Checking the list above gives you an indication of which risk factors may have been relevant in the development of your eating disorder, indicating areas to explore when trying to understand yourself and make changes toward recovery.

4. IT'S YOUR BIOLOGICAL MAKEUP, NOT THE BIOLOGICAL MAKEUP OF THE FOOD YOU EAT, THAT CONTRIBUTES TO THE DEVELOPMENT OF AN EATING DISORDER.

Having one or more of the risk factors does not necessarily mean you will develop an eating disorder. What happens is that a " perfect storm" is created when biological factors come together with cultural factors and other psychological stressors. A helpful way to explain this phenomenon is, "Our Genes load the gun and the environment pulls the trigger."

Research indicates that certain genetic factors *increase your vulnerability* to developing an eating disorder. If you have a family member or relative who has an eating disorder, your risk of developing one increases. This cannot be explained as learned behavior, because as researcher Cynthia Bulik and others have shown, identical twins have a higher rate of both developing eating disorders than fraternal twins. We have yet to fully understand the nature of this genetic predisposition. What Michael Strober, eating disorder expert and researcher, and others have found is that certain genetically transmitted *temperament* traits such as anxiety, perfectionism, obsessive-compulsive tendencies, harm or risk avoidance, sensitivity to rejection, or lack of impulse control, increase susceptibility to developing an eating disorder and thus are risk factors of a biological nature. Bottom line, there are traits and tendencies that make you more vulnerable to developing an eating disorder, but the absence of these doesn't guarantee that you won't.

TRAITS AS LIABILITY OR ASSET

You might have already had a thought like, "Well I know I am obsessive, so what do I do?" People often admit to us they were worried because they knew they had certain traits like compulsivity or perfectionism, and they knew these traits were not going to go away. The goal is to understand your traits and tendencies so that you can use them to work to your benefit. Even though your genes shape your temperament, traits, and tendencies, they do not determine your destiny. When you understand your temperament and accept who you are, you can learn to channel your traits to work for you rather than against you. Traits like perfectionism or compulsivity can be positive if they are channeled properly and kept in balance. For example, perfectionism can work for you when doing math problems or building a computer, but becomes problematic when trying to learn a new skill or be creative. When applied to eating and your body, perfectionism is never good. Becoming aware of your traits, keeping them in balance, and channeling them in a positive direction is actually affirming of who you truly are, and will help you gain acceptance of yourself. This is one reason why we say recovery is a way of getting yourself back rather than just giving something up.

LIST OF TRAITS AS LIABILITY OR ASSET

LIABILITY	ASSET
Perfectionistic	Tenacious
Obsessive	Thorough
Anxious	Energetic
Impulsive	Spontaneous
Critical	Discerning
Manipulative	Strategic
Stubborn	Determined
Controlling	Directive
Compulsive	Driven
Avoidant	Careful
Reckless	Fearless

WRITING ASSIGNMENT: YOUR TRAITS—ASSETS OR LIABILITIES?

Look at the list of traits and choose two that fit you. List how the trait is a liability, how it gets in your way, and is a problem for you. Next list the ways the same trait has helped you and can be a positive factor in your life. It is important to go through all your traits like this at some point. You can add journaling about them on your Goals Sheet. (Tip: It may help to think of feedback you have received from others about these particular traits.)

Personal Reflection: CAROLYN

My trait as a liability: Controlling. Being controlling has worked against me many times. When I was younger I bossed kids around, telling them what to do. I would get upset when people didn't act the way I thought they should. A story I tell all the time is one Halloween when I was five and in kindergarten. All the kids came dressed up like a fairy princess, ladybug, or Superman. I was beside myself because they just were not doing it right! They were supposed to be in scary costumes because it was Halloween! I was the only one who got it right by wearing a witch outfit. I tried to tell them that they were all wrong, and of course the other kids were mad at me and my day was ruined. As I grew up, I found it hard to do projects with people because I wanted everyone to do it like I did and became frustrated. I tend to want control of situations, and when I'm not in control I can get overly scared and avoidant. Being controlling has caused problems in my relationships when I want to get my point across to a fault. And of course when I started dieting, my need for control took over and I took things to an extreme and got an eating disorder.

The same trait as asset: Directive. I am able to take charge in many situations and get things done. People look to me as a leader in various circumstances, which has helped me work with clients, train staff, lead workshops, and was important in creating the treatment centers I founded, Monte Nido. I could not have done any of this without this trait.

1. My trait as a liability: _____
   _____

   The same trait as an asset: _____
   _____

2. My trait as a liability: _____
   _____

   The same trait as an asset: _____
   _____

Your traits usually play out similarly in various arenas. For example, the way you think about and act with food is likely to be similar to the way you think about and act with people. For instance, if you are fearful of eating new foods you are probably fearful of new people and relationships. It can be useful to be scrutinizing, but too much fear will cause rigidity and get in your way of having new and fun experiences. On the other hand, if you are impulsive, or as we like to say, *spontaneous*, you will probably experience yourself this way with food and with people. Being spontaneous is a benefit when situations change and you have to adjust quickly. Spontaneous people are fun to be with. However, acting impulsively can cause you to hurt yourself or others if you become reckless or irresponsible. A client with bulimia shared how her impulsivity affected her relationships when she exclaimed, "I binge and purge men!"

ASSIGNMENT: HOW IS MY RELATIONSHIP TO FOOD LIKE MY RELATIONSHIP TO PEOPLE OR TO LIFE?

Write down the ways in which how you relate to food is similar to how you relate to people or to life. Even if you have already done this assignment in the 8 Keys *book, you will continue to learn by doing it again.*

_____
_____
_____
_____
_____

Repeating this exercise periodically throughout your recovery can give you valuable information. It is important to note that improving your relationship with people can help improve your relationship with food, and the same is true that improving your relationship with food will most likely improve your relationship with people. This means that making changes in either area is most likely to benefit both.

KEEPING YOUR TRAITS IN CHECK

Accepting your traits and channeling them effectively into assets is one aspect of working with your individual qualities. You also need to keep your traits in check by not letting them get out of balance and rule your life. Even a good thing such as using perfectionistic traits for math problems can turn bad if you stay in your room day after day to get a perfect score.

Carolyn: *Channeling my perfectionism into my work is better than when it was directed toward an eating disorder, but even this leads to me becoming off balance causing stress and affecting my relationships.*

All perfectionism not kept in check will lead to an unbalanced and stressful life. Self-awareness and self-reflection are important so you notice when you are out of balance and can correct it.

The following are examples and suggestions for how to keep some traits in check.

Impulsive/Spontaneous:

Find ways to add structure and accountability in your life. Make sure at least two people in your life agree with you before making a big decision. Make some boundaries or specific guidelines for spending money. In essence, find ways to give yourself plenty of time before making decisions and use others to help you with accountability. See Key 6 for ideas on rewards and consequences that might help you.

Obsessive/Thorough:

Practice letting go of things, leaving things alone, letting things unfold, and learn when it's time to walk away from a task even if it is uncomfortable. Practice thinking in terms of "good enough" or even "good enough for now," and let others help you know when they are appropriate to use. Adjust your expectations and make sure they are reasonable to others, not just to you. Learn when to "go for the silver" instead of the gold. Challenge yourself by doing things less than perfectly on purpose. Leave the house in clothes that don't match, don't wear any makeup, or try other things that help to keep your obsessive trait in check and not ruling you, or your life.

Anxious/Energetic:

Energy is good, but even when directed in a positive way, if it's too much, it will be draining to yourself, as well as others. Learn effective breathing exercises that work to calm your body (e.g., taking a few moments to focus on your breath, and breathing out for two counts more than you breathe in). Find activities like yoga or meditation that might be hard for you, but make a commitment to at least try. When you are with others, let someone else go first, and notice if you are doing most, or all, of the talking. Focus on staying present when others are talking, and notice when your mind wanders to what you want to say instead of really listening. Try to spend a few moments a day when you can sit quietly doing nothing.

Controlling/Directive:

You are going to find it hard not being in control, but eventually you will see how your life will improve when you can keep this trait in check. Notice when you start to take over to help in a situation; stop and ask yourself if you really want or need to do this. Learn to delegate and accept the help of others, or better yet, let someone else be in control. Be willing for things not to be done your way. Tell significant others that you are willing and even want them to make some decisions, like where to go for dinner or on vacation. Tell friends you are working on being less controlling (directive) and ask them to point out to you in a kind way when you are doing it and when they notice you keeping it in check.

Avoidant/Careful:

Coming up with a way to discern between what requires caution and what you should avoid is very helpful. Asking yourself questions like, "Is this an actual threat to me, or am I just afraid of the unknown?" and "Are others I trust suggesting I avoid this, or am I deciding it's too scary on my own?" might be helpful. If you know you are in a situation where you have gone beyond appropriately careful and are just avoidant, find something to do that involves taking a risk, even a small one. Try doing something you've never done before, or put yourself in a situation that you would normally stay away from. Talk to a stranger, go into a new unfamiliar store, wear something daring. Start small so you don't get overwhelmed, which could make you become even more cautious. If you are too scared to do any of those things, find someone to do something risky with you.

ASSIGNMENT: STEPS TO KEEP YOUR TRAITS IN CHECK

Choose one of your traits and write things you can do to begin to keep the trait in check, and how you will help yourself be accountable. Add the other traits when appropriate to your weekly Goals Sheet in order to do this for all of them.

Trait:_____

Steps I will take to keep it in check:_____

How I will be accountable:_____

FROM RISK FACTORS TO PIECES OF YOUR PUZZLE

Understanding your eating disorder is like putting together your personal jigsaw puzzle. Many different pieces make up the whole picture, and some contribute way more to the picture than others. You don't need every piece to see the picture, but key pieces can bring the image into focus. Looking at some real issues commonly identified by our clients may help you recognize pieces of your own puzzle. The Real Issues printed in the *8 Keys* book and adapted from Carolyn's first book, *Your Dieting Daughter* (Costin, 1997), is also provided here so you can personalize it by writing in your own examples.

ASSIGNMENT: PIECES OF MY PUZZLE (THE REAL ISSUES)

Read through the Real Issues and write down personal examples under each category you relate to. Add any additional issues that apply to you but are not listed here.

The Real Issues _____

1. *Poor self-esteem:* _____
   I'm not likable. _____

2. *Need for distraction:* _____
   When I'm bingeing or throwing up, I don't think about anything else. _____

3. *Fill up emptiness:* _____
   All my eating disorder rituals help me fill up a void in my life. _____

4. *Belief in a myth:* _____
   I will only be happy and successful if I am thin. _____
   _____

5. *Drive for perfection:* _____
   I have to be the best at everything, whether it is taking a test or dieting. ____
   _____

6. *High-achievement oriented:* _____
   I feel constant internal pressure to work hard and achieve. _____
   _____

7. *Desire to be special/unique:* _____
   I get a lot of attention for my willpower over food. _____
   _____

8. *Need to be in control:* _____
   I have to be in control of my body, and what goes in and out of it. _____
   _____

9. *Wants power over self, others, family, life:* _____
   My eating disorder gives me power over my body. _____
   _____

10. *Wants respect and admiration:* _____
    I got respect from my peers when I lost weight. _____
    _____

11. *Has a hard time expressing feelings:* _____
    I don't know how to express my anger, so I binge and purge. _____
    _____

12. *"Safe place to go"/doesn't have coping skills:* _____
    My eating disorder is a "special world" created to keep all the "bad" out. ____
    _____

13. *Lack of trust in self and others:* _____
    I don't trust people so I isolate from them with my eating disorder. _____
    _____

14. *Terrified of not measuring up:* _____
I won't have anything if I don't have my eating disorder. _____
_____

15. _____
_____
_____

16. _____
_____
_____

WRITING ASSIGNMENT: EXPLORING YOUR ISSUES

Go back through the Real Issues List and choose one that really stands out as a problem for you. Explore this issue further by answering the following questions.

Issue: _____
_____

How this issue contributes to my eating disorder: _____
_____
_____

How I feel about working on this issue or changing it: _____
_____
_____

What do others say about the thoughts I have in this area? (Hint: If you don't know, ask a few people). _____
_____
_____

Practice an Eating Disorder Self vs. Healthy Self Dialogue discussing this issue and what you can or can't do about it. (Hint: What would you say to a friend?)

Eating Disorder Self: _____
_____

Healthy Self: _____

_____

Eating Disorder Self: _____

_____

Healthy Self: _____

_____

Eating Disorder Self: _____

_____

Healthy Self: _____

_____

Two measurable goals I have in this area are (you can put these on your Goals Sheet):

_____

_____

_____

Share this assignment with others to get feedback and ideas.
Once you have gone through this for one issue, do it for all the others when you are ready.

WRITING ASSIGNMENT: EXPLORING YOUR UNIQUE EATING DISORDER

Answer the following questions designed to help you think further about the development of your eating disorder and how your behaviors might be helping you deal with underlying issues.

What are some of the ways I hold myself back from getting better? _____

_____

_____

_____

What am I afraid of giving up if I let go of my eating disorder? _____

What steps have I been reluctant to take? _____

What was my excuse the last time I engaged in an eating disorder behavior? ___

How does my eating disorder help me with any of my issues? _____

How did I deal with these issues before I had an eating disorder? _____

How well do I see the eating disorder working for me overall at this point in my life? _____

What price am I paying (negative consequences) for my behaviors? _____

ASSIGNMENT: TAKE ANOTHER LOOK

Now that you have gone through this Key, go back to the first assignment and look over what you wrote. Have you learned anything new about the reasons you may have developed an eating disorder? _____

SOME FINAL THOUGHTS

Hopefully, you now have a better understanding of what contributed to your eating disorder and might be continuing to perpetuate it. Though it might be hard to put all the pieces of your puzzle together, learning some of the pieces can be important and helpful, but it's not necessary. You don't need to know why you got sick in order to get well. People recover without ever understanding why they got an eating disorder. In fact, even though it might make getting better easier for some, focusing on "why" can cause people to get stuck. Knowing "how" to get better is far more important than knowing why you became ill. Cognitive behavioral therapy (CBT), one of the few recognized "evidenced-based" treatments for bulimia, focuses on "how" to get better by dealing directly with your thoughts and feelings and how they affect your behavior. When you learn how to work with your thoughts, recognize distortions, and challenge them, you can break free from the behaviors related to them. When you can feel your feelings and regulate your emotions, knowing that they are not you and will pass, you are free from the need to use destructive behaviors to cope with those feelings. These are the skills you will be working on in Key 4.

KEY 4
FEEL YOUR FEELINGS, CHALLENGE YOUR THOUGHTS

> *"You are not your thoughts; you are aware of your thoughts. You are not your emotions; you feel your emotions. You are not your body; you look at it in the mirror and experience this world through its eyes and ears. You are the conscious being who is aware that you are aware of all these inner and outer things."*
> —MICHAEL SINGER, FROM THE UNTETHERED SOUL

Learning to become aware of, and separate yourself from, your thoughts and feelings will change your life. It will help you identify and discriminate between the thoughts you need to let pass on through and those you need to pay attention to and perhaps challenge. When you can step back and be the observing witness, you will be able to accept, tolerate, and feel your feelings without always having to act on them. It's your thoughts, feelings, and the subsequent actions—not what happens to you—that ultimately shape your well-being and happiness.

If you have an eating disorder, on some level you use eating disorder behaviors to cope with, distract from, or otherwise deal with your thoughts or feelings. This might not ring true for you if you have had your eating disorder for a long time, because the behaviors become habitual and automatic. When this happens, the eating disorder becomes a way of maintaining homeostasis, or getting through the day, as opposed to a behavior triggered by a thought or feeling. Like any repetitive behavior, restricting food or bingeing and purging, if repeated over time, creates new neural pathways, in essence training your brain to react differently. Behaviors that once required a stimulus or effort eventually become more instinctive and habitual, such that it is hard to even identify any thoughts and feelings as "triggers." Furthermore, you don't realize all the things you might be thinking or feeling because the eating disorder keeps them out of your awareness. If you are in such a place, one way to discover your thoughts and feelings is to stop, or even delay, your eating disorder behaviors, and things will start to come up. Of course, this is hard to do.

ASSIGNMENT: WHAT THOUGHTS AND FEELINGS DOES MY EATING DISORDER HELP ME COPE WITH?

Think back on the last time you engaged in an eating disorder behavior. See if you can come up with what you were thinking and feeling that might have contributed to the behaviors. If you can't come up with anything, ask yourself what you think you would have felt had you not gone through with engaging in the behavior. Often the behaviors are used to prevent or keep away feelings, even before they're clearly identified or understood. If you can't come up with anything, try not engaging in the behavior, or delaying it, to see what thoughts and feelings arise. Be sure to describe whether you were able to identify thoughts and feelings that were there before you engaged in the behavior or those that came up as a result of not engaging in it.

My eating disorder behavior: _____

_____

Thoughts: _____

_____

_____

Feelings: _____

_____

_____

If you were able to identify thoughts and feelings prior to your behavior or as a result of not engaging in the behavior, you are already beginning to see how these might be affecting your actions. If not, working through this Key will help.

ASSIGNMENT: COPING AND EATING DISORDER BEHAVIORS

1. *How do you think you coped with your thoughts and feelings before you had an eating disorder?* _____
   _____
   _____

2. *How do you think other people cope with similar kinds of thoughts and feelings?* _____
   _____
   _____

3. *What happens, or are you afraid will happen, if you don't use your eating disorder behaviors to cope?* _____
   _____
   _____

THE CHAIN—THOUGHT/FEELING/URGE/ACTION
THOUGHTS AND FEELINGS

You might be surprised to realize how many of your behaviors are triggered by your thoughts and feelings. Most of our clients feel unclear about how their thoughts and feelings lead to their behavior, or what can be done about it. Deconstructing the chain of events that leads to your eating disorder behaviors can help you take a step back from them and become aware of a process that, right now, seems merely habitual or automatic. Thoughts and feelings lead to urges to take some kind of action. How you handle your thoughts, feelings, and urges determines what kind of action you take. Those actions will either keep you sick or help you get well.

Urges

Urges are strong, visceral feelings that are hard to control. They are created by a combination of thoughts and feelings that produce a strong desire to act in some way. Learning to deal with your thoughts and feelings allows you to curb or even prevent many urges from happening. Over time, you will learn how to *surf the urges* and get through them without having to act on them. *Surfing the urge* means learning to accept and feel your feelings—observing the urge to act rising within you, and, instead of acting, riding out the urge until it lessens, even goes away. A key that you might easily miss is the acceptance part. Accept your feelings without judgment and accept you having the urge to act on them. Just notice and be curious about the urge rather than judging it, trying to get rid of it or make it go away. Wanting to get rid of the urge is the path to engaging in an eating disorder behavior because that has become the easiest way. Giving in to urges feels like the one thing that will make them disappear, but in reality, it "feeds" them and serves as reinforcement for another cycle. Does this sound familiar? "I'll just do it this one last time and then I will stop." Acting on urges reinforces the pattern; accepting but not acting on your urges will help extinguish them altogether.

Actions

Though it might be hard for you to believe, you can learn how to *respond* to thoughts, feelings, and urges rather than *react*. Certain reactions, like purging after eating a "scary" or "forbidden" food, might seem out of your control, but you can learn to respond differently and eventually retrain your brain such that your urges to purge lessen and then disappear. The process is the same for every difficult behavior change, including weighing yourself or counting calories. Learning how to manage your thoughts and feelings better, and understanding how to separate yourself from them so you can think more rationally, makes it easier to stop automatically reacting with your eating disorder behaviors. Over time, your urges will subside.

THOUGHT/FEELING/URGE/ACTION—EATING DISORDER VS. HEALTHY SELF

Look at the following chain of events that can lead to engaging in either an eating disorder behavior or a healthy alternative one.

Eating Disorder Self:
    Thought
        She cancelled our plans. Now I'm alone. She doesn't like me or care about me.
    Feeling
        Sad, hurt, angry, lonely, fat, and ugly

Urge
   I want to binge to stuff down the hurt and anger, fill the loneliness, and numb out.
Action
   I go to the kitchen and start stuffing down food.

Notice the automatic conclusion the Eating Disorder Self jumped to, and the reaction that occurs as a result.

Healthy Self:
Thought
   She cancelled our plans. It's hard to be alone. I wonder why she cancelled.
Feeling
   Sad, disappointed, hurt
Urge
   Feel the urge to cry and call her to express how I feel.
Action
   Cry, call a friend or someone else to talk over whether I should call her and ask her why she cancelled, or tell her how I feel after I am calmer and less emotional.

Notice in the scenario above that when her healthy self is in charge, she responds to the situation by feeling her feelings and seeking more information, rather than assuming the worst. She also knows how to take care of herself. She takes responsibility for calming herself down and reaches out to a friend for support in helping her to respond rather than react. It is important to note that sometimes you may discover that your assumptions are right—that the person did reject you, and you actually have good reason to feel hurt. However, when you experience the pain of rejection or betrayal, engaging in your eating disorder behavior will never help you resolve what you are hurting over, though it may provide the illusion of helping by temporarily alleviating pain. It will be tempting to use familiar behaviors to cope, but using your healthy self by employing alternative coping methods to deal with pain and hurt will lead to a true resolution rather than temporary distraction.

The two scenarios above show how a situation might be handled by either your Eating Disorder Self or your Healthy Self. There are many variations that can take place along this chain of events. For example, let's say you are at a point in your recovery where you can notice your thoughts and feelings and not assume things, but you still get the urge to binge because you feel bored and alone. You can take care of yourself by feeling your feelings, observing the urges you have, letting them pass through you, and figuring out a new way to respond instead of automatically giving in to them. Again, the bottom line is that having an urge does not mean you need to act on it for the urge (and any underlying feelings) to go away. The urges and feelings will fade and pass, because that is what feelings do.

ASSIGNMENT: WRITE YOUR OWN THOUGHT/FEELING/URGE/ACTION CHAIN

Using a recent event that led to an eating disorder behavior, write your own chain of events that led to your use of the behavior.

Event:
_____
_____

Thought:
_____
_____

Feelings:
_____
_____

Urge:
_____
_____

Action:
_____
_____

Now, see if you can write down the same behavior chain as if your Healthy Self were in control, all the way through the action step. (Tip: If you are struggling, imagine what someone else you know would do, or what you might tell someone else to do in the same situation.)

Event:
_____
_____

Thought:
_____
_____

Feelings:
_____
_____

Urge:
_____
_____

Action:
_____
_____

Thoughts

Thoughts are powerful, but we all give our thoughts too much power without even realizing it. Like the rest of us, you are likely to confuse your thoughts with the truth. Just because you think something doesn't mean it's true. Becoming aware of your thoughts and learning to question and challenge them will help you behave differently. Cognitive behavioral therapy (CBT) is based on this premise, and is often the first treatment of choice for use with bulimia, and is similarly useful with other eating disorders, as well as many other psychological issues. Learning to become aware of your thought patterns and distorted or negative thinking will help you challenge these thoughts and respond to them in more effective ways.

We always ask our clients, "What do, or did, you tell yourself about that?"

in order to help them formulate their thoughts about a situation. Doing this helps you step back from your thoughts, evaluate them, and determine if they need to be acted on, challenged, or dismissed. For example, if you were upset because you tried on pants that didn't fit, we would ask, "What did you say to yourself about that?" When you take time to look at the cascade of thoughts that come up, you begin to see how the thoughts shape what happens next, and you recognize the importance of challenging or letting them go.

ASSIGNMENT: SELF-TALK. WHAT WOULD YOU TELL YOURSELF IF . . .?

Look at the following situations, and write what you think you might tell yourself if this happened to you.

A sales clerk at a dress shop tells you that you need a bigger size.
    I would tell myself: _____
_____

You eat a cookie even though you are trying not to eat any sweets.
    I would tell myself: _____
_____

You binge even though you promised yourself you wouldn't.
    I would tell myself: _____
_____

You feel full.
    I would tell myself: _____
_____

You get a bad grade or perform something poorly.
    I would tell myself: _____
_____

Look over your responses to the above assignment. You should be getting the picture now regarding how your thoughts contribute to your unhappiness and the actions you take as a result. With these few examples, you should be able to see how easily you make assumptions, exaggerate, personalize, or think in all-or-nothing terms. These are some of the most common cognitive (thought) distortions and always lead to suffering. It's important to understand that you do this in an attempt to protect yourself from feeling hurt, disappointment, rejection, failure, or some other pain, but it only works temporarily, if at all, and creates further suffering.

ASSIGNMENT: WHAT I SAY TO OTHERS VS. MYSELF

Seeing the discrepancy between how you talk to and think about yourself and how you talk to and think about others can help illuminate your distorted thinking habits. Go back to the previous assignment. Under each question about what you would tell yourself, write what you would tell someone else you cared about. Do not say something you don't believe—that wouldn't help your friend and it won't help you. Then, answer the following questions:

Why would you talk to yourself so differently than you would a loved one?
_____
_____
_____

Why do you think something is true for you, but not for someone else?
_____
_____
_____

What would happen if you talked to others the way you talk to yourself?
_____
_____
_____

What are you afraid would happen if you talked to yourself the way you talk to others?
_____
_____
_____

Thoughts just pop into our minds. Many thoughts will be healthy and balanced, but in times of stress or emotional upset, your thoughts will often become distorted in predictable ways. It is important to learn which thoughts or cognitive distortions are common to you. Thinking in extremes and using words like "always," "never," "everyone," and "nobody" are red flags for distorted thoughts. Rarely are these extreme statements true.

Cognitive Distortions

In our *8 Keys* book, we provide a list of common cognitive distortions adapted from *Feeling Good* by David Burns (1980). A list is provided here with space after each one for you to write a personal example.

ASSIGNMENT: YOUR PERSONAL COGNITIVE DISTORTIONS

This assignment is to help you identify the ways in which you distort things. Look at each cognitive distortion and see if you can come up with a personal example of something you have thought or said that fits. You might have something to write in every category, or just a few. (Tip: If you are struggling to come up with examples, ask someone you trust to give you examples of ways they think you are distorted, or skip it and come back to this assignment at a later time.)

1. *All-or-nothing thinking:* _____
   _____

2. *Over-generalization:* _____
   _____
   _____

3. *Discounting the positives:* _____
   _____
   _____

4. *Emotional reasoning (if you feel something, it must be real or true):* _____
   _____
   _____

5. *Mind reading (you think you know what people are thinking or feeling):* ___
   _____
   _____

6. *Personalizing (you take things that happen personally, as if done intentionally):*
   _____
   _____

7. *Blaming:* _____
   _____
   _____

8. *Magnification or minimization:* _____
   _____
   _____

9. *Mental filter (not being able to take in the good and the bad, i.e., filtering out things that don't fit with your preconceived ideas):* _____
   _____
   _____

10. *"Shoulding" yourself:* _____
    _____
    _____

11. *Labeling (a behavior becomes an identity, i.e., I overate, I am "an overeater"):*
    _____
    _____

We want you to take time to do these assignments because awareness is necessary in order to change anything; you need to see the problem if you want to fix it. Once you are aware, you can begin to challenge and change old patterns. Even if you have been thinking a certain way for a long time, your brain has the capacity to learn to think differently. Remember that each time you counteract a negative, distorted, or extreme thought with a more appropriate or balanced one, you are practicing a skill and creating new neural pathways that will make this easier over time.

Challenging Your Thoughts

Learning to challenge your thoughts is a crucial skill—not only for dealing with your Eating Disorder Voice, but also for challenging what we call the "critical voice," the voice that is often still hanging around and causing trouble after the eating disorder is gone. You can't always control the first thought that pops into your head, but you can learn to manage or work with subsequent thoughts to help you find a more accurate and balanced way of thinking.

ASSIGNMENT: RESPONDING TO YOUR DISTORTED THOUGHTS

In the space below, write down three examples from the assignment you did earlier regarding your personal cognitive distortions. Respond to these thoughts using the skills you learned in Key 2, bringing out your healthy self to challenge, counteract, balance, or dismiss distorted thoughts.

Cognitive distortion: _____
_____

Healthy self-response: _____
_____
_____

Cognitive distortion: _____
_____

Healthy self-response: _____
_____
_____

Cognitive distortion: _____
_____

Healthy self-response: _____
_____
_____

ASSIGNMENT: DIALOGUE WITH YOUR COGNITIVE DISTORTIONS

This assignment is just like having a dialogue between your Eating Disorder Self and Healthy Self, the difference being that the thought or cognitive distortion may not be about food or weight, or even eating disorder related (i.e., "I am hopeless," "I should be able to do this on my own," or "nobody can help me."). The goal is to have a back-and-forth dialogue between your healthy self and these kinds of thoughts, similar to how you learned to challenge eating disorder thoughts such as, "If I eat this I will get fat" in Key 2. Remember to always end the dialogue with a healthy self-response. This would be a good assignment to put on your weekly Goals Sheet because distorted thoughts continue to arise for a long time during the course of recovery, and challenging them is an ongoing process.

Cognitive distortion: _____
_____

Healthy self-response: _____
_____
_____

Response back to your Healthy Self (probably trying to argue with or to dismiss the healthy response—yes, but . . .): _____
_____

Healthy Self: _____
_____

Response: _____
_____
_____

Healthy Self: _____
_____

Response: _____
_____
_____

Don't get discouraged if the dialogue is hard to do, if you feel stuck, or if the cognitive distortion seems stronger or more believable; you are still gaining valuable information. This kind of dialogue takes practice, but each time you do one, you learn things and strengthen your ability to respond from your Healthy Self. If it feels strained or uncomfortable, do it anyway, but don't make up things that are not true. For example, if you say, "I love my body" when you don't, we find that will just make this seem like a busywork assignment, not meaningful, and you can even feel resentful. Better to say, "I accept my body for now," or "I know I need to care for my body." Another example: Don't say, "No one would ever intentionally hurt my feelings," because in life this might happen. Better to say, "I don't know if this was done on purpose or not," or "Whether or not he meant it on purpose, my feelings were hurt."

You will get sick of us saying this, but if you get stuck, remember to think of things that you would say to someone else. Again, this gets easier as your Healthy Self gets stronger.

Although writing these dialogues may seemed forced now, what will happen is that by practicing them in this way you will begin to have them happen in your head. They will require less and less effort until your healthy responses become almost as automatic as the unhelpful thoughts once were.

FREEING YOURSELF FROM THE VOICE INSIDE YOUR HEAD

It's easy to confuse the voice inside your head with *you*. True growth, healing, and freedom can happen when you realize that, really, none of your thoughts are *you*. Even though you are working on strengthening your healthy voice, that isn't *you* either. *You* are the one aware of and observing all voices. Realizing you are not the voices you hear in your mind will help you free yourself from them.

Most of your thoughts are not all that important and just come into your mind without much notice. Your thoughts, even strong ones, affect no one else, but have the power to make you feel better or worse about the past, present, and future. The real cause of suffering isn't what happens to you, it's the meaning your mind makes of what happens to you. Sometimes your thoughts are just your mind chattering on about things, and sometimes your thoughts have a charge or energy to them that can build up to where you feel it in your body. Other times you may feel energy build up in your body and not know the cause, which creates all kinds of thoughts, and you can spend a lot of time and effort trying to make sense of the feeling. In these situations, it is helpful to have a way to get rid of energy that is building up or has built up in your body. When you are able to let go of excess energy and get your body back to neutral, it is a wonderful shortcut that eliminates having to spend a lot of time figuring out the reason why you are upset. Sometimes this shortcut is all you need to do to feel better and move on. You don't always have to "figure everything out."

Chatter

Pay attention and you will notice the voice in your head narrating unnecessarily. This is your mind trying to manage your experience of reality and stay in control, much like a backseat driver. Your mind only registers a fragment of all the things you see or experience throughout the day. Certain thoughts and experiences mean more to you than others, and once your mind clings to a thought, the tendency is to understand it, control it, and create meaning out of it.

For example, you might notice a car across the street, and the voice says, "I wonder whose car that is?" "I think I have seen that car before," or, "I hope the driver does not stay there too long blocking my view." Another example is that one day you might feel down and the voice will say, "I am so sad," "Why am I sad?" "My husband makes me sad," " What am I going to do?" and on and on. All this incessant chatter is your mind trying to understand and control things in order to protect you. Most of what you hear from this voice is unnecessary, and at times you might even realize it isn't helping, but getting it to stop is very hard.

Discharging Energy

When something upsetting happens you will feel it in your body. If someone says something hurtful, confusing, or you get into an argument, your body absorbs the experience. If you are not aware of feelings in your body, take a minute and think about a time when you were really hurt or upset. Really put yourself there and play the movie of what happened in your mind. Notice any body sensations you are having while thinking about this painful memory? An emotion is the combination of a thought and a body sensation. Think about how your body feels when it's filled with energy during an argument. You have learned to call this energy or emotion "anger." Notice how your mind will try to discharge the energy with more thoughts.

"I can't believe she did that to me."

"I'm going to be alone for the rest of my life."

"He is so mean and unfair, I hate him."

"What did he mean by that? Why did he say that?"

These thoughts fuel your emotions and cause a cascade of feelings, leading to having more thoughts and more energy. The initial thoughts are usually followed by, "What am I going to do about it" thoughts, which are followed by strong urges to act in some way, making it is easy to become caught in a cycle of resorting to unhealthy or unproductive behaviors. Everyone has these kinds of thought cycles, but people with eating disorders often have urges that sound like, "Screw him, I'm going to go binge," or "I need to purge now," or "I'll show her, I won't eat."

The way out of useless mind chatter is to take a moment to remember that you are not your thoughts, but rather the one who is aware of them. Become the observer and notice them. By doing so, you create some distance between yourself and the thoughts, allowing you to challenge them, let them pass, remember they are just thoughts, and make a more rational choice about what you should or shouldn't do.

ASSIGNMENT: BECOME AN OBSERVER OF YOUR THOUGHTS

For one full day, try to just notice the many thoughts you have about everything. Check in whenever you notice where your mind takes you: when you are getting up, taking a shower, driving in your car, making dinner. How negative or positive are your thoughts? Are they judgmental and critical of yourself or others? Are they exaggerated? Do they promote fear? Are any reassuring or compassionate? Are any really helpful? What happens when you try to not have any thoughts? Do the best you can to write about your experience.

_____
_____
_____
_____

We think you will agree that if someone followed you around all day, talking to you the way you talk to yourself, you would say they were intrusive, mean, overbearing, and extremely critical. You would want to get this person out of your life, and we would encourage you to do just that.

There are many practices often thought of as spiritual, such as meditation, mindfulness, and yoga, which are designed to help you learn to separate or free yourself from your mind. These practices can help you learn to identify your thoughts and let them pass, knowing they are not *you*. When you can do this, the negative, critical voice that fuels your eating disorder will lose its power. Other resources to help you start learning to observe and free yourself from your thoughts are *The Untethered Soul* by Michael Singer, *Waking Up* by Sam Harris, and *Mindsight* by Dan Siegel. Carolyn's new book, *Yoga and Eating Disorders: Ancient Healing for a Modern Illness*, discusses how yoga helps free the mind, reconnect body and soul, and heal from an eating disorder. We will return to this topic in Key 8.

Feelings

Given that your feelings are a driving force behind many of your behaviors, it is important to have the awareness and skills to navigate, understand, and respond to the feelings rather than react to them. It might be hard for you to imagine, but you can learn to feel and accept your feelings without judgment. You can also learn to let them go, releasing their energy from your body.

Feelings are important and bring richness to your life. Ideally, your feelings alert you to things in life that need and deserve attention. If you avoid or keep your feelings out of your awareness, you won't know what you need to do to help yourself. If you don't know whether you are lonely or tired, you won't know whether you need to connect with someone or take a nap. Conversely, if your feelings take over and overwhelm you, you will probably make choices that in retrospect will seem irrational once the emotional charge has died down.

It is important to learn how to respond to feelings in a helpful way, or how to let them go so they don't take over and wreak havoc in your life. We got so much feedback from readers on the feeling section in Key 4 of our *8 Keys* book that we decided to share some of them here, followed by our responses.

"I read Key 4 of your book and I just don't understand what you mean by "Feel your feelings."

We mean just that. Don't try to stop your feelings or shut them down. Don't assume that some feelings are bad and you should not have them. You can't control how you feel, so don't judge yourself for your feelings. Feelings are experienced in your body as well as your mind. Your mind creates thoughts to go along with the feeling you experience in your body. If you feel sad, just notice where you feel it in your body—sit with it and allow it. This is the quickest way through. If you feel sad, talk about it or cry. Allowing yourself to feel your feelings will help them to dissipate and get out of your body. It is also helpful to notice if there are conditions that change your feelings, like being tired, hungry, sick, or under the influence of drugs or alcohol.

"When I grew up, my feelings were not allowed so I learned to shut them down. It is automatic for me and I'm not sure if I can be taught to 'feel my feelings.'"

Many of our clients have learned to shut down their feelings and need help allowing the feelings to just be. We realize it is hard when you have trained yourself not to feel, but you can get this back. Your body is going to help in this process. When you shut down, you know it; you have physical and even mental markers and signals telling you that you need to shut down, and letting you know when you do. You can begin to explore those, and interrupt the shut-down process. You will hear us say over and over that describing what is happening in your body helps you get in touch with what you are feeling because feelings have a physical component. Even describing what "shut down" feels like in your body is a way to begin.

"I hate feeling. I despise vulnerability. I've spent years trying to shut off that part of me. After a year of therapy I still try to find a way to 'work around' this issue of feelings."

First we would ask that you get clear about why you hate feeling. There are many positive feelings, such as joy or relief, and you probably don't hate feeling those (though we know some might say they don't like positive feelings either). The point we want to make is that as a human being, it is inevitable that you have feelings, and if you try to shut yourself off from negative ones, you impair you ability to feel positive also. But in reality, you will have feelings; learning how to handle them is the key.

Feeling vulnerable is uncomfortable for most people, so you are not alone. It might help to understand the purpose of vulnerability. Simply put, without it, it is hard for others to connect with you. Avoiding vulnerability doesn't make you strong, in fact it takes courage and strength to allow yourself to feel vulnerable. When you are vulnerable and those around can see your humanness, their own vulnerability is awakened, allowing a connection on a more intimate level. Connection is a basic human need, so avoiding it not only won't protect you from harm or being hurt, but it will actually set you up for it. Without authentic human connections you are still vulnerable—vulnerable to addictions and compulsive behaviors. We can't survive without connection, so if not connecting to people, you seek it through substances or behaviors. In order to recover, it's important to take small steps in allowing yourself to be vulnerable. Taking a risk, like finding the safest person you know and telling them how you feel about something, while at the same time stating your fear around doing so, is a start. It is important to note that vulnerability means fear of something. *Assignment: Make a list of what you think might happen if you are vulnerable. We realize that since being vulnerable promotes connection and intimacy, working on this area may bring up past wounds that need healing.*

_____

_____

"How do you know what your feelings are in the first place? What if you can't identify them?"

One way to identify a feeling is to check in with yourself and notice what you are feeling in your body, and what you feel like doing about it. For example, if your fists are clenched, your face hot, and you want to scream or hit someone, this is usually called anger. If your heart is pounding and you feel like running away, you are probably scared. The terms anger and scared don't really matter though because they are just shortcuts we have all learned to use in order to describe what happens to us when our body takes on the energy of our thoughts. Your body is a guide to your feelings. You have probably had the experience of someone saying, "I'm not angry," but the way they are standing—the position of their arms, and the tone, tempo, and volume of their voice—indicates otherwise. Which do you trust, the verbal or the nonverbal information?

Sometimes people don't stay with their feelings long enough to identify them or they know what they are feeling but invalidate it because it seems physically or emotionally intolerable. Sitting quietly and checking in with your body, noticing what is going on inside you without judgment or running from it, is the first step in identifying feelings and will help you move beyond them, getting your body back to neutral.

For various reasons, all of us are more comfortable with some feelings than others. For example, Carolyn is far more comfortable with sadness than anger, and Gwen is more comfortable with anger and scared of being sad. Looking into our two different reactions and responses to these feelings might help you explore your own feelings and reactions to them.

Personal Reflection: CAROLYN

I don't remember expressing anger very much as a child. I can remember some times where it seems I was probably mad, but it quickly morphed into being sad.

To this day, any anger I have will quickly turn into sadness, and I cry. This has had both positive and negative results. Discharging the energy through crying can reduce the pressure I feel, but can also create a tendency to put up with inappropriate behavior for too long in both personal and work relationships. Once I figured out that this is what was happening, I learned how to get my pattern to work for me. I now know that it is okay for me to transform anger into sadness, and to use the sadness to motivate me to act. I can feel sad and let the energy out by crying, *and* I can tell the other person what I think is wrong or not working for me in a way he or she can (usually) hear. Now that I understand it, I think this pattern is useful; I believe sadness is underneath anger anyway, and I find that people respond better when confronted without angry energy. This is *truth without judgment*, which is discussed in Key 8.

Personal Reflection: GWEN

In the past I felt so uncomfortable with sadness that it was hard for me to even admit to myself when I was sad, or to express it. Today I still feel uncomfortable showing sadness, but I can feel it and talk about it. As a kid, sadness scared me. If I felt it coming on, I would deny it, make a joke, or distract myself. If this didn't work and the sadness broke through into my awareness, I would get very scared. Growing up, the overall mood in our home was tense. My dad was angry a lot and if he was home, his anger permeated everything, which made the rest of us tense and sad. My mom seemed the most affected by his anger, and her sadness made her seem vulnerable and alone. I desperately wanted to cheer up those around me and to make them laugh. To me, it seemed like sadness never went away once you let it in, so I was determined not to let it in and do what I could to keep it away from others too. I ran from sadness as much as I could and I know my eating disorder was one of the ways I kept sadness and other difficult feelings away. The problem in never expressing my sadness was that nobody ever knew I needed help, comfort, or compassion, so I felt very alone and scared if I ever felt sad, which made it even harder to deal with and more scary to feel.

Anger didn't bother me nearly as much because there was at least power in it. I wasn't scared or intimidated by anger because although my father was angry most of the time, he wasn't physically abusive or out of control when angry. I didn't like feeling angry, but it sometimes felt like fuel, and sometimes I needed that fuel to help me do things I was afraid to do, like saying how I felt even though it might upset someone else. My fear of rejection and judgment was so strong that it took anger for me to override the fear and push me into action.

ASSIGNMENT: WHAT DO YOU FEEL WHEN . . .?

When people say or do something mean or hurtful to you, what do you usually feel? Try to describe your physical sensations in your body and the reaction you have.

_____
_____
_____

Think of a recent situation that upset, frustrated, or disappointed you. How did your body experience it? Did you get angry or sad? Did you feel guilty or embarrassed? Is there a way in which you would like to respond differently in the future?

_____
_____
_____
_____

If you are worried about not knowing what you feel, we have found that stopping yourself from engaging in an eating disorder behavior will cause feelings to come up. Whatever they are, and wherever they came from, you can begin there and use the techniques we describe in this Key to work with those feelings.

ASSIGNMENT: WHAT FEELINGS COME UP WHEN I INTERRUPT A BEHAVIOR?

The next time you want to engage in an eating disorder behavior, stop yourself from doing it or delay it by setting a timer or doing something to distract yourself. Write about all the feelings that surface when you interrupt the behavior.

When I interrupted my behavior, I noticed these feelings:
_____
_____
_____

ASSIGNMENT: IDENTIFYING DIFFICULT FEELINGS

Below is a list of feelings that many of our clients commonly share having difficulty with. They say they are unable to allow themselves to feel the feeling, they berate themselves for feeling it, or the feeling results in negative or destructive behaviors. Read through the list and put a check by the feelings that you find particularly difficult to deal with. Add any others that fit for you, but aren't on the list.

____ Rejection   ____ Failure   ____ Shame   ____ Unworthy   ____ Lonely
____ Fear   ____ Anger   ____ Insecure   ____ Guilty   ____ Sad
____ Disappointment   ____ Overwhelmed   ____ Hurt   ____ Jealous
____ Out of control   ____ Powerless   ____ Vulnerable   ____ Intimacy
____ Success   ____ Sexual   ____ Incapable   ____ Anxious
____   ____   ____   ____

ASSIGNMENT: EXPLORING DIFFICULT FEELINGS

From the list of difficult feelings you checked, pick two that are particularly difficult for you right now. Write each feeling and then explore by answering the questions that follow.

Feeling #1: _____

_____

_____

When is the first time you remember feeling it? _____

_____

Does a significant memory stand out regarding this feeling? _____

_____

_____

How was (or is) this feeling expressed and responded to in your family? _____

_____

What does it mean about you to have this feeling? _____

_____

_____

What do you tell yourself about this feeling or having it? _____

_____

_____

What are all the things you do in reaction to having this feeling? _____

_____

_____

Are you afraid of what will actually happen if you experience the feeling, or are you afraid you can't tolerate or survive feeling it? (Hint: Think of failure as an example.) _____

_____

_____

_____

What are you afraid others will think (or do) if they know you have this feeling?

How do you think others who have this feeling handle it?

What does it feel like, or where do you feel this in your body?

What are actions you can take to counteract the bodily sensations?

Feeling #2:

When is the first time you remember feeling it?

Does a significant memory stand out regarding this feeling?

How was (or is) this feeling expressed and responded to in your family?

What does it mean about you to have this feeling?

What do you tell yourself about this feeling or having it?

What are all the things you do in reaction to having this feeling? _____
_____
_____

Are you afraid of what will actually happen if you experience the feeling, or are you afraid you can't tolerate or survive feeling it? (Hint: Think of failure as an example.) _____
_____
_____
_____

What are you afraid others will think (or do) if they know you have this feeling?
_____
_____

How do you think others who have this feeling handle it? _____
_____
_____

What does it feel like, or where do you feel this in your body? _____
_____
_____
_____

What are actions you can take to counteract the bodily sensations? _____
_____
_____
_____

The more you look directly into rather than avoid feelings you find difficult, the more you will be able to recognize, understand, accept, and handle them. Facing and embracing the difficult feelings allows you to let them go.

The following quote is from a client exploring his feelings around shame:

"My parents were very strict with us and praised me for self-discipline and taking the hardest road possible. Any digressions for the sake of fun, pleasure, self-care, or relaxation were seen as indulgent, lazy, selfish, and evidence I wasn't a good person and would be punished for it down the road somehow. I felt *ashamed of my desires, needs, and feelings. I secretly wanted to have fun and just lay around sometimes. To this day, if someone comes in and 'catches me' lying around doing nothing, I feel the shame in my body and I start apologizing and explaining, making sure the person knows I haven't been there for long. Any pleasure seems to trigger shame in me now. I'm afraid to date because sexual pleasure makes me feel guilty and ashamed even though I know it is normal and even healthy. Then to make it worse, I feel ashamed that I haven't had a relationship or any experience with sex. I can't win!*

I am working on this in therapy and have learned that my eating disorder helps me deal with my shame. When I deny myself things I want, or have the self-discipline to restrict food and lose weight, it makes me feel that I'm controlling myself from indulgence or pleasure seeking, or from people thinking I'm a selfish person.

I am now starting to see that my eating disorder helps me feel like I'm keeping a shameful, gluttonous self from coming out but at the same time creates shame because I'm ashamed of the behaviors I am doing to myself and what that says about me."

Like this client, many people go out of their way to avoid, deny, or escape from feeling shame. You can see from the example that having an eating disorder makes things even more complicated because the behaviors themselves can cause shame.

Feel Your Feelings

Trying to protect yourself from your feelings does not solve anything, and it doesn't work. If you don't allow yourself to acknowledge and feel your feelings, they get stuck inside and create other problems, making them harder to transform or let go of. You can spend endless amounts of time and energy trying to avoid or deny your feelings, and because of that, they actually run your life. For example, if you have to protect yourself from feeling disappointed, you will be afraid of and avoid things where there is any chance of disappointment. Disappointment then runs your life. But if you learn to accept feeling disappointment as a part of life—acknowledging when it happens and allowing it in—you will be able to let it go.

The first step is learning to identify your feelings by discovering and accepting what is happening in your body, noticing that a feeling is something that has come in and can also go out. You learn to separate yourself from your feelings. All the assignments in this Key are geared to practicing these skills and will make a huge difference in both your relationships and your overall well-being.

OVER IDENTIFYING WITH YOUR FEELINGS

Just as you are not your thoughts, you are not your feelings. As we've said, your feelings are a combination of thoughts and body sensations. This is why you need both mind and body techniques to help you deal with them.

To begin to separate yourself from your feelings, it helps to understand the language you use to describe your feelings. For example, rather than saying, to yourself or to others, "I *am* sad," practice saying, "I *feel* sad," or, "I am *filled* with sadness." This semantic adjustment might seem silly at first, but it will help you relate to sadness as a temporary experience. Simply saying, "I *am* sad" indicates a trait you have rather than a state you are in, and indicates that sad is what you *are* rather than something you are *feeling*. For the same reason, it is important for us to say that someone *has* anorexia or bulimia rather than someone *is anorexic* or *is bulimic*. It is important to use language that helps separate you from your illness, and the same is true for separating yourself from your feelings.

TRANSFORMING YOUR FEELINGS AND GETTING THEM OUT OF YOUR BODY

There are many ways to regulate and experience your feelings without becoming overwhelmed or derailed by them. Separating your *self* from your *feelings* and getting them out of your body means you can regulate them and put them in proper perspective in order to make good decisions.

Saying you are angry and describing all the reasons why without learning to reduce the feeling of anger in the body will not help much. Have you ever noticed the stance that people's bodies take when they are experiencing a feeling? Your body takes certain stances that are associated with your feelings. For example, when you feel afraid, your breathing may become short or you might get rigid with tense shoulders that hike up toward your ears. You can lessen the feelings of fear by lowering your shoulders, loosening up, and taking some deep breaths. By putting your body in the position it would be in if it was calm and taking slow, deep breaths, your parasympathetic nervous system will kick in, and actually help your body calm down.

Because your feelings are felt as body sensations, describing what you are feeling in your body, as well as identifying your feelings, will help tame both the mind and the body.

If your feelings are confusing or difficult to tolerate, try to stay present and feel them anyway, even if only for a little while. Staying present can be challenging. Practice by deep breathing, relaxing, and focusing on what you're experiencing in your body. Sometimes you may not know the reason for your feelings. Learning how to manage or transform the physical experience of your feelings in your body might be the only thing you can do in the moment to help yourself.

To help you understand how to transform feelings, we will focus on anger, as it is usually easy to recognize. A variety of body sensations are associated with feeling angry. Some report heat rising in the neck, head, stomach, or all over, and many people actually turn red from the heat. People commonly use phrases like, "You need to cool off," or "cool down" when talking to someone who is angry. In fact, you will find that using an ice pack on your neck, or cold washcloth on your face when you get angry actually helps to calm you down and get anger out of your body. Taking the heat out of your body lessens the feeling of anger, which then helps you return to neutral so you can think more clearly and respond in a way that serves you.

Taking long and deep breaths is one of the easiest—and often most effective—ways to transform and discharge distressing feelings from the body, including anger. Others find physical activity the best way to "blow off steam." Everyone is different, so learning what helps you is important.

ASSIGNMENT: FEELING AND TRANSFORMING YOUR ANGER

Think of the last few times you were angry. Without using words like angry or mad, describe what anger feels like in your body. Remember to focus on your body sensations, not your feelings. (Tip: some people feel their jaws clench, some feel their shoulders get tight or hunched, or their hands tighten; most feel some kind of heat.)

When I am angry, my body . . . _____

Things I can do to reduce or transform those sensations: _____

ASSIGNMENT: TRANSFORMING OTHER FEELINGS

Look at the three feelings listed here. Next to each one, write what your body feels like when you are experiencing that feeling. Then list counter behaviors you could do to transform the emotion and bring your body back to neutral.

Shame. My body experiences: _____

Behaviors I could do to transform it: _____

Sadness. My body experiences: _____

Behaviors I could do to transform it: _____

Guilt. My body experiences: _____

Behaviors I could do to transform it: _____

The next time you experience one of these feelings, try doing the things you wrote down and see if they make a difference. You might notice a difference right away, but go easy on yourself as this takes practice and time.

ASSIGNMENT: PRACTICE WHEN THE IRON IS WARM, NOT HOT

It is helpful to practice getting your body back to neutral when your emotions aren't extreme. Try an experience right now. Use your awareness to scan your body and notice any areas or places where you are holding your body in a tense way, like hunching your shoulders or tightly crossing your legs or craning your neck. Just try to change anything you notice by slowly unclenching, uncrossing, and loosening up the noticeable areas. Observe how you feel. This can be done in traffic, during an argument, lying in bed, or wherever you find yourself needing to neutralize a feeling. With practice, you will be able to do this whenever you want, even if the iron is hot (when the emotions are intense).

Feeling Worse While Getting Better

As you progress in your recovery, your feelings will become more noticeable or seem more intense. Reconnecting with the myriad feelings that have been covered up for so long may, at first, make you feel worse. Recovery involves learning to feel your feelings without using your eating disorder or any other destructive ways of escaping or masking them. People, not just those with eating disorders, do all kinds of things to avoid, suppress, or distract from their feelings. Stealing, self-harm, and other compulsive behaviors and addictions are also common struggles of people who have not learned how to deal with their feelings or let others in to help them.

Sometimes You Just Need a Break

Despite the importance of dealing with your feelings, sometimes distracting yourself from the feelings you're having is useful. It is important to note that distraction is different from avoidance. Non-harmful forms of distraction can be used to divert your attention for a while if you feel there is nothing else you can really do about the situation, or until you are in a calmer, more rational state of mind. You might go for a walk or play basketball. You might comfort yourself by taking a bath or listening to music. If your feelings are very intense, it may be easier to comfort yourself after some other form of distraction. Intense feelings may also require a distraction that matches the intensity of the feeling. For example, if you are extremely angry, taking a bath and relaxing might be too hard, while gardening or cleaning out your closet might work perfectly. The bath will probably feel better after something like this.

ASSIGNMENT: WHAT ACTIVE DISTRACTIONS CAN YOU USE?

Everyone is different, and what provides a good distraction for one person might bore another (think sports or shopping). Write down some things you think would be good distractions for you when you need to use them.

1. _____
2. _____
3. _____
4. _____

ASSIGNMENT: WHAT COMFORTS AND SOOTHES YOU?

Take a moment and think about what kinds of things or sensations feel comforting or soothing to you. Some ideas include a hot bath, a massage, sitting by a fire, listening to music, or reading. Write down a few ways to self-soothe that appeal to you.

1. _____
2. _____
3. _____
4. _____

Have Compassion for Yourself

Self-compassion is a critical ingredient when dealing with your thoughts and feelings. You probably find it far easier to be compassionate toward others than to yourself. Recovery requires you to explore your life, your thoughts, your behaviors, your problems and feelings, and then practice new skills. Self-observation is required, but if it leads only to self-reproach or judgment, it can end up making you feel worse about yourself instead of better.

Treat yourself with the kind of compassion you would show anyone else going through your situation. We venture to guess that you would not berate others for their feelings, or suggest to others in similar situations as yours that they starve, binge, purge, or self-harm to deal with their feelings. If you are like most of our clients, you not only feel compassion for others, but can also offer good advice when they need help. Why would you treat yourself any differently?

ASSIGNMENT: ASSESS YOUR SELF-COMPASSION

Read each statement listed below and put a check next to all that apply.

____ 1. *I often feel undeserving.*
____ 2. *I have a hard time accepting and sharing my flaws.*
____ 3. *When something bad happens, I blame myself.*
____ 4. *I treat others better than I treat myself.*
____ 5. *I feel bad practicing self-care.*
____ 6. *I am judgmental of myself.*
____ 7. *I have a hard time forgiving myself.*

Scoring:

Add up how many check marks you have. Total: _____

Newsflash: If you are like most of our clients, you need to turn some attention to how you think about, talk to, and treat yourself. Even if you only checked one item, you could use some help practicing self-compassion and self-care.

The good news is that self-compassion is something we learn, not something we have or don't have. While you can learn self-compassion, your old habits are well entrenched, so it takes continued practice to achieve it. That might sound discouraging, but it is no different than practicing patience, meditation, playing an instrument, or yoga. The more we practice something, the better we are at it.

We will come back to self-compassion in Key 6, but we suggest you also explore other resources. Here are two books to start with:

Self-Compassion by Kristen Neff

The Mindful Path to Self-Compassion by Chris Germer

ASSIGNMENT: COMPASSION MANTRA

Read the following simple mantra or prayer below. Copy it down and keep it with you to take out and read when you are suffering.

This is a moment of suffering
Suffering is a part of life
May I be kind to myself in this moment
May I be compassionate with myself through this pain

This mantra is really about acceptance, which is a good starting point for developing self-compassion. Accepting where you are right now without judgment and kindly helping yourself to do better is how you would treat any other human being in your situation. It is important to recognize you are a human being too, and you need to give to yourself what you give others.

Putting It All Together

The connection between your thoughts, feelings, and behaviors can be very difficult to detect at first, but will become clearer overtime. With practice, becoming a witness to your thoughts and challenging them as well as accepting, tolerating, and transforming your feelings, will get increasingly easier. You might find challenging your thoughts helps in making better decisions right away, or you might first find yourself getting lost in an endless mind battle. You might need to attend more to transforming the feelings in your body in order to respond in a healthier way. It is up to you to try out the ideas we share and find what works best for you.

PERSONAL REFLECTIONS: STRATEGIES FOR HANDLING THOUGHTS AND FEELINGS

Learning to manage feelings is something we all work on and struggle with to some extent. When trying to come up with examples of how to deal with difficult feelings, we realized that we both have different strategies and decided it might be helpful to share these with you.

Anger

Gwen: The first thing I do when I want to transform anger is to try to understand what feeling is underneath the anger so I know what I need to do to help myself. The feelings under my anger are almost always hurt, guilt, or fear. I tend to be a very cerebral person, so working with my thoughts and feelings helps me. My strategies for each are a bit different, so identifying what is under my anger is crucial. If I realize fear is under my anger, I take some deep breaths and reassure myself that everything will be okay. I remind myself that anger doesn't help me and can make others around me feel attacked or blamed, which isn't what I want. I will usually take responsibility for this out loud, which helps me as well as anyone around me.

If I realize that guilt is lurking under my anger, I take a look at my boundaries. If I am setting boundaries, like saying no, and feeling guilty about it, I know my *guilt* isn't really guilt, but actually *anxiety* and will go away quickly. If I feel angry because I'm not setting boundaries so others are doing things I don't like, I remind myself that it is my job to teach people how to treat me and if I'm not doing that, it's not really fair to be angry at them. Regardless of what feeling is under my anger, to transform it, I always try to take responsibility for any part that is mine, see the other person's perspective and search for any reason to feel compassion toward that person. Compassion seems to quell anger pretty quickly for me. If I am still angry after that, I let some time pass because I know I tend to let go of anger after a few days, even when I want to hold onto it. I intentionally do not allow myself to engage until time has passed and my emotions have lessened. I often say to myself, "If it's a good idea to say this today, it will still be a good idea three days from now." Eventually, if I still think it's necessary and appropriate, I will set up a time to talk and hopefully resolve the conflict.

Carolyn: I had a wonderful, loving mom who allowed me to express myself freely. I felt heard and validated. However, there was an exception to this that I did not even know about until I was an adult. After I developed an eating disorder, my mother told me that she had not been comfortable with anger and found it particularly difficult in females. She actually apologized to me, saying, "When you were young and fought with your brother it was uncomfortable for me to see anger in a little girl. I actually treated you and your brother differently in regards to this. I would grab you and pull you away from the situation."

This helped me understand that my reaction of turning anger to sadness, as discussed earlier, must have been, at least partially, influenced by my mother's discomfort with anger. In the long run, I have found this very useful because hurt and sadness are the primary emotions underneath anger, and the sooner you get to them, the better.

The first thing I do when I feel angry is stop and pay attention to my body. I feel myself want to get still and feel what I feel. Most of the time what happens next is that I feel sad and I cry. This clears the negative energy, paving the way for me to discuss my feelings calmly. Sometimes the anger stays with me and I know I need to get it out of my body before I can be productive. Trying to think about another person's perspective, or see my own part in the situation, will be too influenced by what my body is feeling. Therefore, I try to do something to cool off, calm down, and get my body back to neutral before trying to figure things out or communicate my feelings. I might listen to music or go for a walk in nature. Occasionally I want to talk to someone to help me discharge the anger, and if so, I try to prepare the person for my angry energy. I have always found it helps both the other person as well as myself when I give warning before using them to discharge my emotions.

Sadness

Gwen: As I disclosed earlier, sadness is a hard one for me, but I have developed self-talk to help myself. If I am very sad, I reassure myself that I'm just experiencing sadness and I will be okay. I will get through this even though it doesn't feel like it. Sometimes I want to be alone, but if that goes on more than a day or so, I force myself to reach out to friends and tell them I am struggling even if I don't want to talk about why at the time. I make a deal with myself to say yes if asked to see a movie or visit with friends, and I usually do so even if I don't feel like it because I know getting out will be helpful. I try to allow myself to cry if I want or need that, and I also try to do something physical, like walks or dancing, because I know it helps more than I ever expect it will. One of the best antidotes I use for sadness or any difficult emotion is humor. Watching a funny movie or going to a comedy show works wonders. Laughter is good medicine.

Carolyn: I can remember learning that it is okay to feel sad, cry, and be vulnerable, and that nothing bad really ever comes of it. I remember when I figured out that people who saw me vulnerable seemed to get closer to me, not further away. I realized people wanted to interact with me and help me more when I was sad rather than angry, like my mother, as shared earlier. And I know what to do with sadness—I cry. Crying makes me feel better, and I am not afraid to cry in front of anyone. I once saw the Dalai Lama cry in front of 7,000 people during a lecture he was giving. He stopped for a moment, sobbed, and started talking again. I saw the sad energy leave his body; I saw him returning himself back to neutral. I was already good at expressing sadness, but seeing him helped me get even better about it.

When you cry tears of sadness, you release cortisol, the stress hormone that builds up in our bodies, so of course you feel better afterwards. When you cut an onion, the tears that come have a completely different chemical composition. After discharging my cortisol through tears, I might then do something enjoyable to help me feel better, or if there is something I need to do to handle the situation that made me sad, I can start dealing with it. If you ever feel bad about crying, want to justify your tears, or just educate someone about the importance of shedding tears, say, "Excuse me, I have to get rid of some excess cortisol."

Hurt

Gwen: Another very hard one, and I have no problem recognizing it. As I said above, when I get hurt, I often get angry too. The first thing I do is try to determine if I'm hurt because someone did something hurtful, or if they just did something they wanted and I am hurt for reasons that make me feel like I am back in junior high. I can tell because I feel embarrassed to admit it. When this happens, talking about my feelings with someone else (not the person who hurt me) is usually enough to help me feel better. Intentionality also means a lot to me. If I know someone didn't mean to hurt me, I usually let it go pretty quickly, but if I believe someone doesn't care about me or intentionally hurt me, holding onto my hurt and anger feels protective, so letting go is a much longer process.

Before I started recovery, I would rarely, if ever, admit I felt hurt. Carolyn really helped me learn to communicate my feelings in a way that elicits more understanding than defensiveness in others, and she also helped me to learn to tolerate the vulnerability that comes along with having more honest and authentic relationships.

Carolyn: No one likes to feel hurt. Most of us usually turn it into anger or sadness and if you have read the rest of the workbook, you already know I will most likely turn it into sadness. Aside from what I said earlier regarding how I deal with sadness, when I am hurt, I practice *truth without judgment*. No matter how scared I am about getting hurt even more, I get myself to talk to the person who hurt me, whether it was on purpose or not, telling him or her the truth about how I feel without becoming negative or judgmental (we discuss this further in Key 8). I might have to let some time pass so I don't have strong feelings in my body when I communicate. Then I am better able to say what I want to say without blaming or demanding or using any negativity or anger.

Shame

Gwen: I decided to write about shame because it is an extremely difficult feeling for most people to deal with and not often talked about. Body shame in particular has been around since before the onset of my eating disorder and has lingered on and rears its ugly head at certain, often unpredictable, times. Sometimes it happens when I catch an unflattering angle of myself in the mirror, or I see a picture of myself that was taken when I wasn't aware so I didn't have a chance to *smooth or arrange my clothes to ensure certain parts are covered*. It has happened when I see a group picture someone has posted where I'm the one who just happens to be closest to the camera so I appear not only larger than I actually am, but larger than everyone else as well, and I get a painfully familiar slap-in-the-face-feeling of body shame.

    I cringe and imagine everyone looking at it and seeing how huge I am. I feel a rush of hot energy creeping up my body that makes me want to delete, cover, or hide the source of my shameful feelings. I'm flooded with confusing feelings of fear, anger, and self-reproach. For this reason, I often don't enjoy having my picture taken and I feel annoyed at anyone who posts a bad picture of me. I used to try to "fix" my feeling by throwing myself into a weight-loss spiral. Now I just take a breath, remove the picture from my line of vision, and of course, blame the person who took the photo . . . big improvement.

The roots of my body shame started very early in my life when my mother began obsessively and relentlessly dieting, making comments about her weight and body as well as mine and everyone else's. Due to my chronic dieting and my even more chronic breaking of my diet, I had steadily gained weight slowly throughout high school. By senior year I was feeling pretty bad about myself and very ashamed of my body. During this same time, I suffered my first painful heartbreak, so feelings of rejection and betrayal were present and compounded my feelings of shame.

Talking about my feelings, feeling vulnerable, and leaning on friends for support was not something I knew how to do at that time in my life, so I just pretended I was fine when I was not. This is the emotional and physical condition I was in when I went off to college to have *the time of my life.* Instead of thriving in college, I isolated and fell into a major depression. I didn't know what to do to help myself or to take care of myself through these very painful feelings. Who could have known that my decision to go on yet another new diet, combined with that mixture of deeply painful feelings, along with having no support system, would be the perfect storm for my eating disorder to develop? Losing weight helped me to feel *better* about myself. It was intoxicating because it worked. And then of course, it didn't work, but by the time it became obvious to others, I was already entrenched and was more terrified of changing or feeling the way I did before than I was afraid of being sick or dying. I couldn't see past my fear and I couldn't stop, either.

So, now all of these years later, I am not worried or even that surprised when I get slapped with body image shame. For a long time I tried to avoid anything that I thought would trigger my shame because I was afraid it might be too strong for me to deal with, but now I know how to deal with body shame when I feel it.

I take a breath, I remind myself we are all a little broken in our own ways with our own particular heartbreaks. This is mine. I don't judge myself. Over time, these vulnerabilities are woven into our cells and become part of our inner lives and stories. I might always be more sensitive than most to feelings of body shame, but now, instead of planning to "fix" the problem by betraying myself, compromising my health and relationships, or beating myself up, I just choose a roomier blouse and get back to my busy life.

Carolyn: I used to not recognize shame at all. I only associated this feeling with people who had been abused. It took me a long time to realize that the way shame shows up in my life is the deeply distressing feeling I get when someone "catches" me resting or doing something that could be interpreted as slacking or indulgent. I learned to value productivity and devalue any kind of self-care. I never saw my mom buy a nice outfit for herself or go to a makeup counter or get a massage or manicure. To this day, I feel uncomfortable doing things described as self-care, not because I think any of these things are bad or wrong but because of an old message I somehow got regarding what it reflects about me if I do them. To me, self-care meant self-indulgence or being selfish.

Still now, I prefer to say, "I am going to physical therapy" rather than, "I'm getting a massage," and when I do get a massage, I prefer to go with a girlfriend and let her book the appointment. Many of my *vacations* are combined with a work event, or I bring my computer and work on my trip. I recognize this and try to circumvent these feelings, but sometimes they are automatic and just come. I work at feeling them and doing the self-care thing I know is good for me. I tell myself what I tell clients all the time: "Do the harder thing."

Final Thoughts

Learning the skills in this key is a game changer. You might feel overwhelmed by all the information here and wonder if you will be able to accomplish the goals we describe. It helps to think of it like learning to ride a bike or play an instrument—at first, it feels unnatural and difficult, but over time, your fingers get used to the way they need to move on the guitar strings, your body figures out how to hold the violin bow, or you learn to balance without training wheels. This is how you train your brain to create those new neural pathways we discussed in this Key, making what once seemed impossible become automatic.

KEY 5: IT *IS* ABOUT THE FOOD

"The chief pleasure in eating does not consist in costly seasoning, or exquisite flavor, but in yourself." —HORACE (65–8 B.C.), ROMAN LYRIC POET

". . . It is possible to recover without ever gaining insight or dealing with underlying issues that caused your eating disorder, but if you don't change your relationship with food, you cannot recover."
— 8 KEYS TO RECOVERY FROM AN EATING DISORDER

No matter what created the *disorder* in your relationship with food, to get better you will need to put *order* back into the way you think about food, the way you eat, and the relationship between eating and your body. There are many great things in store for you that are beyond what you might imagine. You can return to, or maybe cultivate for the first time, a natural, fun, pleasurable, and soulful relationship with food and eating. You can learn to appreciate your body and nourish it. We realize this kind of relationship with food might sound far-fetched, and you might be full of doubt that you could ever get there, but it is our human nature, so there is no reason you can't. Right now, that part of you has been covered up, repressed, or stolen by the eating disorder. This Key will help you learn how to find the pleasure in eating again and create a new relationship with food, your body, and your life.

If all you needed was information on how much, when, and what to eat, you could have changed your relationship to food already. In order to successfully work through this Key, you will require skills you're learning in all the other Keys. You'll need continued motivation (Key 1) and the ability to challenge your Eating Disorder Self (Key 2). Underlying issues and your thoughts and feelings will get in the way unless you learn to cope with them differently and more effectively (Keys 3 and 4). You will also need practical help with behavior change (Key 6) and the capability of reaching out to others for help (Key 7). Finally, to get to a place where you can cultivate a more meaningful and appreciative relationship with food and your body, you will need mentoring on nourishing both body and soul (Key 8).

To get started, we are going to explore your current relationship with food and how you might like it to be different.

WRITING ASSIGNMENT: YOUR RELATIONSHIP WITH FOOD

The following questions ask you to think about your relationship with food and how it could be different. When answering these questions, set aside any fears, such as losing control, gaining too much weight, or being deprived.

1. *What would you like to do with food that you currently can't do (e.g., eat a variety of foods, eat without feeling anxious or guilty, eat with friends, go to restaurants, eat things you really like)?*

    _____
    _____
    _____
    _____

2. *What behaviors would you like to stop doing with food, but currently can't stop (e.g., counting calories, eating all night, cutting up food into bits, only buying fat-free food, bingeing, purging)?*

    _____
    _____
    _____
    _____

    Tip: If you can't answer the questions above, ask someone close to you to tell you what they would like to see you be able to do with food, or stop doing with food.

3. *If you could have a normal, healthy relationship with food, what would it look like?*

   _____
   _____
   _____
   _____

4. *What would your relationship to food look like if eating had no impact on your weight?*
   If your answer is different from your answer to number 3, why is this the case?

   _____
   _____
   _____
   _____

Rigidity and Chaos with Food

People who have disordered eating fall into three categories in terms of their relationship with food: too rigid, too chaotic, or both. You might easily identify which category you are in, or you might be someone who has vacillated between these three categories. For example, you may have at one time been very chaotic with your food and eating habits and then exerted control over your eating and became too rigid, or the other way around. Your basic temperament affects how you relate to food and how you relate to life. Chances are, the way you approach food is probably similar to how you deal with many other areas in your life, including money, people, or sex. For example, if you are rigid and controlled with food, you are probably pretty controlled with money; if your relationship to food is chaotic, it is likely that your relationships with people would lean toward chaotic as well. Developing more balance and flexibility is the ultimate goal.

ASSIGNMENT: ARE YOU RIGID, CHAOTIC, OR BOTH?

Write about your current relationship with food in terms of chaos and rigidity. If you are too rigid, give examples, such as how you deal with portions, food rules, etc. If you are chaotic, give examples of your chaotic thinking or behaviors around food. If you are currently switching back and forth between rigidity and chaos, write about that. My relationship with food right now can best be described as:

_____
_____

Examples: _____
_____
_____
_____

There is no doubt that developing a more balanced, flexible relationship with food will be challenging, but over time it will more become natural. We are all born intuitively knowing how to eat. If you have ever watched healthy babies breast- or bottle-feeding, you have seen they have no problem knowing when they are hungry and will communicate it until fed, and they also know when they are full and will stop eating. They have no concerns about calories or thoughts about better-tasting alternatives to satisfy the feeling they experience as hunger. Nobody has to teach healthy babies how to do this because they are born intuitive eaters. Very young children usually stay connected to this innate, or intuitive knowledge about when and how much to eat. They don't eat by rules, think about their weight, or feel guilty for eating things they love. They don't binge to fill up a psychological emptiness. They don't count calories or follow a meal plan.

As we get older, this simple and natural relationship to food gets much more complicated. Not only are we faced with a multitude of food choices and develop food preferences, we are also exposed to vast amounts of information, ideas, myths, and opinions about food; what is considered healthy vs. not healthy, fattening vs. nonfattening, good vs. bad. All this interferes with or inhibits our innate or gut intuition as a guide to hunger and fullness.

It would be so easy if we could just tell you to go back to the way you were as a child and eat intuitively again, but in addition to all your thoughts and opinions that get in the way, if your relationship with food has been damaged by repeated dieting, eating disorder behaviors, or overriding your hunger or fullness, your body signals or your interpretation of them are not reliable.

Once your inner guide has been ignored long enough, these signals can go haywire or disappear all together, making it too hard to "trust your gut."

If you have lost trust in your innate ability to make decisions about food, it makes sense to look for external sources of guidance, and information (think diet programs, weight loss books, and nutrition companies). The problem is these external guidelines can't be right for everyone because everyone has different needs, and they can be based on faulty information and lead you even more astray. You might be able to find appropriate guidelines, but then find yourself taking things to the extreme, such as thinking, "If low fat is good, then no fat must be better." It is likely that you have taken bits of information from here and there and created your own "food rules" that get you into trouble rather than help you create a healthy structure and balance around food.

Food Rules

If you are a seasoned dieter, or restrictive with food, you most likely have developed rules related to food and weight that you try to follow, even though you might not ever have thought of it this way, told anyone, or written them down anywhere. If your eating is chaotic, you probably have many of these rules in your head as well, which you vow to follow but find yourself falling right back into chaos day after day.

You develop these rules to keep yourself in line or feel "safer" around eating. Food rules are created to help alleviate the mistrust and lack of control you feel about your own appetite, desires, and decisions. Food rules usually sound something like, "Do not eat over _____ calories a day," "Purge anything that isn't on the safe list," "Don't eat starches or carbs," or "Only eat 'clean' or organic food." The "Thin Commandments" in our original 8 *Keys* book is compiled from years of listening to clients talk about their food rules.

You may have developed your rules consciously or not, but becoming aware of what they are, slowly challenging them, and creating different, more balanced, and flexible guidelines for yourself will lead to recovery.

WRITING ASSIGNMENT: LISTING AND EXPLORING YOUR FOOD RULES

Write down the food rules you follow, or try to follow, or think you should be following.

1. _____

2. _____

3. _____

4. _____

5. _____

From the above list, choose one rule you are willing to explore in this workbook and then answer the following questions. Then, you can use your weekly Goals Sheet and journal to go through the rest of your list of rules.

Rule: _____

Reason for the rule: _____

How did I come up with this rule? _____

Do I plan on following this rule forever? _____

What happens if I break the rule? _____

Is this rule based on facts or fears? _____

How does this rule inhibit relationships? _____

How does this rule enhance them? _____

Do other people have to follow this rule to be okay, and if not, why do I? _____

Does this rule allow for flexibility, such as being sick, or being more active? _____

Does this rule allow for special occasions or holidays? _____

Would I tell anyone else to follow this rule? Why or why not? _____

What do I gain by following this rule? _____

What am I giving up by following this rule? _____

What am I giving up by not following this rule? _____

What would it take for me to give up this rule? _____

ASSIGNMENT: CHALLENGING YOUR FOOD RULES

To break your patterns, you will need to start challenging your food rules. In the space below, write two rules you are willing to begin working on.

1. _____
2. _____

Use your weekly Goals Sheet to start challenging your food rules. There you can list the rule you want to work on and how you are going to start to change it. You might need to read the rest of this Key and Key 6 on behavior change before you begin to make changes. Keep in mind that even if you take small steps, eventually you will get where you want to go. The more you can challenge your current food rules, the faster you will get there, but everyone is different, so go at a pace you can tolerate.

CHANGING YOUR RELATIONSHIP WITH FOOD

Letting go of eating disorder behaviors and finding balance with your food takes awareness, education, guidance, practice, and of course patience. You will also need some idea about what to do, what to expect, and some trust that you will be okay. It will be easier for you to challenge and change what you are currently doing if you have something new to replace it with. Well-meaning people in your life have probably suggested, "just eat," "stop worrying so much," or "listen to your body." But you probably need more specific guidelines in order to change. This Key gives you a new eating philosophy with guidelines, rather than rules, which provide both guidance and freedom to make your own decisions about what, when, and how much to eat.

CONSCIOUS EATING

Conscious Eating is a powerful alternative to restrictive food rules and chaotic eating behaviors. Eating consciously means using knowledge, awareness, and desire to guide you about when, what, and how much to eat. Conscious Eating includes being aware of, and learning to respond to, your body signals of hunger and fullness, incorporating accurate and relevant nutritional information, and giving yourself permission to eat foods you truly enjoy.

The philosophy is simple, but at first it won't be easy to do because it will differ from what you are doing now, and you might have a hard time trusting it will really work. Initially, if you want or need more structure, you may choose to follow a meal plan, which is explained later on in this Key. However, if you are the kind of person who likes more freedom, and you know that a meal plan would likely trigger resistance or rebellion, the Conscious Eating guidelines will give you structure without imposing control. Regardless of where you are,

Conscious Eating can bring you a healthy and balanced relationship with food you can continue for the rest of your life.

THE TEN CONSCIOUS EATING GUIDELINES

1. Be conscious of your hunger. Eat when moderately hungry, don't wait until you are famished.
2. Eat regularly. Do not skip meals (eating at least every four hours).
3. Allow yourself to eat all foods (unless you are allergic or have some other serious health issue).
4. Eat what you truly want and like while being conscious of how foods make you feel, what you may need more of in your diet, and relevant health issues (for example, candy may not be a good conscious choice if you have diabetes or if you haven't eaten any protein all day).
5. All calories are equivalent when it comes to weight gain. In other words, eating a 100-calorie cookie will not make you fatter than eating a 100-calorie apple. (See an exception, explained below.*)
6. For meals, eat a balance of protein, fat, and carbohydrates. (Your body needs all of these to function properly and efficiently. Deprivation of foods or nutrients leads to physical and psychological problems and can actually trigger eating disorder behaviors.)
7. Stay conscious of your fullness and your satisfaction. (You can eat a lot and not be satisfied. Texture and taste of food are important for satisfaction, and eating enough is important so your body registers the experience of being comfortably full. The goal is to feel full and satisfied, but not physically uncomfortable in any way.)
8. If you overeat, which is normal to do sometimes, reassure yourself that your body can handle the excess food. You can wait until you are hungry again and then you are back on track.
9. Enjoy food and the pleasure of eating. (Try to be mindful while preparing and eating food. Turn eating into dining using candles, nice dishes, and flowers on the table. Enjoy meals with friends.)
10. Make conscious choices to avoid foods (types or amounts) that make you feel *physically* bad after eating them. (i.e., caffeine makes you irritable and jittery, popcorn or raw vegetables hurt your stomach.)

The exception to guideline number 5, that all calories are equal in terms of weight gain, is related to problems with insulin. Insulin is necessary to transport glucose (blood sugar) from the food you eat into your cells to be used as fuel or stored as fat. People who have insulin resistance or problems regulating insulin may need to eat differently or take insulin, or both, to ensure proper glucose metabolism. However, unless a physician has diagnosed you with high blood sugar, diabetes, or insulin resistance, this exception does not apply to you.

ASSIGNMENT: CONSCIOUS EATING ASSESSMENT

Assignment: Read over the Conscious Eating Guidelines and then for each one, rate yourself on a scale of 1 (you do not follow the guideline) to 10 (you follow the guideline all the time). Try to give an explanation for your answer.

1. I'm conscious of my hunger. I eat when I'm hungry and don't purposely wait until I am starving.
   How I rate 1 to 10: _____
   Explanation: _____
   _____

2. I eat regularly and do not purposely skip meals, or snacks.
   How I rate 1 to 10: _____
   Explanation: _____
   _____

3. I allow myself to eat all foods and don't exclude food out of fear. (This does not include foods you are allergic to or can't eat due to a diagnosed health condition.)
   How I rate 1 to 10: _____
   Explanation: _____
   _____

4. I eat what I want while taking into account nutrition information such as getting enough protein or calories.
   How I rate 1 to 10: _____
   Explanation: _____
   _____

5. *Even though some foods have greater nutritional value than others and are "healthier," I recognize that all calories are equal when it comes to gaining weight and that no certain food can make me gain weight, but certain eating habits can.*
   How I rate 1 to 10: _____
   Explanation: _____
   _____

6. *For most meals, I eat a balance of protein, fat, and carbohydrates.*
   How I rate 1 to 10: _____
   Explanation: _____
   _____

7. *I am conscious of when I am full and satisfied, and for the most part do not overeat past this point.*
   How I rate 1 to 10: _____
   Explanation: _____
   _____

8. *If I do overeat (which is normal to do sometimes) I don't make myself compensate for it or beat myself up, but accept it as a natural human thing to do from time to time.*
   How I rate 1 to 10: _____
   Explanation: _____
   _____

9. *I enjoy food and the pleasure of eating.*
   How I rate 1 to 10: _____
   Explanation: _____
   _____

10. *I make conscious choices to avoid foods or amounts that make me physically feel bad or ill after eating them.*
    How I rate 1 to 10: _____
    Explanation: _____
    _____

Add Up Your Total Conscious Eating Score: _____ *out of 100*

See where you fall on the scoring scale below and read the information associated with your score.

Scoring

1 to 20, severely compromised:

> *If your score is 20 or below, you probably already are aware that you have a distorted, unhealthy, compromised relationship with food. Your body and your psyche are suffering from this relationship. Your thoughts and behaviors around food are either too rigid, too chaotic, or both. Your eating is likely guided by fears, misconceptions, emotions, or external rules. You will need help knowing where to get started, but don't be upset. You are where you are. We were once there too. We changed and so can you.*

21 to 40, unhealthy:

> *A score in this range indicates that your relationship with food is problematic and not a healthy one. There might be some areas where you score higher than others, or you might score low on all the guidelines but in either case you will need guidance and support to help get you on the road to becoming a Conscious Eater. As we say to everyone, it is important to assess yourself and be honest with those trying to help you. Look over your ratings on each guideline and see where you think you might want to start.*

41 to 60, out of balance:

> *People in this range are out of balance when it comes to their thoughts and behaviors around food. You may have some very good ideas about eating, and yet many of your actions are misguided or unhealthy. If your score is in the 40s, you are far from being a conscious eater and will need a lot of help and practice. If you are closer to 60, you are making several Conscious Eating decisions, but something is in the way. Go back and determine if you are scoring low in all areas or your overall score is low because you follow some guidelines well, but others hardly at all. This will help you decide if you need to target specific guidelines, or work on all of them.*

61 to 80, somewhat Conscious Eater:

If you are in this category, there are areas that need attention but you are already a somewhat Conscious Eater. Of course if your score is closer to 60 there will be more to improve on than if it is closer to 80, but in either case it will be helpful for you to carefully go over the Conscious Eating guidelines and see where you can make changes.

81 to 100, Conscious Eater:

Your score indicates that you are a Conscious Eater. You don't have to follow the guidelines perfectly to be a Conscious Eater. Your score means you are, for the most part, eating with awareness of your body, your appetite, your hunger and fullness signals, and taking into consideration knowledge of nutrition in order to eat a proper, balanced diet. Even with this score it may be good to periodically check in with yourself and see how you are doing. With our busy lifestyles and the drama that can exist around food and weight in this culture, looking over the Conscious Eating Guidelines can be a good way to keep in touch with yourself and see if your relationship with food is where you want it to be.

Hopefully your Conscious Eating Assessment has highlighted where you stand and clarified areas for improvement regarding your relationship with food. If you feel overwhelmed or need help to begin making changes, working with a therapist, dietitian, or other professional might help you get over what's holding you back. Whether doing this on your own or with help, you can put Conscious Eating into practice. See what a few clients have to say:

"For years I have not had a healthy relationship with food. Answering the Conscious Eating Assessment honestly was eye-opening. Seeing the new patterns that needed to be developed and practiced daily sunk in as something I knew I had to do in order to heal."

"Completing the Conscious Eating Assessment helped me realize just how bad my relationship with food really is. After so many years with an eating disorder, certain things just became normal and quite routine. Answering the questions honestly and sharing them with my therapist helped me accept the guidance I need for healing and recovery. The assessment now serves as *a checklist of sorts, helping me keep on track while I'm learning how to be a Conscious Eater."*

"Before I took the Conscious Eating quiz, I assumed I was not a Conscious Eater at all because I am at a point where I need to follow a meal plan and eat 100 percent of it—leaving no room for my eating disorder to negotiate. Taking the quiz, I learned that I am a lot more aware than I give myself credit for, and it helped me with the frustration I was feeling for not being further along."

Putting Conscious Eating into Practice

Becoming a Conscious Eater means learning to stay connected to your bodily sensations of hunger and fullness, taking into consideration useful health and nutritional information to make appropriate and satisfying choices for yourself, while staying present and conscious of the people and the conversations around you. If your brain is hijacked by an eating disorder, you can't do that because having an eating disorder transforms normal, healthy body signals into stressful, anxiety-provoking feelings. Although it can be very tempting to believe information you read, or hear from others, the truth is that your body is very wise and will give you the best and most accurate information about when, how much, and even what to eat if you take care of it and learn to listen to its signals. The more you diet, follow rules, count calories, or compare yourself to others, the more disconnected you will feel and the less you will trust your body and the less your body will trust you. Remember, your body doesn't know you are intentionally depriving it, so it does what it can to slow down your metabolism and digestion so that you can hold onto as many calories as possible. The way to get it to speed up again is to eat. Eating communicates to your body that there is food around so you don't need any help conserving energy.

Even if initially you need a meal plan to help normalize your body and retrain yourself to feel and respond to hunger and fullness, you can rebuild trust with your body as you start listening and responding to it again.

ASSIGNMENT: FOLLOW THE CONSCIOUS EATING GUIDELINES FOR ONE DAY

Using your Goals Sheet, pick one day to try Conscious Eating. Hopefully, knowing you only have to do it for one day will alleviate some of your fears or resistance. "One day at a time" is a common and helpful mantra when trying to change a behavior. Write about your experience in your journal, and if you want, let us know how it goes by visiting our Facebook page, "8 Keys to Recovery From an Eating Disorder Group" and sharing your experience. You might get useful feedback or even be able to help and inspire others.

The Hunger Scale

Reconnecting with and learning to pay attention to your hunger and fullness is a very important part of Conscious Eating, which is why the hunger scale is part of keeping a food journal. The hunger scale is a continuum which starts at 1 for extremely hungry and ends at 10 for extremely full. The following is a brief description of each number:

Hunger				Neutral				Fullness	
1	2	3	4	5	6	7	8	9	10

1. Extremely hungry, lightheaded, headache, no energy.
2. Still overly hungry, irritable, stomach growling, constant thoughts of food.
3. Hungry for a meal, sensing hunger, thinking about food and what would be good to eat. (This is the target hunger level.)
4. A little bit hungry, a snack would do, or making plans for eating soon.
5. Neutral: Don't feel hungry or full.
6. A little bit full, not quite satisfied, have not eaten enough
7. Satisfied and comfortably full. (This is the target fullness level.)
8. A bit too full, a little uncomfortable. This is normal to do sometimes.
9. Overly full, uncomfortable (like on holiday or if unconsciously eating).
10. Extremely full, painful, (likely after an episode of binge eating).

You might find yourself resisting the hunger/fullness scale. It might make you overly conscious or rigid, or you might not truly understand the difference between an 8 and a 9. It is important to note that knowing your exact hunger level on a scale from 1 to 10 is not critical. What is critical is paying attention to your body and not letting yourself get too hungry or too full. The hunger and fullness scale can help reacquaint you with your body cues.

About Food Journals

We often suggest using food journals, at least for a period of time. The purpose of keeping a food journal is to increase your awareness and help you, or others who may be helping you, keep track of things so when you look back you can see what worked and what didn't. All our suggestions are meant to help you reach your goals, so if you notice a lot of resistance coming up, try to use some of the skills from Key 4 and just allow the feelings to be there, accept them, and let them go. Try this for one day even if you are afraid. We suggest your food journal contain the following information.

Food Journal

1. Date and time of day.
2. Description of food eaten.
3. Amount of food eaten. (Be general or specific depending on needs.)
4. Hunger level before eating.
5. Fullness level after eating.
6. Feelings or thoughts.
7. Urges to binge or purge and any bingeing or purging behavior.

Lessons learned: _____

_____

_____

Food Journal Example

Time	Food and Amount	Hunger / Fullness	Feelings	Urge-Binge/ Purge
7:00 A.M.	cereal/milk,1/2 banana	2–7	hopeful	N/N
10:10 A.M.	scone, latte	4–8	anxious, fat	Y/P
1:15 P.M.	tuna sandwich, apple	3–7	happy, nervous	N/N

4:30 P.M.	a few Crackers	4–4	anxious	N/N
8:45 P.M.	4 tacos, beans, salad, chips	2–9	anxious, guilty, full	Y/P
10:20 P.M.	cottage cheese, 1 peach	5–7	sad, determined	N/N

What I learned: *I'm not really ready to challenge myself with a scary snack like a scone and latte. It made me feel anxious and fat even though I was hungry. I freaked out after and purged. I also realize that only eating crackers for afternoon snack is not enough and a setup for getting way too hungry, especially since I waited too long to eat dinner. I ended up eating way too much and then purged again. I also did not reach out for help after purging earlier in the day, which I need to do to help me get back on track.*

ASSIGNMENT: PERSONAL FOOD JOURNAL

You will need to make copies of the Food Journal we supply in this workbook, or make your own and copy. To start with, use the Food Journal sheets to keep track of your food and feelings for a day, a few days, or more. We highly recommend you add "Filling Out My Food Journal" to your Goals Sheet and keep doing this assignment for a while. You will discover patterns and stumbling blocks and determine how best to target your food journaling to be of help.

ASSIGNMENT: NOTICING YOUR EATING PATTERNS

Look over a few days or a week of your food journal. Notice what patterns emerge; what feelings got in the way, which food decisions made things harder for you, and which ones worked out well. These insights will provide valuable information about what, how, when, and where you can make adjustments to move forward in recovery.

Here are a few questions you can ask yourself when reviewing your food journal.

> Are some times of the day harder than others?
> Do you ever reach out to people for help?
> Does eating with others help you?
> Do you often let too much time elapse between eating?

How does your hunger level affect how much you eat?

Is it harder to stop eating when you start off overly hungry?

Do you under eat to "balance" over eating?

Do you find yourself at the extreme ends of the hunger scale more often than not?

Do you binge when tired or angry, or any other clear emotional trigger?

Do your explanations give you clues about where or how you are stuck?

Write a summary of what you have learned from your food journal:

_____

_____

_____

MAKING FOOD BEHAVIOR GOALS

Once you gather information about yourself, it is easier to target specific goals. Throughout this Key and the other Keys we continue to ask you to make goals for yourself and use the weekly Goals Sheet to write them down to keep track of them and your progress. We realize that even if you have information about yourself and know what to do, it might still be hard to make specific goals, especially if you are not used to it or you are afraid, ambivalent, or resistant. Below is a list of common goals that might help you get started.

Examples of Food Behavior Goals

1. Add one new food you don't usually eat as a snack this week.
2. Eliminate using measuring cups or spoons, and use your best judgment to portion your meal or snack. (If you rely on measuring devices all the time, start with one snack or meal.)
3. Use a timer, and when you feel the urge to binge or purge, set the timer and don't allow yourself to binge or purge before the timer runs out (then increase the time on the timer).
4. Eat a meal at a restaurant where you would normally binge or binge and purge. Keep the meal.
5. Write in your journal before a binge about why you do and don't want to do it.

6. Call three people before you binge, tell them why you do and don't want to binge.
7. Add a specific amount of a starch (bread, chips, potato, etc.) to your dinner.
8. Try a dessert you have not allowed yourself to eat for a long time, eat at least half of it.
9. Buy groceries at least twice a week to have food in the house, making it easier to eat.
10. Make specific plans with a friend, telling them how they can help you during or after the meal.

ASSIGNMENT: MY FOOD GOALS

Now that you have read more than halfway through this Key and (hopefully) have done a few assignments, you probably have some idea about what areas are in need of change. Take a few moments and list some goals that make sense for you. Remember to make them specific, and clear enough so you can measure your progress. You don't have to tackle them all at once. These items can be slowly added to your weekly Goals Sheet.

1. _____
2. _____
3. _____
4. _____
5. _____
6. _____
7. _____
8. _____
9. _____
10. _____

ABOUT MEAL PLANS

A meal plan can be helpful and is sometimes necessary for making changes in your eating behavior. You might feel too overwhelmed trying to decide what to eat throughout the day and need the structure of a meal plan. You might be afraid to trust yourself to eat the right amount of food if it's not specified or written down. If you are unsure if a meal plan is a good idea for you, there are several indicators listed in the next assignment that can help you decide.

ASSIGNMENT: INDICATIONS I NEED A MEAL PLAN

Read through the list of Indications and put an x next to the ones that apply to you.

Indications a meal plan is needed:

_____ *You are out of touch with nutrition information and serving sizes.*

_____ *You have no idea of the amount of food you need.*

_____ *You don't feel or don't trust your hunger and fullness signals.*

_____ *You feel safer knowing ahead of time what you need to eat.*

_____ *You need to gain weight, but are afraid of adding too much food.*

_____ *You are too afraid to eat what you need or want.*

_____ *Your anxiety or compulsivity makes it too hard to make decisions in the moment.*

_____ *You are too entrenched in your current eating behaviors to try anything else.*

_____ *You work well with structure (it aids your success and doesn't cause rebellion).*

_____ *You have tried to get better without a meal plan and it has not worked.*

Even checking one item might indicate a need for a meal plan. If you checked off a few items, this is a strong indication that a meal plan is needed to help you get your food on track.

MAKING A MEAL PLAN

Everyone has different nutritional and caloric needs, so creating a meal plan is a very individualized endeavor, which is why we suggest getting professional advice, but if you are not able or ready to go to a professional, hopefully you can find someone else in your life who would be willing to help you with support and accountability. (Even voicing your commitments or intentions to another person increases the likelihood that you will follow through.) You can use the Conscious Eating Guidelines to help you make and follow a meal plan as a first step in working toward becoming a conscious eater. Eventually conscious eating becomes natural to you and meal plans unnecessary.

Meal Plan Example

Breakfast: 2 eggs, 1 piece of toast, 1 teaspoon butter, jam, 1 orange.
Snack: 1 Clif protein bar.
Lunch: Turkey/mayo sandwich (4 ounces turkey), 1 cup cut-up veggies, and 1 cookie.
Snack: 3 pieces of string cheese, 15 Wheat Thins.
Dinner: Veggie burger with cheese and bun, green salad with 1 tablespoon dressing, and ¼ avocado.
Snack: 1 cup of low-fat ice cream.

The above meal plan is just an example and not meant for you to follow. It is included to show what a specific, concise plan looks like. The plan is easy for you or anyone else you've chosen for support and accountability, to see what you need to eat and determine whether or not you ate it. For best results, keep it simple, balanced, and specific enough for you to follow with some challenges, but not too many too soon. If it is too easy, it will not help you grow and change. If it is too difficult, you might get frustrated and give up. Remember, being dependent on a meal plan is not the ultimate goal, but rather a step toward being able to eat consciously without one.

Here is what a few recovered clients have to say about the process of going from using a meal plan to becoming a conscious eater:

> *"While in treatment, and gaining weight, I needed to follow a meal plan. I was not aware of my hunger and fullness cues and usually felt uncomfortably full after eating anything. Sometimes I felt hungry and full at the same time! It was all very confusing and I could not imagine following the Conscious Eating Guidelines without a specific plan, but they taught me that, even following my meal plan, I could be doing it consciously and therefore be a Conscious Eater. I thought my body was broken, and in a sense it was. It wasn't until I was weight-restored and regularly followed a meal plan for months that I could transition to a more intuitive way of eating using the conscious eating guidelines with no need for a meal plan."*

"One year after leaving intensive treatment I was still very afraid of food and weight gain, and so I tended to eat a narrow range of foods. As my weight gain stabilized, I became more comfortable branching out a bit and trying new things, but still within the constraints of a meal plan. I worked on being a conscious eater while following my meal plan, and over time I felt my brain begin to change. I became less anxious and obsessive and gained increasing comfort with food. As I progressed in recovery, I started a new job and began making friends, and the meal plan didn't always fit in with my work schedule or social life. The meal plan began to feel like a burden rather than a safety zone. I wanted a bigger, freer life and realized that I needed to try conscious eating without a meal plan."

"Initially, I was afraid to follow my hunger cues. I thought that if I ate when I was hungry, I would never stop eating. I didn't trust that my body would tell me when it had enough. Part of my fear stemmed from the way my body responded to restriction during my eating disorder—I was hungry all the time, even though I would rarely admit it. With my dietitian's help, I began integrating conscious eating into my meal plan, noticing when I was hungry and full, as well as the degrees of hunger and fullness. I paid attention to which foods I enjoyed, rather than which foods made me feel safe. I experimented with going outside the meal plan, such as having brunch with friends. My initial forays outside my meal plan, using Conscious Eating principles, reassured me that my weight wouldn't skyrocket because I was able to eat French fries with my friends and not get fat. I began to trust my hunger and fullness signals. If I had a big breakfast, I wasn't as hungry for lunch. Conscious Eating allowed me to let go of counting calories or exchanges and worrying over how eating certain foods would impact my weight. As long as I continue to respond appropriately to my body, I can trust it to tell me when it is hungry and when it has had enough. I've been fully recovered for a few years now and continue to eat this way. For me, Conscious Eating was a major turning point on the path from being in recovery to being recovered."

THERAPEUTIC MEAL SESSIONS

You might find that you repeatedly make goals and plans to challenge or change a behavior, and you just can't get yourself to do it. Instead of giving up, we encourage you to try having a therapeutic meal session with someone else you trust who is aware of your goals or intentions and can support you. Often, the best person for this is a professional you trust. If you are seeing a therapist or dietitian, one of them might be willing to do a meal session with you, but most have never have done these and might not understand what they are, or their value. We have found that many professionals just do not feel comfortable doing meal sessions. You might consider sharing this section or the entire Key with your professional and then see if he or she is open to scheduling a meal session. You might also consider looking into seeing a dietitian or meal coach who specifically provides meal sessions.

Meal sessions are helpful in so many ways that we can't imagine not doing them with our clients. If someone keeps making a goal to have a piece of pizza each week and can't seem to do it, having a meal session can change everything. Having food or a meal with our clients provides them with a trusted, safe, but also authoritative figure, who can be necessary to accomplish a difficult and sometimes even phobic task. A meal buddy, professional or otherwise, can help you eat the appropriate amount, stay with you afterwards to protect you from bingeing or purging, and help process whatever feelings might arise. Meal sessions are the fastest way we know of to bring your food issues to the surface, challenge and overcome your fears, and ultimately change your relationship to food. Eating a meal with someone can also help illuminate things unlikely to come up in a traditional talk therapy session. Meal sessions are not meant to "catch" you at anything, but they can provide you help and support in the moment when your food fears, rituals, and behaviors, such as cutting up your food into bits, ordering salad with no dressing for dinner, or getting up to purge after a pasta meal, are most likely to express themselves. The goal is to help you through these things, not to shame you.

Personal Reflection: GWEN

There were many key moments that led me, or "pushed" me to the next step in my recovery. One of those occurred during the first meal session I ever had. I had already been through a serious medical scare and although it was hard for a doctor to say for sure what caused it, I knew it was my eating disorder. It scared me enough to go to a dietitian, even though I doubted it would help. I assumed she would tell me to eat more of this or do that and I would agree, but not be able to. This is exactly what happened, so she suggested I do a meal session with her and start seeing a therapist. A meal session sounded scary, uncomfortable, and strange, but somehow she convinced me to try.

On my way to the restaurant, I was thinking, "This isn't going to be helpful." I knew I wasn't going to act like I did when I was by myself. I was going to fake it through this lunch by ordering and eating normally. At first, it seemed like my plan was working. I was making small talk and really trying to keep my cool and appear unruffled while scanning the menu for something I could eat that would be considered *normal*. I felt my anxiety increasing, but instead of talking about that, I just said I was getting the chicken sandwich and shut the menu.

When the meal came, I felt overwhelmed immediately but determined to get through it. Quickly, my anxiety skyrocketed, and my attempts to hide it were not working. I started talking, or rather rambling. I picked up the sandwich in front of me and tried to hide my shaking hands. I don't even know how to describe what occurred in the next five minutes, but the embarrassment of it haunted me for years whenever I thought about it. While my mind was racing, my heart was pounding, and my mouth was rambling, my hands were literally pulling apart that sandwich, ripping it apart. Even to this day, as I write this, I can feel my chest tighten and my heart quicken. I was terrified, embarrassed, confused, and on the verge of having a panic attack. I can't say how long this went on, but at some point, the dietitian reached over and held my hands to hold them still and said, "Stop." Her voice was calm, but authoritative, in a way that broke through my panic. I stopped. Then, my eyes filled with tears and at that moment, I felt something crack inside me. The illusion I was living under had shattered and the reality of how sick, scared, and out of control I had become was blaringly obvious. Having a witness made it feel almost unbearable. I could not even fake it through one lunch and I was scared.

Everything changed after that meal session. I went for a couple more sessions with the dietitian and therapist, and then I agreed to go into treatment. It was clear to everyone, including me, I was sicker and more entrenched than anyone had realized and I needed more help. Because this dietitian understood eating disorders as well as she did, she was able to help and contain me in a very frightening moment, and that moment led to my getting the help I really needed. As difficult as it was then, I am grateful to her.

ADVANCED MEAL SESSIONS

Most meal sessions are done to provide good role modeling: eating in a healthy way to help clients do the same. There is another kind of meal session we do that is at an entirely different level. We realized that after a while our clients needed to step up the nature of their meals sessions in order to deal with real-world situations. You have probably experienced eating with others who inadvertently do or say things about food or dieting that are difficult or triggering to you. In these "advanced meal sessions," we intentionally set up triggering situations to help desensitize clients to the real world without resorting to their eating disorders. For example, what would you do if your friend, roommate, or co-worker ordered a salad with no dressing and talked about her new diet?

Advanced meal sessions (and other kinds of advanced sessions, like going to a gym or buying clothes) can help you learn how to tolerate your feelings and build the resilience you'll need to do the right thing for yourself, even if you are triggered by something, or someone, which *will* happen.

Planning these sessions is collaborative, and we only do them when a client is willing and ready. Even though clients know in advance that we will be doing something triggering at the meal session, we don't tell them exactly what it is, so they aren't completely ready for it. The opportunity to practice tolerating and responding to these kinds of situations when it is not actually happening, but it *is* happening, seems to provide a safe, but challenging halfway step that helps being able to do it in real life. It can be pretty funny as well, and a little humor around food is helpful. Clients can't help but laugh listening to us ordering the diet plate, or saying some of the triggering things we say to them.

If you have a therapist or a dietitian, ask if he or she would be willing to do this with you, however, you can also do this with a willing friend or family member, but be careful whom you choose. You can tell the support person what their role is so he or she is prepared to challenge you by intentionally triggering you in some way, or you can provide a list with a few and let it be a surprise.

Examples of triggering situations we have used in advanced meal or food sessions:

1. Go out to lunch and have the support person make comments on what or how much you are eating.
2. Order first at a restaurant and then have the support person order much less food.
3. Go out to eat where the support person doesn't order carbs and discusses how bad they are.
4. Eat a challenging meal while the support person asks about the calories in everything and then barely eats.
5. Have someone come to the grocery store with you, and whenever you choose an item, they point out a lower-calorie version.

If you aren't ready for this yet, that is okay. In fact, we refer to them as "advanced meal sessions" because they are. You need to be ready and when you are, these experiences are very valuable.

ASSIGNMENT: TRIGGERING MEAL CHALLENGES

Find a person who will help you with a triggering meal challenge. Ask them to go to a meal with you and do things that will likely trigger you, but not tell you ahead of time.

Tell your support person that he or she has to come up with things that could happen to you in the real world. For example, push the food around on their plate, get up from the meal several times, or order plain grilled fish when you order a pizza. Are you getting the picture?

List a few of your own food challenges or triggering ideas to give your support person:

1. _____
2. _____
3. _____
4. _____
5. _____

Write about your triggering meal experience. Include what happened, how you handled it, and what you learned by it. _____

_____

_____

_____

_____

_____

Personal Reflection: GWEN

Last week, I had a "challenge meal session" with my client Mimi. When she began treatment, Mimi was afraid to eat in restaurants or even in front of others. Today she is able to eat at any restaurant, and is doing well in her recovery, but when eating with friends she often under eats or slides backwards in some way. Mimi's intention for the meal outing was to make it challenging for herself by ordering something she loves but has been too afraid to order (panini) and she also agreed that I could add a few "advanced" challenges as well.

After she ordered her lunch, and it was my turn, I ordered a small salad, no croutons, with diet dressing on the side. She knew ahead of time that I was going to challenge her, but she didn't know exactly what I would do or say. Even though she knew I was only doing it to trigger her, it was still very difficult for her to tolerate and she was uncomfortable, but not so uncomfortable she couldn't get through it and eat her food. The situation was just enough to challenge her and give her the opportunity to practice responding from her Healthy Self. We processed her thoughts and feelings and came up with healthy self-statements she could say at other times when this happens. Here are the things she came up with:

1. I've already been down that road. I know where it leads and I don't want that anymore.
2. I don't want to let others control what I eat.
3. If I just eat what she is eating, I will be hungry in an hour and there won't be any food.
4. I don't know how hungry others are, or what others have eaten today, or will eat. Comparing makes no sense.
5. Others are on their own path. I need to remember to stay on mine.
6. What others eat is none of my business. I need to keep my eyes on my own plate.

KEY 5: IT IS ABOUT THE FOOD

From Mimi:

"Even though I knew Gwen was going to trigger me at the lunch outing, it still freaked me out. It was SO triggering. My eating disorder voice was screaming at me. I felt irritable and anxious, and I wasn't sure if I was going to be able to eat what I ordered when it came. Talking about it helped. It took me out of my head, anyway. Knowing it was part of the therapy made it a lot easier. I knew it was practice for me. My mom is always ordering a half salad, and I get so mad at her because it makes me scared and then I don't want to eat anything and we start arguing and things get ugly. This gave me the experience of feeling all of those feelings and then being able to still do what I needed to do for myself.

This was literally the first time I have ever been able to do that, and it gave me hope that I can do it next time with someone else. I am almost looking forward to it, just to prove to others and myself I have progressed. I know I said I never wanted to do that again, but I changed my mind. I think I am ready for another challenge meal session."
—MS

SOUL FOOD

As we said earlier, all the other Keys will help you change your relationship with food. Key 8 will help you understand why, and how to bring soul into it. If you just needed nutrition from food, you could eat like astronauts and get your food from tubes that contain the essential nutrients. The process of preparing and eating food offers us endless opportunities for connecting with ourselves, others, and the world around us, and is a source for *pleasure, connection, creativity, miraculous wonder, and soulfulness.*

Pleasure: We have hunger and we have appetite. If you are a normal person and have been without food for days, you are hunger driven and would likely eat almost anything. You don't ask yourself, "Hmm, what am I hungry for?" Your biology drives you to find food, any food, so you can survive. But appetite is about desire. Food gives endless pleasure to our senses—smell, taste, and even touch. We do not seek to help you just satisfy your physical hunger, but to appreciate and fulfill your appetite, your desire, that will fully return when you heal your relationship to food.

Creativity: Food can be alchemy. Have you ever watched a great chef cook? Actually, anyone who cooks is an alchemist, but watching a great chef is mind-blowing, hence the popularity of cooking shows. Try making a soufflé or a special sauce or baking the perfect pie crust. Being able to take ingredients, put food together, and come up with meals that taste and look great takes a lot of creativity. Knowing when to follow a recipe and when to wing it with a little more of this or less of that is wonderfully creative.

Personal Reflection: CAROLYN

I am not a good cook, nor was my mother. I did not learn creativity in this arena. Then there's Gwen, who can go into a kitchen and make a great dish out of all kinds of leftovers, after I have claimed, "There's nothing to eat in here." However, I was in Italy recently on a family vacation, and we took a cooking class where we made our own ravioli and tiramisu. I was amazed at how into it I was. It took hours but was incredibly enlightening, fun, creative, and joyful, especially to do together with my family. Since cooking is not my best suit, I get creative around the ambience of meals, adding interesting centerpieces to the table, nice plateware, and silverware, candles, and music. We encourage you to try making the food or the ambience special and see how it makes you feel.

Miraculous Wonder: The fact that food becomes you is miraculous. It's hard to even wrap your mind around the fact that you can plant a seed, which with water and sunlight becomes a tomato or an apple that you eat, and it becomes *you*. We suggest planting something, caring for it, watching it grow, and then enjoy eating it and knowing it is becoming you. Without the nutrients food provides, things can go bad, really bad. You can become exhausted, bleed inside your joints causing severe pain, develop red-and-blue spots and dark patches on your skin, bleed around your gums and teeth to the point where your teeth fall out, and become jaundiced . . . all for lacking just one nutrient, Vitamin C. Vitamin C deficiency, also called scurvy, leads to all those symptoms. If you take any time to explore what nutrients are and what they do to make our bodies work the way they do, you too will know miraculous wonders.

Connection: "Let's go out to dinner," "Meet me for lunch," "You want to grab a bite?" "Come over to our house for dinner," "Are you going to the BBQ?" There are millions of these phrases being said every minute of every day that reveal the connection between food and relationships. We probably don't have to tell you that if you can't participate in eating with others, your social life changes drastically. Food and community are at the heart and soul of relationships.

Soulfulness: By doing any of the things discussed in this section, you will be bringing soul into your life with food. If you grow it, create it, bless it, and dine on it rather than just consume it; add candles, flowers, and music to it; go outside and watch the sunset while eating it; all this brings soul into your relationship with food.

Our goal is that you do not just see food as a way to survive but as a conduit to experience all the things we have just described. Right now, the idea of this kind of relationship with food might seem remote or unattainable. So now we share meal blessings written by two former clients, both of whom had the worst relationship with food you can imagine. When the eating disorder is no longer ruling your life, you will be amazed at what you also will be able to do with and say about food.

Meal Blessings

Food
Thank you for being light to my heart.
Thank you for being energy so I can be
And thank you for how good you taste
And for how you smell
And for how you delight my soul.
Food . . . I pay attention to you on purpose
to thank you for sustaining me.
I love this life
You transform your energy into mine.
Thank you.
—Amen EV

"As I am about to eat, I bless the food for its ability to sustain me
I honor the journey it has made so far and the journey it will take inside of me
I thank you food for giving up your life and for the pleasure you are about to give
So that I can live mine.
I am no longer blind to the miracle that you are
I no longer resist what you have to offer
The soul in me recognizes the soul in you
And we become one."
—GB

LEARNING TO ACCEPT YOUR NATURAL BODY WEIGHT

As we like to say, there are only two ways to deal with anything, including your natural body weight and shape, acceptance or resistance. Resistance to the reality of "what is" causes endless suffering and interferes with your ability to make the best choices for yourself. We are all born with a genetically predisposed weight and shape. You may not like your body and you may want to change it, but there is only so much you can do without endless amounts of effort and compromising your health or happiness, or both.

If you are above your natural weight: You might be thinking, *I can't accept my body at this weight*. Even though this will be hard for you to hear, not accepting your body is like not accepting gravity. It is what it is, right here, right now, even if for you it is overweight. Your resistance to your body isn't the motivator you might think it is, and it is directly interfering with your feelings about yourself and your ability to make good decisions.

Accepting your body does not mean accepting the situation that got you where you are. You can change your situation by changing your eating habits. For example, if bingeing has caused you to gain weight, you can stop bingeing and your weight will go back into your normal range. Not accepting, or "resisting" where your body is right now does not change anything; it only causes more suffering, more self-reproach, and keeps you stuck in whatever cycle has currently taken over.

If you are under your natural weight: You might be thinking, *Okay, you want me to accept my weight . . . I do, now please let me keep it that way*. Accepting your body right now, as it is, means accepting reality, and if you are underweight it means accepting that. Acceptance means not trying to resist the truth about your body, for example, pretending you weigh more or hiding under big clothes. You will ultimately decide whether or not to change, but acceptance of where you are now is important.

Acceptance means freeing the mind from resistance, paving the way for you to move forward, making the necessary changes in your eating situation that will bring about your health, natural weight, and recovery. The goal should never be about weight anyway—that just gets in the way. The goal is for you to be able to eat the foods you need to eat to be healthy, the freedom to eat the foods you enjoy, and to be able to eat with others. Being able to do those things will bring you peace, contentment, and happiness. Focusing on weight will not help you get there.

What would it look like if you were to accept where your body is right now? Remember, acceptance of this doesn't mean that you have to like it, or affect whether or not you change it in the future. But if you want to change, accepting where you are will guide you to turn your attention to where your relationship with food needs to heal. You may have forgotten what it feels like to be at your natural weight, or maybe you aren't even sure where that is for you. There are several physical, social, and psychological indicators that can help determine if you are in your natural weight range. The following assignments will help you take a look at these and assess where you are.

ASSIGNMENT: PHYSICAL INDICATORS OF A HEALTHY WEIGHT RANGE

Put an X in front of each item that describes your current physical situation.

_____ *Weight range is maintained without engaging in eating-disordered behaviors (for example, restricting, bingeing, purging, or compulsive exercise).*

_____ *Regular menstruation, ovulation, and hormone levels (age-appropriate).*

_____ *Normal blood pressure, heart rate, and body temperature.*

_____ *Normal blood chemistry values such as electrolytes, blood counts, liver function, thyroid, etc.*

_____ *Normal bone density for age.*

_____ *Normal levels of energy (not exhausted, shaky, or agitated all day).*

_____ *Normal (or at least some) sex drive.*

_____ *Ability to concentrate and focus (reading, movies, work, school).*

_____ *Ability to identify and respond to the body's hunger or fullness signals.*

Look at the areas that you did not check. Any one of these can be an indicator that your body is trying to compensate for unhealthy eating habits or weight. If there are any categories that you can't answer, for example, you don't know if your blood chemistry panel or your bone density is normal, then it is important to find out. Of course, there might be other explanations for why you would have low energy or issues with your blood pressure, but chances are they are the result or consequence of your eating disorder.

ASSIGNMENT: PSYCHOLOGICAL AND SOCIAL INDICATORS YOU ARE IN A HEALTHY WEIGHT RANGE

Put an X in front of each item that describes your current situation.

_____ *Don't avoid foods simply for fear of getting fat.*
_____ *Normal social life with authentic, in-person relationships (not just online).*
_____ *No (or extremely minimal) obsessive thoughts, cravings, or urges to binge.*
_____ *Can choose freely what to eat both when alone and with others.*
_____ *Do not hide food or lie about eating.*
_____ *No issues eating at restaurants, friend's houses, parties, and on vacations.*
_____ *Do not have to eat according to certain food rules or rituals.*
_____ *No erratic mood swings.*
_____ *Ability to focus on social interaction while eating with people.*
_____ *I detect and appropriately respond to my body's hunger or fullness signals.*

It might seem confusing to you that the items on this list are indicators of being in your healthy weight range. What we have found is that if you can say "yes" to the items on this list, it indicates you are probably eating normally and therefore in a healthy weight range. The more items you left unchecked, the stronger the indication that you aren't eating normally and therefore are less likely to be in a healthy weight range. Go over the indicators that didn't get a check mark, and come up with one or two goals you can put on your Goals Sheet, which will help you take steps towards checking them all off.

Goal: _____

_____

Goal: _____

_____

GETTING RID OF THE SCALE

Weighing yourself is not helpful. In Key 5 of our book, we discuss the reasons why we believe you should get rid of your scale in great detail. If you are addicted to weighing because you are underweight and afraid of gaining weight, then weighing is a sure way to sabotage your efforts and recovery. You will wince, recoil, and suffer at the sign of the slightest weight gain, even if you know this is the goal. You will be afraid it is going too fast, or you are gaining too much, and you will react. This pattern will cause you to gain and lose the same few pounds endlessly.

If you are addicted to the scale because you are above your natural weight and want to lose weight, you must let go of weight loss as goal. This does not mean you will have to stay at your current weight forever if it isn't your healthy weight. It does mean that you can't focus on weight loss and recovery at the same time, no matter what you weigh. Recovery and weight loss are two goals that interfere with each other. For example, if you want to lose weight and you have bulimia or binge eating disorder and spend a week binge free, that is a major success. However, if you get on the scale and have not lost weight, you may feel so disappointed you give up, thinking all your efforts are not paying off. Over and over, we have seen the desire to lose weight impede recovery. Remember, accepting where your body is right now does not mean you cannot enact healthy things to create change.

We are not saying that your weight has no bearing or does not matter. We are not saying, "Who cares what you weigh, just be happy." We are not saying that no one should weigh you or keep track of what is happening with your weight. On the contrary, if you have anorexia it is important for a health professional to weigh you to make sure you are making progress and to reassure you it's not happening too fast. What we are saying is, no matter what the diagnosis or why you think weighing yourself is helpful, trust us and get rid of the scale and let go of weighing yourself.

LET GO OF WEIGHING YOURSELF

Read the above heading many times. Post it around your house. It may seem impossible or contrary to what you have heard in other philosophies such as Cognitive Behavioral Therapy or Family Based Treatment, both of which promote routine weighing and knowing your weight. We have found with our collective 50-some years of experience that weighing is not conducive to recovery. We believe that weaning our clients off the scale is another huge aspect of our success with helping so many people become fully recovered.

In the *8 Keys* book, we included a lot of information on why weighing is contraindicated to recovery, including a conversation we had about weighing when Gwen was in treatment at Monte Nido. Readers have told us that this information was very useful in helping them give up the scale so if you have not read it, you might consider doing so. You're welcome . . . You will thank us later.

Quotes from clients who never thought they could stop weighing:

"I tried for years to recover from my eating disorder, but the whole time I was weighing myself, sometimes daily, sometimes multiple times a day. I could not believe it when Carolyn suggested that I stop weighing myself and explained how it was getting in the way. I worked with her for a year before giving up my scale. It was only after that when I started to really make progress. Now I know that the scale kept me sick for a lot longer than I needed to be. Everywhere I go, I notice scales and I shudder at how I used to be possessed and trapped by them. At least now I'm free." —CR

"When my therapist told me to stop weighing, I panicked. I was terrified and thought my anxiety would skyrocket. How else would I know how I should feel, what I should eat? The first three days were hard. I thought about it a lot. But after that, it was a huge relief. I needed some consistent reassurance during my recovery that my weight was okay, but that was enough because I trusted the people helping me. I will never go back to weighing again." —AB

"There were times I weighed myself many times a day just to reassure myself I was okay. I used the scale to tell me if it was a good day, a bad day, or an okay

day. If I saw a scale I had to get on it, but it always ended badly because I was never happy with what I saw and I always reacted with my eating disorder. I had to bring in my scale to my therapist, because otherwise I couldn't stop weighing. If you would have asked me if would ever be able to break this habit, I would have said no, but I did it and it was a major turning point for me and now I'm fully recovered and have no use for a scale."

—RL

Final Thoughts

Learning to eat differently and creating a new relationship with food will be trying and difficult, but will become natural with time. It will also be well worth it. A good relationship with food will help you live a much longer and much more enjoyable life. Your body really does need its fuel (food) to be healthy and happy. As we have discussed in this Key, food is life, alchemy, and pleasure, and eating is one of the most natural and enjoyable ways we have for connecting with others. Challenging the Eating Disorder self, breaking your old rules, keeping a food journal, making a meal plan, and learning about conscious eating are important and challenging, but also very attainable steps toward recovery. If you have not done any of the assignments in this Key yet, please reconsider, and try starting somewhere, even if it is a small step.

Don't get discouraged. If you find making changes too hard and need additional help, the next Key might be what you need. Key 6 is designed to help you with strategies for behavior change and will also assist in identifying and transforming not only your overt eating disorder behaviors, but others lurking around that you might not realize are there.

KEY 6
CHANGING YOUR BEHAVIORS

"Some people prefer the certainty of misery rather than the uncertainty of change."

"Better the devil you know, than the devil you don't know."

There is no way around it. You will have to make changes in order to get better. You have to let go of some things, try new things, take risks, feel uncomfortable, accept that it will feel worse before it feels better, and believe that things can be different.

There are so many things to change that it can seem overwhelming. This makes sense because you are trying to change how you approach life, not just food. Practicing what you learned in Key 4 can help lessen reactivity. When difficult thoughts and feelings arise, allow yourself to feel whatever is there, challenge them, or simply let them pass on through.

Key 6 is about helping with the difficult process of changing behaviors. To begin with, it is important to clarify which behaviors we are talking about here. There are the overt eating disorder behaviors like bingeing, purging, or restricting that will have to change in order for you to recover, but there are also many other behaviors that, while not always recognized as eating disorder behaviors, are just as likely to sabotage your recovery if you don't stop doing them. Weighing, counting calories, and excessive exercise are a few examples. These are usually behaviors that millions of people do with no serious consequences, yet for those with eating disorders these behaviors can be a slippery slope that will interfere with long-term recovery. The assignments in this key are designed to address both the overt and other recovery sabotaging behaviors.

Tip: Using the Goals Sheet will help you target and keep track of what behaviors you are working on each week. This keeps tasks more concrete and manageable and helps to keep you accountable.

ASSIGNMENT: WHY IS IT HARD TO CHANGE?

You are reading this book because some part of you would like to change. We know that change is difficult and obstacles get in the way, but you're the best person to ascertain why changing has been or is hard for you. Take some time to think about and write down the reasons you think changing your eating disorder behaviors is hard for you.

_____
_____
_____
_____
_____

WHY CHANGE?

If change were easy you would have done it already. Changing your behaviors is difficult for all the reasons you listed in the previous assignment, and then some. Knowing the reasons why you want to change is important, but usually not enough to make it happen. Chances are you know your behavior is dangerous to your physical and mental health and wellbeing. For example, you have probably heard that restricting lowers your metabolism, making it even harder to deal with your weight. You may know about the consequences of laxative abuse, including permanent damage of your colon and a possible colostomy bag. You probably have read about the long-term effects of vomiting. If you haven't heard or read about the risks and complications of your behaviors and you want more information, you can find it online or read Key 6 of the *8 Keys* book. Chances are you do know that what you are doing is harmful and at some point will have negative and perhaps serious and irreversible consequences, and you probably still find it extremely hard to stop. Understanding *what* behaviors you need to change, and *why* you want to change is helpful, but usually these aren't enough. This Key will help you learn *how* to make difficult changes in your life.

CHANGING YOUR "OVERT" EATING DISORDER BEHAVIORS

To start this work on change, the first step is targeting your specific overt behaviors. For example, you might not binge during the day, but binge at night; you might be eating three meals, but not enough at each meal; maybe you only purge after eating out, or take laxatives on the weekends. The idea is to target your behaviors and be as specific as possible. After you have done that, you can work on them one at a time, or even a few at once, depending on what works best for you and what is possible given your level of motivation and support.

ASSIGNMENT: MY OVERT EATING DISORDER BEHAVIORS

List 10 overt eating disorder behaviors. Remember to be very specific (e.g., I skip breakfast, I never eat desserts, I binge and purge whenever I go out to a restaurant). It is likely that these are not your only behaviors needing change, but you can start with this list. Use the weekly Goals Sheet to focus on one or more of your behaviors at a time.

1. _____
2. _____
3. _____
4. _____
5. _____
6. _____
7. _____
8. _____
9. _____
10. _____

RECOVERY-SABOTAGING BEHAVIORS

Most likely, there are many other behaviors you engage in that aren't as obvious or overtly eating disordered, but they contribute to and will keep you stuck in your eating disorder. While it is true that many people without eating disorders can engage in these behaviors without it becoming "unhealthy," if you have an eating disorder, these very same behaviors will sabotage your progress in recovery. You might find yourself strongly resisting the idea of giving up some of these related behaviors or not understanding or believing they will sabotage your recovery. Try to put that aside for now and look at the following list.

ASSIGNMENT: CHECKLIST OF RECOVERY-SABOTAGING BEHAVIORS

Review this list and put a check next to any of the behaviors you engage in and add any others you can think of.

_____ *Compulsive exercise.*
_____ *Counting calories (or fat grams or carbohydrates).*
_____ *Reading food labels.*
_____ *Measuring or weighing your food.*
_____ *Chewing and spitting out food.*
_____ *Food rituals (cutting food into bits, chewing excessively, eating only on small dishes).*
_____ *Comparing yourself to others either in real life or in magazines or on television*
_____ *Body checking and measuring.*
_____ *Keeping clothes that fit only when you are underweight.*
_____ *Fasting, cleanses, or detox diets.*
_____ *Diet pills.*
_____ *Only eating vegan food.*
_____ *Only eating organic or raw foods.*
_____ *Weighing yourself.*
_____ *Other.* _____
_____ *Other.* _____
_____ *Other.* _____

RESISTANCE TO CHANGE IS NORMAL

There will be many reasons for your resistance to change, and you will likely feel more resistant to making some changes over others. Review the list of your overt eating disorder behaviors and your recovery-sabotaging behaviors and ponder these questions. Do you notice or feel resistance at even the idea of changing them? Do you feel differently about changing the overt behaviors than you do about the others? Notice the various thoughts and feelings that come up and get in the way of you trying to change.

If you simply *do not want to change*, we ask you to just read this Key with an open mind. Perhaps something we say will help you think or feel differently. In any case, if you decide you want to at least explore the idea of change, you can begin some of the assignments and see what happens. In the end, it is always your decision whether or not to proceed.

ASSIGNMENT: RESISTANCE TO CHANGING MY OVERT EATING DISORDER BEHAVIORS

Assuming at least a part of you would like to change, select two of your overt behaviors listed and write down what you think is in the way of making any changes. This exercise will help to illuminate any beliefs, thoughts, or fears, which have now become obstacles in your recovery. Thoughts like, "I am not strong enough to change" can create feelings of hopelessness and helplessness, which can keep you from even trying. If every answer is, "I'm afraid of gaining weight or getting fat," write that down and then add to your answer what you are afraid will happen if you gain weight. A helpful question to ask yourself might be, "And if that happens, then what"?

1. My overt behavior: _____
   What gets in the way of change: _____
   _____
   _____

2. My overt behavior: _____
   What gets in the way of change: _____
   _____
   _____

ASSIGNMENT: RESISTANCE TO CHANGING RECOVERY-SABOTAGING BEHAVIORS

Assuming at least a part of you would like to change, select two of your recovery-sabotaging behaviors you checked off or listed that you would like to change and write down what you think is in the way of you being able to make changes.

Again, think of any beliefs or fears you are aware of and try to add what you are afraid will happen if your fear comes true. (And if that happens, then what?)

1. *Recovery-sabotaging behavior:* _____
   _____
   _____
   _____

   What gets in the way of change: _____
   _____
   _____
   _____
   _____

2. *Recovery-sabotaging behavior:* _____
   _____
   _____
   _____

   What gets in the way of change: _____
   _____
   _____
   _____
   _____

Look at any differences in your resistance to change between your overt vs. recovery-sabotaging behaviors. Is there anything that stands out for you?
_____
_____

Look over your reasons why you are afraid to change. We are sure you can come up with a number of reasons why change is too hard, not right, or not going to work for you. Since we can't be there to respond personally to your answers, we have included a list of the common reasons we hear from clients about why they can't or don't want to change, followed by our responses.

COMMON REASONS FOR RESISTANCE

All our clients have resistance or ambivalence regarding change. We expect this and are ready for it. The following list contains some of the most common reasons clients have given about why they are resistance to change. The truth is we had many of these thoughts too, before we changed our own eating disorder behaviors.

_____ 1. *"I don't feel ready to change."*
_____ 2. *"I don't know how or where to even start."*
_____ 3. *"I am too afraid of what will happen if I change."*
_____ 4. *"I don't think I am strong enough to change."*
_____ 5. *"My behaviors are just automatic now and out of my control."*
_____ 6. *"I don't have the tolerance or patience to change."*
_____ 7. *"Some people can change, but I can't."*
_____ 8. *"I don't think that what it takes to change is worth it."*
_____ 9. *"I am not worth it."*
_____ 10. *"If I change one thing, people will expect me to change more."*
_____ 11. *"My behavior is not that bad,"* or *"My behavior is way better than it used to be."*
_____ 12. *"Why should I change this? Other people do it all the time."*

ASSIGNMENT: MY REASONS FOR RESISTANCE TO CHANGE

Put an X in front of any of the reasons for resistance that you personally relate to from the previous list. Then find the number you picked and read our response.

1. **"I don't feel ready to change."**
If you wait until you are "ready," change may never happen. No one ever feels totally ready because there is fear and ambivalence involved. Changing a behavior involves taking risks, and there will be times when you will need to go out of your comfort zone. It is a process that takes time and practice.

2. **"I don't know how or where to even start."**
Start small. Take baby steps like delaying a binge 20 minutes rather than trying not to binge. Small steps can be the best, and often the only way to make difficult changes. You might not think delaying a binge is that helpful, but it is

helping you become increasingly more in control. Take a risk and try it. If you feel the urge to binge, set a timer and delay the binge 3 to 5 minutes to start, then gradually longer. When you do this, you strengthen the part of you that doesn't want to binge (your Healthy Self). Oftentimes, if you are able to delay a behavior for 15 to 20 minutes, the strong urge subsides and getting through it becomes easier.

Another example of a small risk is eating a challenging food, which is a food your Eating Disorder Self might call "scary" or "fattening." We know it probably feels too hard to just start eating it, or to trust that you can just eat a normal amount. One way you can start small is by just allowing yourself to have one bite. If you don't lose control or *get fat* from that one bite, perhaps you can take two bites the next day, and then three the next. If you don't trust yourself to actually take the bite or eat a bite without bingeing, ask someone to be there with you. You don't have to change anything all at once. If you take the time, you can figure out a small way to go in a new direction.

3. *"I am too afraid of what will happen if I change."*
Fear of the unknown is understandable. The best way to deal with fear of the unknown is to gather information to make the unknown more known. You can find a professional or a recovered person and talk to him or her about what is likely to happen when you make changes in whatever you are thinking about changing. The key to change is learning to break it down into small steps so that the change is not so dramatic and you can begin to get a sense of safety in knowing that nothing horrible will happen.

4. *"I don't think I am strong enough to change."*
Remember, your eating disorder can't be stronger than you. You give it all its power, so if you are strong enough to engage in the behavior, you can channel that energy into being strong enough to not do so . . . even if it takes time to make that happen. Eventually, not engaging in your behaviors will take no effort at all. Think about a time before you had your eating disorder. Did it take strength not to restrict, binge, or purge?

5. "My behaviors are just automatic now and out of my control."

Things do get to the point where they feel automatic. There was a time when we both thought there was no way we would be able to change our behaviors. However, since behaviors become automatic over time, the same process applies to getting better. If you can slowly decrease your behavior and get to the point of stopping it altogether, then over time not doing it will become automatic. Another idea we suggest to clients is to do at least one thing before engaging in the behavior. You might call a friend, journal, or write out a dialogue between your Eating Disorder Self and Healthy Self. When you try to interrupt the cycle, your Healthy Self comes forward and gets a little taste of being in control, even if only for a brief period of time.

6. "I don't have the tolerance or patience to change."

Learning to tolerate difficult feelings is a crucial life skill, as is patience. Nobody is born with these skills, and everyone has to work on them. Having realistic expectations and thinking of recovery like a hike to the top of a mountain instead of a sprint might be useful. It most likely took you a long time to get to this place, so be realistic and fair to yourself, and realize it is going to take you awhile to get out. Six months from now will be here before you know it. You will have to wait for the time to pass, regardless of how you choose to spend it—in your eating disorder or working on recovery. It's up to you.

7. "Some people can change, but I can't."

There is no such thing as not being able to change. There are some things you might not be able to change, but how you manage your food isn't one of them. It might be difficult and scary to change your behaviors and get well, but it is not impossible.

8. "I don't think that what it takes to change is worth it."

At first, it's hard to feel like changing is worth it because you are going to feel worse before you feel better. Until you recover, you can't really know if it's worth it. We can say we have yet to find a recovered person who says that it wasn't worth it. We know that changing takes a bit of faith in the alternative, but unless you do it, you will not know. We do feel confident saying that staying in your eating disorder is for sure not worth it.

9. *"I am not worth it."*
You might feel you are not worth it, or say you don't deserve to get better. What would you say to anyone else who said that to you? We are pretty sure you would tell anyone else that they are worth it and deserve to get better, even if you didn't know all the reasons they had for thinking otherwise.

You might have reasons for feeling unworthy that date back to before the eating disorder, but having an eating disorder shrouds your self-worth, complicating things even further. Ask yourself why you are not worth it. Do those same reasons make others unworthy? Ask yourself, "What does someone have to do in order to be worth it?" When you really examine this, you will probably agree that no one has to do anything to be worthy of changing and improving his or her life.

10. *"If I change one thing, people will expect me to change more."*
Change is always going to be up to you. Expectations from others can feel bad and make changing harder. The people who care about you might see you change something and get hopeful or excited and become overly eager to see more. They may see you change one thing and think that change is easy or you are now "on your way." You might be afraid of failing or disappointing others. Consider letting your friends, family, therapist, or whoever you are concerned might have these expectations know how you are feeling, what's helpful or not helpful to say. How else would they know?

11. *"My behavior is not that bad," or "My behavior is way better than it used to be."*
This type of rationalizing is not relevant. Rather than compare yourself to how you were before to justify what you are doing now, compare yourself to how you want to be or being recovered. This will help motivate you to keep moving forward and not settle for a small life. Ask yourself, "Is my behavior something I really want to continue, is it in my best interest? Can I have the life I really want? Can I feel good about myself?" Even if you are better off now than at some other time, why settle for living life less sick when you can be all well?

Usually behaviors wax and wane and get progressively worse over time. It's good to acknowledge progress and where you have been, but often what you are doing is still unhealthy, mentally and physically. One client who stopped bingeing and purging said she "only chews and spits now," which she thought was healthier and not that bad for her. As we explored her behavior more, it became apparent that it was just as compulsive, shameful, secretive, and as in the way of her relationships as her bulimia had been.

12. *"Why should I change this? Other people do it all the time."*
First of all, you don't have to change anything. The idea is to change things that have caused you problems or will get in the way of *you* getting better. People who don't have eating disorders can do certain behaviors like skip a meal or weigh themselves, and it does not cause them any problems. That can be difficult to see and accept, but if they don't have an eating disorder, these behaviors are not problematic. If you had skin cancer, it would be best for you to change your behavior by avoiding the sun and wearing hats and sunscreen every moment. Seeing others out enjoying the beach without having to take these precautions would be very difficult and might seem unfair, but going out in the sun because others do it all the time and are okay would be reckless.

13. *"I'll gain weight and I can't tolerate that."*
This one is last because it is one we hear almost every time we ask the question and is often the code for a deeper fear or belief. There are actually two beliefs here. Some people have to gain weight to get well, but the belief that you can't tolerate it is just that—a belief. Learning to tolerate uncomfortable feelings, like the knowledge that you need to gain weight, or gained some weight, is not much different than learning to tolerate any other uncomfortable feeling you need to accept in order to live a normal and full life. Think about it, if you couldn't tolerate the reality that your dog will die one day, it would be almost impossible to enjoy or even have a pet. We all learn to tolerate certain truths or feelings so we can get through the day and enjoy our lives. We all have to find a way to tolerate the reality that we can't protect our loved ones, we all die one day, bad things happen to good people, and many others. Although you might believe you can't tolerate weight gain, it's not true. As counterintuitive as it might seem, tolerating your healthy weight is not only possible, it actually gets easier with time rather than harder. Body size and body image are

not correlated in the way you might believe they are. If that were true, all the underweight people with anorexia would have better body image than normal weight or overweight people, and that is simply not the case at all.

SPECIFIC RECOVERY-SABOTAGING BEHAVIORS

Compulsive Exercise

One of the most commonly "justified" behaviors is compulsive exercise. It is easy to defend a behavior that we are all told is good for us, and even critical for optimum health, but too much of a good thing is bad. The question is when does this good thing go bad? In short, you know you are a compulsive exerciser when your exercise isn't a choice anymore. Instead of your workouts being about health and fitness, you feel obligated to do it, driven by fear and unable to slow down or stop in spite of adverse consequences to your physical, emotional, or social life.

ASSIGNMENT: SIGNS OF COMPULSIVE EXERCISE

Look at the list and check all that apply.

- _____ *You judge a day as "good" or "bad" based on how much you exercised.*
- _____ *You base your self-worth on how much you exercise.*
- _____ *You never take a break from exercise.*
- _____ *You exercise even though you are injured.*
- _____ *You arrange work and social obligations around exercise.*
- _____ *You cancel family or social engagements to exercise.*
- _____ *You become irritable or anxious when something interferes with your exercise.*
- _____ *You sometimes wish you could stop but are unable to.*
- _____ *You know that others are worried about how much you exercise.*
- _____ *You always have to do more and rarely feel satisfied with what you have done.*
- _____ *You exercise to compensate for overeating (or just eating).*

Even if you checked only one item on the list, it indicates a need to look further into your exercise behavior to be sure that it is not interfering with your recovery.

CHANGING YOUR EXERCISE BEHAVIOR

Over-exercising is always bad for your body. Injuries, bone loss, and hormone imbalance are just a few problems that can arise. Psychological aspects are also present and need attention; we almost always see issues of intimacy, as well as anxiety and rigid thinking in our clients who over-exercise. Think about it.

Do you turn to exercise when troubled or under stress, rather than seeking help from others?

Do people who love you complain about your exercise interfering with the relationship?

ASSIGNMENT: GETTING FEEDBACK FROM OTHERS

Ask someone close to you what he or she truly feels about your exercise behaviors. Try to stay receptive and just listen without interrupting or getting defensive. Then, come up with one goal for this week that involves stopping, reducing, or changing an exercise habit. If you have already heard a lot from the people around you and you know you need to change, you can make a goal now. Ask someone for support to help you, e.g., perhaps they can go for a walk with you to prevent you from running, or someone can go to the beach with you on a rest day you need to give yourself.

My exercise goal: _____
_____

Who or what can help me accomplish this: _____
_____
_____

Counting Calories, Fat Grams, Carbohydrates, etc.

Counting calories, fat grams, or anything else may start out making you feel safe or in control, but over time it can become an obsession that you can't stop. Most people admit that they wish they could stop but think it is impossible. We both remember having those same concerns, yet neither of us counts up calories or anything else today, automatically or otherwise.

ASSIGNMENT: MY COUNTING BEHAVIOR

Write down any counting behavior you have, and then pick one small goal that you could work on to start making a change in this area.

My counting behaviors: _____
_____

One small step I will take in this area: _____
_____

Who or what can help you with this change? _____
_____

Tips for Change:
1. Do not write any numbers down!
2. *Stop looking* at labels, calories, or fat grams in the foods you are eating.
3. Take a Sharpie marker and black out all the information on the food you buy, or ask someone else to do it for you.
4. Eat a food that you don't know the calories of.

If you eat even one new food and don't know how many calories it has, you won't know your total daily calories, and the system that is holding your brain hostage will start to break down. Of course there will be foods for which you already know the calorie count, but there are always new foods to try that give you the opportunity to free yourself.

FOOD RITUALS

Food rituals are behaviors you engage in routinely that make you "feel safer" while eating food. They can include: eating the exact same food prepared the same way, eating at the same time every day, cutting up food into tiny bites, eating food only in a certain order, or always eating in the same or a certain size dish.

ASSIGNMENT: MY FOOD RITUALS

Write any current food rituals. _____
_____
_____

Select one food ritual to work on. _____
_____

Who or what can help you with this change? _____
_____

Tips for Change: Your brain will be resistant to changing, but as soon as you start to break the ritual, even a tiny bit, it will start to loosen up, and each subsequent mealtime or snack will be easier. Expect it to feel scary and create a lot of anxiety at first. While working on letting go of food rituals, make the commitment not to create new ones.

Comparing (Especially Your Body) to Others

> *"Comparison is the thief of joy."* —THEODORE ROOSEVELT

Comparing yourself to other people is not helpful and will be a source of dissatisfaction and pain. You will always be able to find someone who has something you don't have and you want, for example, a thinner body, better skin, longer hair, trimmer thighs, a flatter stomach, whatever it is. You can't be them. You can only be you, and your body will have its own parameters based on your unique genes. It is very difficult to stop comparing yourself to others when our culture promotes it, but as you know it leads to constant suffering. What is worse, if you are like most of our clients, you compare yourself to Photoshopped models in magazines rather than those who read them, or the celebrities in the movies rather than those in the theater watching, or your yoga teacher rather than the people taking the class.

Even if you find someone more beautiful or fit, so what? Where did you get the idea that you had to be the most or best at everything? Or that everyone and everything is on a ranking system? You will always be able to find people who have more of what you want and less of what you want. Continually comparing yourself to others and coming up short is wasting your precious energy. The better use of your energy is to work on making improvements that are suitable and healthy for you and that do not require you to compromise your wellbeing. Becoming your best self means comparing yourself to yourself and not to anyone else.

> *"Every block of stone has a statue inside it and it is the task of the sculptor to discover it." You are only in charge of your stone and you need to learn to tend to it with care and compassion."* —MICHELANGELO

ASSIGNMENT: REDIRECTING COMPARISON

Take a week to notice your tendency to compare yourself to others. When you catch yourself comparing yourself to another person, stop and redirect the thought to yourself. Write down something positive about yourself, something you like about yourself or your life you would not want to lose. If that feels too hard, practice writing "So what?" Try one example below.

Comparison: _____

_____

Positive thought redirection: _____

_____

_____

ASSIGNMENT: A THREE-STEP GUIDE TO HELP CHANGE A BEHAVIOR

We suggest you use your journal and a weekly Goals Sheet to do the following three-step behavior change process. This assignment will take over a week to complete because the first week is just observing and tracking the behavior.

Step 1: Tracking the behavior.

Choose a behavior you want to change: _____

_____

For a week in your journal keep track of the behavior: how often, when, where, and how it occurs. Include any thoughts or feelings you notice happening before the behavior, during, and after.

Step 2: Take one or more small steps.

Looking over your notes on tracking your behavior. See if you can come up with small and specific steps you can do that might help you decrease the behavior. The following are some ideas taken from our clients.

- *I will cover the full-length mirror in my bedroom.*
- *I will not buy magazines that contain pictures that are triggering.*
- *I will not go to fast food drive-through restaurants.*
- *I will stop writing down my calories.*
- *I will eat dinner with my children and not wait to eat later.*
- *I will give my scale to my therapist.*

Choose one or more steps you will take to cut down on or avoid the behavior you selected above. Tip: Make sure to list concrete, observable things.

Steps I will take to help me. (List the behavior again here.)

_____
_____
_____

Step 3: Noticing the difference.

Did taking small steps help or not? Write down what happened and what you might need to do next, or what other steps might make it easier or more successful for you. Write about how you feel when you are engaging in the behavior you are working on changing, and how you feel when you are able to stop yourself. If you are able to stop your behavior for a few days, do your feelings change? Notice again in a week. You might even be able to write about what it feels like in your life to be letting go of the behavior altogether. Remember, at first you will feel very anxious not following through on your urges to do the behavior. If you give it time, you will start to see that both your urges and your anxiety decrease, which makes stopping the behavior easier as time goes on.

_____
_____
_____
_____

Even if you continue doing a behavior you set out to change, don't worry. It takes time to completely change an entrenched behavior, but even very small changes add up. Over time, your awareness will allow you to honestly evaluate how this behavior is actually affecting you. You may think that engaging in the behavior provides reassurance or relief from fear or anxiety, but that is always short lived. Eventually, the anxiety comes back and the urge to do the behavior is there again.

You will discover that after the initial anxiety and distress that comes from changing these self-sabotaging behaviors subsides, you will feel relieved to be free from them.

Strategies to Help You Change

There are several other strategies that helped us and help our clients make changes. You can try these and see if one or more work to help you. Don't be fooled into thinking that it has to work the first time you try it. It might take a few times for a certain technique to help. You will learn from trying. Some of these tips are also included in other Keys. Skip anything you find redundant but sometimes reading things again can serve as a helpful reinforcement.

Tips for change:

1. **Write an Eating Disorder Self/Healthy Self dialogue before engaging in the behavior.**
Go over the information in Key 2. Remember that when doing this assignment it is important to note that you are asked to write the dialogue "before" engaging in the behavior rather than "instead of" engaging in it. We do not care if you do engage in the behavior at this point. You might stop the behavior but the main point here is to get access to the part of you that wants to do the behavior and the part that would like to stop.

2. **Communicate with at least three people before engaging in the behavior.**
When you have to reach out to others, chances are this will bring your Healthy Self forward, so already it is giving the Eating Disorder Self the backseat, even if only for a few moments. When you call people or text them, they might be

able to distract you long enough to get through your urge even if they don't know why you are calling. You can also tell them exactly why you are reaching out. It can be particularly useful to let certain people know ahead of time that you might reach out to them when you are trying to stop an eating disorder behavior. Just talking to, or being with people can help, but sometimes the people in your life have a number of really good things to say that might help you see the circumstances differently.

3. **Journal or write a letter to yourself or someone else before the behavior.**
People are not always going to be there for you, so it's good to learn how to use your journal and yourself as a therapist or best friend. Getting things out on paper can distract you and can inform you. If you are anxious, this is especially helpful as it helps calm down your amygdala, the part of your brain that experiences anxiety.

4. **Set a timer to delay the behavior.**
This is a great tool to help you get successive control of a behavior. For example, if you are trying to stop bingeing, you can take a small step by using your cell phone or a kitchen timer and when it goes off you can then go binge if you still want to. You can gradually increase the amount of time you set on the timer to 10 minutes, then 30 minutes, and you will find that you can delay a binge this way for longer periods of time. Often, after a long enough delay, the urge lessens or simply goes away. We have known people who used this technique and ending up successfully stopping bingeing. The key is that you are in control, and no one else is making you do it. But start with a small amount of time. Even if you are tempted, don't try 20 minutes right away. You will be more successful if you start small and work up to longer time periods.

5. **Use a transitional object.**
A transitional object is a term that was originally developed in relation to childhood attachment. The term was used to describe an object that would substitute as a "stand-in" for a mother's presence when she was not around. For example, a baby blanket or a pacifier are both used as transitional objects that serve to soothe and comfort babies, reminding them of their mother's presence. We have found that it helps to have a small item or "transitional object"

that we can give our clients to have and use outside of our sessions as a sort of link or connection to us and the work we are doing together. We use various transitional objects with our clients such as rocks, sea glass, crystal hearts, key chains, or any number of things, and they can have words written on them or not. The transitional object represents or holds the therapeutic connection, helping clients stay in touch with information discussed in therapy, goals they set, or commitments they made. You can even make your own transitional object using something that would be meaningful to you and could help you stay connected to your goals. One client made a key chain with the word "choice" on it, after a session where we discussed the idea that engaging in her eating disorder behaviors was actually a "choice." Another client took a small rock from the fountain outside the therapy office because it reminded her of her Healthy Self that would become most present during her sessions. Many clients have used angel, goddess, or some other cards with beautiful quotes written on each one. During difficult times, you can either randomly pick a card, or find one that feels right and carry it with you so you can pull it out and read it when you need a reminder.

Clients describe their experiences.

> *"I use the heart you gave me every singe day now. When I wake up I hold it for a few moments to remind myself that I am going to stay open and not close down for fear of being hurt. I carry it in my purse or my pocket and if I feel like I am starting to shut down, which leads to restricting, I get it out and go over the things we discuss in session and how I do not want to keep doing the same old thing. I never thought it would help this much, it's like having a piece of your heart with me."* —AP

> *"I just tried using the rock you gave me and can't believe how it made me feel. I thought about how we chose it together because it was solid and strong and yet smooth and nice to touch, like me. I was mad at my mom about something she did and I just wanted to binge and purge. Then I remembered the rock . . . hard, solid, smooth, strong, but nice. I remembered my promise to at least hold the rock before doing anything. So I went to get it and the weird thing is as soon as I held it, I felt your presence. I felt all the feelings I have in sessions when I am telling you how much I don't want to binge and purge anymore. Until I got the rock in my hand I didn't feel that way."*

ASSIGNMENT: FINDING OR CREATING A TRANSITIONAL OBJECT

It's time for you to get your own transitional object. You can create one for yourself or explain the concept to your therapist, other professional, or someone else you respect, listen to, and find supportive. Look for an object or something that has meaning for you. Once you have chosen your transitional object, write about it below, describing why this particular object has meaning for you and how you think it might help you.

My transitional object: _____
_____
_____
_____

ASSIGNMENT: USING MY TRANSITIONAL OBJECT

As the week goes by, write down times and situations where you either used your transitional object or could have, but didn't. After the situation occurs, write about what happened when you tried using your new tool, or why you didn't use it or you used it and it didn't help. If possible, add whatever changes you can so your transitional object works better for you. Remember, progress means any change in the right direction. If having the transitional object made you more present with yourself or altered your patterns or behaviors in anyway even if it didn't stop your behavior completely, don't get discouraged. Change takes time, and even very subtle changes add up and make a difference.

1. *Situation:* _____
   _____

   What happened: _____
   _____
   _____

   What I could do differently: _____
   _____
   _____

KEY 6: *CHANGING YOUR BEHAVIORS*

2. *Situation:* _____

   _____

   What happened: _____

   _____

   _____

   What I could do differently: _____

   _____

   _____

Take some time to reflect on what you have learned or your experience using a transitional object. You might find that having a friend who also wants to try using a transitional object to stay connected can be helpful.

Personal Reflection: CAROLYN

At some point in my private practice many years ago, I realized that my clients needed something in between sessions to remind them of the work we were doing together. I could not be there with them, but was there something I could give them that they could hold or look at that would soothe or calm them down and help them remember my words in session? It was easy to come up with rocks because I collect them and had a bowl of pretty rocks in my office. One day in session a client was having a particularly hard time and expressed that she was not sure what she would do until the next session. I asked her if she wanted to take one of my rocks home with her as a kind of reminder of our work together. She had seen this bowl of rocks for several months, as it was right on the coffee table during our sessions. She seemed very interested and intrigued and I asked her to pick out one and take it home and maybe put it somewhere she could see or pick it up and hold it when she wanted to get in better touch with the work we were doing together, or the goals she had made, or anything else that helped. The following session she came in so excited. She told me she had used the rock in a few ways. She had taken it to a dinner with her father and kept it in her pocket and thought of me when she had an urge to leave the table and purge. She had left it by her nightstand and when she woke up at night she saw it there and it was comforting. A few times it had even helped her not see the comfort of food in the late-night hours. We were both a bit aston-

ished at how well this worked, and from then on I have been using transitional objects.

My favorite story is the client who came back after taking a rock home and told me, "I put it on the back of the toilet seat and sure enough when I went in there to purge, there you were! And I couldn't do it."

The above stories are really good ones, but don't be disappointed if you try this and the results are not so dramatic. Anything you do will take time, but for transitional objects to be effective you also need to be in a place in your recovery where you want to be reminded of your desire to get better.

6. **Choose a reward or consequence to help you changefor the behavior:**
(This last tip for change is described in the following section.)

Rewards and Consequences

Rewards: If you seriously want to stop a certain behavior, it might work to set up a reward system for yourself. The urge to engage in a behavior can become so strong and so automatic that a vague reward, "wanting to get better", or a long-term reward, "I want to be healthy enough to have children when I get married," are usually not strong enough to help you stop in the moment. Sometimes, however, short-term rewards can make a difference if the reward you come up with is compelling and immediate enough.

The following list contains some of the rewards clients have used:

1. If I eat my meal plan each day, I get to go to the gym.
2. If I have a binge- and purge-free day, I can buy a new pair of shoes.
3. I can get a massage when I have a binge- and purge-free week.
4. If I try a food I'm afraid to eat, I can get my nails done.

We know that you might be thinking, "If this worked, I could have gotten over my eating disorder long ago." We understand that often rewards like this will not work, but sometimes at the right stage of recovery, they can and do help. Some people find using (negative) consequences works better than rewards. Our experience is that people with eating disorders, particularly anorexia, are more highly motivated to avoid consequences than to get rewards. There is even some research to indicate this might have something to do with genetic predisposition.

Consequences: Even if you are seriously motivated to stop a behavior, the habitual nature of it along with the fact that there are no immediate consequences can make it hard to stop. You can probably come up with long-term consequences, but those don't have enough impact to affect you in the moment. The more immediate the consequence, the more likely it is to have an impact. You might know you gain weight if you binge, but you don't see weight being added immediately to your thighs. You might know that restriction of food leads to bone loss, but in the moment, you don't feel your bones losing density after skipping lunch. We ask clients who are ready to stop a behavior to come up with a meaningful consequence they will impose on themselves if they engage in it. We don't push this assignment on clients, or try this with people who are still very ambivalent. This assignment takes a strong desire to stop the behavior, and it helps if there is someone you trust to be accountable to. (You might be able to be accountable to yourself, but it is much harder, so think about who might be able to support you.)

One client shares her experience:

"Even after years of treatment, I was still having trouble with my behaviors around food. Despite all the insight I'd gained, simply putting the food in my mouth was still a frequent struggle . . . and I didn't even really know why. More than anything, it felt like a very very bad habit that I just couldn't break.

"When I went to Carolyn for help, she asked me to name something I really cared about. My answer: Kevin Garnett and the Minnesota Timberwolves. My dad and I grew up watching basketball together and it is a real passion for me. Kevin is my hero and I saw all of his games.

'Perfect,' Carolyn said. 'If and when you restrict, you don't get to watch Kevin's next game.' I was simultaneously horrified and relieved, because I knew she really had me with that idea. I had this funny feeling that this could help me not restrict, and yet I felt a bit trapped now.

For this to work, I had to be willing to stick with the deal, and stay really honest with my therapist and myself. Of course there were much bigger reasons I wanted to recover than simply to watch basketball games, but making the consequence so tangible and immediate really worked for me. The next time I wanted to restrict, I realized I would have to share this and lose my ability to watch the game. I ate. It was hard but I did it." —P.S.

Here are some examples of consequences that worked for our clients.

1. Washing my spouse's car if I purge.
2. Giving $10 a minute to the Republicans if I exercise over one hour. (This from a hard-core Democrat with an exercise disorder.)
3. Paying $5 to my therapist every time I binge. She keeps it in a jar and will give it back to me when I have 2 weeks free of bingeing. After 3 months, if I haven't done it, she gives it to a charity I don't support.
4. If I don't follow my meal plan I have to call my boyfriend, or friend and cancel our plans.

The above consequences are all real examples that helped clients stop entrenched behaviors. They worked because the client was ready and wanted to stop the behavior, but it had become so ingrained, something more immediate to motivate or deter was needed. This technique works best if *you* decide the terms. It is not as effective if someone threatens to do it to you.

ASSIGNMENT: PERSONAL REWARDS AND CONSEQUENCES FOR MY BEHAVIOR

If you feel ready and want to see if a consequence or reward could help, come up with a behavior you want to change, your reward or consequence, and who (if anyone) will help you be accountable.

The behavior I want to change: _____
_____

The reward or consequence I will use: _____
_____

My support person: _____
_____

KEY 6: CHANGING YOUR BEHAVIORS

It is helpful to come up with a few other rewards and consequences you can also use: _____

Rewards: _____

_____

_____

Consequences: _____

_____

_____

HELPFUL QUOTES OR MANTRAS

In Eastern philosophy a mantra is a sound, word, or phrase that is repeated often such as in prayer or meditation that expresses a basic belief. Finding an inspirational quote that has meaning for you can be very helpful and most people use them without even realizing it. You can say these words of wisdom, or helpful mantras or phrases to yourself in times of upset or stress, or in moments of quiet reflection or contemplation.

You might know some already and you can ask other people if they have any helpful or inspirational sayings that help them when things get tough. It can be useful to ask a support person to say these reminders or mantras to you in moments when you are having a hard time. The following list contains some examples we like:

- *"When I let go of what I am, I become what I might be." —Lao Tzu*
- *"Turn your wounds Into wisdom." —Oprah Winfrey*
- *"You never fail until you stop trying." —Albert Einstein*
- *"It is what it is." —Unknown author, Gwen's favorite*
- *"Let go or be dragged." —Unknown author, Gwen's other favorite*
- *"You can't be the judge of your own body." —Carolyn*
- *"It is only with the heart that one can see rightly. What is essential is invisible to the eye." —Antoine de Saint-Exupéry*
- *"Be yourself, everyone else is taken." —Oscar Wilde*
- *"Everything will be okay in the end." —Unknown*
- *"What is my goal and is what I'm doing right now going to help me get there?" —Carolyn Costin*

WRITING ASSIGNMENT: MY PERSONAL MANTRAS

Come up with a few sayings or mantras you find helpful. You can use some from our list, ask several people you respect for their ideas, or look up quotes about inspiration on the Internet. Pick some that are meaningful to you and write them down.

Mantras or sayings I can use: _____
_____
_____
_____

COMPASSION AND CHANGE

Change will bring about all kinds of unrest. You might be hard on yourself, feel like you can't do it, or get angry and want to give up. This is why we often talk about having the kind of compassion for yourself that you most likely demonstrate for others. Think about it, if beating up yourself or criticizing yourself worked, you would surely be well by now.

Self-compassion is not indulgent or letting yourself off the hook. In fact, it is one of the most difficult things to do. Self-compassion is facing and accepting the reality that you are human and you are going to falter, make mistakes, and never be perfect. Self-compassion is about *giving yourself a break* and accepting you are doing the best you can. If you could do better, why wouldn't you be? Practicing self-compassion is having acceptance for yourself as you are right now and talking to yourself in a kind and understanding way. This is a lot harder to do than being compassionate toward others. It takes strength, courage, and maturity to demonstrate compassion for yourself. Buddhists call this *Maitri*, or Loving Kindness to Yourself. Since this is by far one of the hardest things to do, we explore it further in Key 8.

FINAL THOUGHTS

> "Never be afraid to fall apart because it is an opportunity to rebuild yourself the way you wish you had been all along."
> —RAE SMITH

Leaving behind your eating disorder can feel unsettling, unsafe, and bring up a variety of fears, but fear is never a good reason to stay with something harmful and oppressive. Going through the discomfort is the only way it will eventually become more comfortable.

Letting go of anything this time- and energy-consuming will feel like a loss, and it can also be hard to admit to yourself that many good years were wasted on things that didn't really deliver what seemed promised, or the cost for whatever you did get was way too high to pay. You might be tempted to hang on and just try a little harder—or maybe a little longer—to reach certain goals, but at some point, you have to come to terms with the truth of what your eating disorder is *really doing to you* and what it *will never do for you*. Your eating disorder will never really make you more lovable, a better person, or invulnerable to pain. As difficult as this realization is, it will open the door for creating a better life. Once you know the truth, you can never go back into denial or the belief that what you were doing was working or going to work. The best part of *letting go* of your eating disorder is finally being able to *create and hold onto* that which can actually provide you with the love, self-worth, and connection you were seeking all along. You are starting that right now, every time you pick up this book or work on recovery. Having an eating disorder can make you feel very alone, but you don't have to do recovery alone. The next key is about realizing the need for others and learning how to get past any resistance to reaching out for help.

KEY 7
REACH OUT TO PEOPLE RATHER THAN YOUR EATING DISORDER

> *"You may or may not recognize how you use your eating disorder, rather than relationships, to obtain comfort, deal with feelings, or just get through the day. In order to recover and leave your eating disorder behaviors behind, you will need to learn to reach out to people instead."*
>
> — 8 KEYS TO RECOVERY FROM AN EATING DISORDER

A quote from a client

> *"Over time, reaching out to others becomes more natural than using behaviors. Sometimes it was very hard. Those were the times it was most important, because how hard it was indicated how strong my eating disorder was in those moments. Each time I reached out, though, I pushed against the myths my eating disorder was telling me. The more I exercised my Healthy Self by reaching out, the stronger it became. I started to see that, even at times that were easier and I could do it on my own, I didn't always have to. Sometimes, I reached out because I needed to know I wasn't alone in the fight. It became apparent that asking for help wasn't a sign of weakness, but rather one of strength. Reaching out shows vulnerability and a willingness to do what's hard, even when it feels wrong, because engaging in life is more important than hiding in fear."*

Our Need for Connection to Others

Connection is something we all need and are wired to seek. It is an innate driving force in our lives. In Key 3 we discussed many risk factors for the development of an eating disorder, but we believe that an eating disorder can more easily take root where there is a feeling of disconnection. Furthermore, research by Michael Strober and others shows that supportive relationships, whether with friends, family, helping professionals, or mentors, are key to recovery. Whether we realize it or not, when we don't feel truly connected to people, we will search for a substitute to fill that need. The substitutes can come in many forms—alcohol, drugs, sex, or an eating disorder. Accepting your human need for authentic connection, and learning how to get it in a healthy way, will help resolve or lessen your urges to engage in eating disorder behaviors and bring healing and contentment to your life. Maybe you had a very good reason to disconnect from the people around you, or maybe you lost those connections another way, but regardless of how or why you stopped using the people around you for emotional support and connection, the result is the same. Learning to reach out to people will help you begin to change your current dynamic, and you will soon discover how connecting with others can help you break old patterns, feel your feelings, challenge your thoughts, heal underlying issues, and change the current course of your life. Think about it, the more entrenched you became in your behaviors, the less you connected with others, so it makes sense that you need to reverse that pattern to get well.

GETTING BETTER FEELS BAD (AT LEAST AT FIRST)

With almost any other illness, when people start to recover, they feel better. Getting over an eating disorder does not feel good—at least not for a while. When you start improving, for example, restoring weight, stopping a binge, eliminating laxatives, or resisting urges to purge, chances are you will feel worse. Those behaviors are there because, at this point, you feel better engaging in them than not doing so, even if it is because they are habitual or even if you think you want to stop. Also, feelings are apt to arise that those behaviors keep at bay. Feeling those feelings, challenging your thoughts, and changing your behaviors is all hard work. You are bound to feel uncomfortable and overwhelmed. Interrupting a behavior, trying a new food, or getting rid of your scale can make you so uncomfortable that you might wonder if it is even worth it! When getting better makes you feel bad, it is hard to keep going, and you might feel like stopping altogether. Help will come from reaching out to others.

Your first step in reaching out to others might be with a professional, counselor, or other support person, but eventually you need to learn how to reach out to and connect to relationships like friends, family, spouses, and other loved ones.

ASSIGNMENT: HOW ARE YOU AT REACHING OUT TO OTHERS?

Answer the following questions with a "Y" for yes or "N" for no:

_____ *I have a person (or people) who are supportive and can help me with my recovery.*

_____ *I have reached out to at least a few people about my eating disorder.*

_____ *I usually call people when I feel bad, sad, or upset.*

_____ *I understand that reaching out is not a sign of weakness.*

_____ *I ask for help when I feel the need to engage in an eating disorder behavior.*

_____ *I ask for help when I realize I am out of control.*

_____ *I think of others as emotional support and ask for help when I need to talk things out.*

_____ *I find a way to let others how they can help me or what I need from them.*

_____ *I reach out to others just to stay connected with people.*

_____ *I do not feel guilty asking others for help.*

If you answered No to a few, or several questions in the previous assignment, you are missing out on a great opportunity for authentic connection in your life and the relief that comes from allowing others to truly know, understand, and help you. Even if you answered No to only one of the above questions, this Key can help you understand your needs, the complexity of your relationship with others, and the benefit of connection in helping you recover.

USING RELATIONSHIPS TO PUT THE EATING DISORDER OUT OF A JOB

Whatever it is you think your eating disorder is going to do for you, it will never help you get what you seek. It will not help you live a happier life, take the place of a friend or loved one, or find true connection. To help you get well, we are going to tell you to take a risk, and turn to people rather than your eating disorder. The moment you want to go to the store and get binge foods, take laxatives, head to a bathroom to purge, or skip lunch, what if you *ignored your Eating Disorder Voice* and *reached out* to someone instead? Reaching out to someone can help alleviate the urge to engage in an eating disorder behavior, sometimes delaying it and sometimes causing the "need" for the behavior to go away. You can also reach out to someone to help you actually engage in a behavior that is good for you, like eating your breakfast or trying a challenging food. There are many ways you can let people help you in your recovery process.

Client quote

> *"I don't know when it became so hard for me to reach out to other people for help. At some point I got the message that I should be able to handle things myself, and asking for help was a sign of weakness. With a lot of help I started reaching out to my therapist, first telling her things I would never have shared with anyone and realizing her acceptance made me feel better. Then taking the risk to tell others, and getting acceptance there too. Then I was encouraged to try reaching out before a binge. This was so hard but once I tried it, I could not believe that people actually were able to help me, either by distracting me, talking through my feelings with me, or just coming to be with me until the urge passed. We need each other, and I had somehow forgotten how helpful other people can be, even when you don't think it could happen.*
>
> —AJ

WHEN TO REACH OUT

There are endless ways that other people can help you. You might want help directly related to stopping a behavior, or maybe accomplishing a challenging task. You might just need a sounding board, or just some human comfort. The following is a short list of some examples you can use as guidelines for when to reach out to others for help:

1. Before engaging in an eating disorder behavior (this at first might just help you understand it, or delay it, but eventually can help to prevent it).
2. After engaging in an eating disorder behavior (to process your feelings and be honest).
3. When having a difficult time about anything (to distract you or help calm you).

4. To help you be accountable for following through with your meal plan.
5. To get support for a meal challenge (difficult or scary food).
6. After succeeding at a recovery goal (to get validation and acknowledgment).
7. To hear a friendly voice in order to distract from a painful feeling or thought.
8. To help you feel connected.

> "I remember being so frustrated in therapy because I kept bingeing even though I was making progress in so many other areas, including relationships and having more fun. I could understand why I wanted to engage in my eating disorder behaviors when I was angry, or bored, but I found myself continually stopping for binge food on the way home from being out and having a great time after connecting with friends. After talking about it and exploring my feelings, I realized that what was triggering my urge to binge was a feeling of emptiness and disconnection that came over me after I had been with people. It was like I was afraid that I would not experience it again, or the difference between being with them and alone was too drastic. My therapist suggested that after getting together with people, I try calling a friend on the drive home to help make the transition less severe. It turned out that just connecting with someone on the way home was enough to help me pass up the grocery store. I didn't have to talk about my eating disorder, what I was feeling, or even say that I was struggling. I just needed to connect a little so I didn't feel a void that needed filling. Now, it's part of my plan. On my way home, I call a friend to discuss the night's events." —SM

ASSIGNMENT: WHEN I NEED TO REACH OUT

Take a moment to think about your current daily routine, your behaviors, and situations that can be problematic for you. Write down some situations where it might help you to reach out to someone.

_____
_____
_____
_____

RESISTANCE TO REACHING OUT

Chances are you have resistance to reaching out to others for help. If you are like most of our clients you have several reasons why you don't want to do it, can't do it, or why you think it won't help. In our 8 *Keys* book we listed 14 of the main reasons clients have given us for why they don't reach out. There are many thoughts and feelings that get in the way, but your fears are usually far greater than the reality. Reaching out to people does not mean things will always work out great, all your needs will be met, or just by doing so your eating disorder will go away. In fact, it is likely that at times you will be disappointed by people, they might not help, or someone might even make you feel worse. Like everything, it takes practice communicating what you need and finding the right people to reach out to. However, remember we only discuss 8 Keys to recovery and this is Key 7, so we obviously believe it is critical. See how the following client got herself to take the first step.

> *"The biggest obstacle for me in terms of reaching out to my friends or family when I am struggling is embarrassment. My ego or pride gets in the way. I am known as the independent, together one. I am the one people reach out to or go to when things get bad. So if I'm the one who needs help, I am afraid that people will stop seeing me that way or trusting me. If people know I am barely hanging on to my lunch, how will they trust me to be there for them?*
>
> *"However, I did reach out this week and it paid off. Driving home from work, I was tired, hungry, and a bit overwhelmed. My mind was all over the place. I wanted to restrict and to binge, and they both felt right and wrong at the same time. Then I started thinking that maybe what I wanted had nothing to do with food. I tried to figure out what my symptoms were telling me, like I had talked about in therapy so many times. I realized I needed and wanted both connection and escape, which seemed confusing at first. I felt alone and empty of love and connection, but full of stress and feelings from the day. In a light bulb moment I realized that my eating disorder was not really a solution for this. I called my sister and talked with her on the way home. I told her about all the stress at work, and listened about her day as well. We laughed at sister stuff that reminded me of being a kid. She tentatively asked how I was doing, and I felt my wall go up and was about to lie and tell her I was doing great, but instead I spoke through the wall and*

told her I actually called her because I was struggling, but that talking to her had helped. She told me that it was the first time she felt let in and how good it made her feel that I chose her to reach out to. Feeling this deeper connection to her defused my stress even more. I no longer felt the need to use food to manage my feelings. I got home, made dinner, took a bath, and felt both proud of myself and hopeful."

ASSIGNMENT: REASONS I DON'T REACH OUT

Look at the list of reasons for not reaching out and put an "X" in front of the ones you relate to. At the end, add any reasons you have for not reaching out that are not included on this list.

Reasons for not reaching out:

_____ *I don't want people to know how much I need help.*
_____ *I am ashamed.*
_____ *By the time I realize I am in trouble, it is too late.*
_____ *I would not know what to say.*
_____ *I don't see how talking helps.*
_____ *I don't have anyone to call.*
_____ *People won't know what to say.*
_____ *People have not been there for me in the past.*
_____ *I don't want to burden people.*
_____ *I am afraid to rely on others because they will not always be around.*
_____ *I am not sure I want to be stopped.*
_____ *I will feel worse if I try and it does not help.*
_____ *I tried it and it did not work.*
_____ *I should be able to handle things on my own.*

_____
_____
_____

ASSIGNMENT: COUNTERING YOUR REASONS FOR NOT REACHING OUT

In the 8 Keys book we provide counterarguments for each of the reasons listed above for not reaching out. In this workbook we are asking you to come up with the counterarguments for all the reasons for not reaching out, including any you added. Counteracting the reasons why people don't reach out helps reinforce your Healthy Self, and will make it easier to reach out when the time comes, even if it seems hard now. (Tip: If you need help, read our counterarguments in the original book, or think about what you would tell someone else, or ask others what they might say as a counterargument.)

1. *I don't want people to know how much help I need.*
   Counterargument: _____
   _____

2. *I am ashamed of my behaviors.*
   Counterargument: _____
   _____

3. *By the time I realize I am in trouble it is too late to call someone.*
   Counterargument: _____
   _____

4. *I would not know what to say.*
   Counterargument: _____
   _____

5. *I don't see how talking helps.*
   Counterargument: _____
   _____

6. *I don't have anyone I can call.*
   Counterargument: _____
   _____

7. *I don't think people will know what to say to me.*
   Counterargument: _____
   _____

8. *People have not been there for me in the past.*
   Counterargument: _____
   _____

9. *I don't want to burden my friends.*
   Counterargument: _____
   _____

10. *I am afraid to rely on others because they will not always be around.*
    Counterargument: _____
    _____

11. *I am not sure I want to be stopped.*
    Counterargument: _____
    _____

12. *I will feel worse if I reach out and it does not help.*
    Counterargument: _____
    _____

13. *I tried reaching out and it did not work.*
    Counterargument: _____
    _____

14. *I should be able to handle things on my own.*
    Counterargument: _____
    _____

15. _____
    Counterargument: _____
    _____

16. _____
    Counterargument: _____
    _____

17. _____
    Counterargument: _____
    _____

Client quote

"I so did not want to be a burden asking others for help all the time. It took me a while to learn that I wasn't a burden for reaching out, I was a burden for having an eating disorder! When I started asking others for help, people actually told me that they preferred that to the silence my illness had created. I know it is hard to believe, but it was my authentic relationships with people that truly began to replace the relationship I had with my eating disorder."

—LP

CHOOSING WHOM TO REACH OUT TO AND HOW

To whom you choose to reach out is an important part of the equation. Not everyone will be able to respond in a way that works for you. Some people will not know what to say, will not be available when you need them, or will get easily frustrated. It can help to talk to the people in your life you think would make good support people for you, tell them you feel that way about them, and ask if they are willing to help you. You can discuss how you might reach out to them at certain times and for what. You can describe things you think would be helpful for them to say or do, or you can just tell them that being there for you as a safe, comforting listener is enough. You will need to find out what works best for you with which people. You can even reach out and get help from others without ever having to tell anyone anything. Some clients just call friends to distract themselves from their urges without ever saying why they called. Other clients have called a friend when wanting to purge and said, "I feel like purging, can you talk to me for a while?" With no preparation at all, you might find yourself able to ask your partner, a parent, or a friend, "Will you eat dinner with me because it will make it easier for me to eat?" There are endless ways to let other people in to help. Think about the people in your life and what might work in your situation.

ASSIGNMENT: WHO ARE MY GO-TO PEOPLE?

It might be hard, and you can probably come up with many excuses, but write down a few people in your life you might try reaching out to.

_____
_____
_____

TARGETING SPECIFIC EATING DISORDER URGES AND BEHAVIORS

Reaching out can help stop you from engaging in a specific behavior in the moment. If you have done the assignments in this Key, you have listed situations or behaviors where you could use support, come up with arguments to counter why you don't reach out, and made a list of who you might use as support. It is time to give reaching out in a specific way, for a specific reason, a try.

ASSIGNMENT: MY SPECIFIC PLANS FOR REACHING OUT TO STOP A BEHAVIOR

List four of your current eating disorder behaviors (or certain situations that likely result in your using behaviors), the person you will reach out to, the method you will use to reach out, and what the person can do to help.

Behavior/ situation	Support Person	Method of reaching out	What I need
Ex. Binging	My sister	Texting	Text me or call me back and talk
Ex. Skipping dinner	My best friend	asking to eat together	Just be there and eat with me

1. _____
2. _____
3. _____
4. _____

Use your Goals Sheet and target one or two of the behaviors you want to work on for the week. Evaluate how things are going as the week progresses, and make any changes you think could help improve things. You can continue targeting one specific behavior until you feel it has gotten better, you can add other behaviors, or target all eating disorder behaviors as indicators that you need to and will reach out. Eventually, reaching out will become natural and a way you take care of yourself, and you will not need a Goals Sheet to do it or keep track of.

Keep in mind that reaching out before acting out might help you avoid engaging in a behavior, but it might not. Don't give up. It can take a while to figure out what and who works best for you. Even if it doesn't work in the beginning or only delays or reduces the time spent, or the intensity of the behavior, that is a start. If you keep at it, it will help. You might find what other clients have to say about this helpful:

Quotes from clients

"At first, reaching out was terrifying. I was afraid of what the person would think. I didn't want to be judged. I didn't want to seem selfish, and asking for help felt like that. I didn't want to seem incompetent, and it seemed like reaching out showed that I knew what the right answer was but I couldn't get myself to do the simplest things. I thought, 'If I can text/call/say this, I should be able to do it on my own.' However, I realized I couldn't do it on my own . . . because, if I could have, I would have gotten better on my own. So, I tried reaching out first to my therapist and dietitian, then to friends. At first it did not always change my behavior, but somehow as I did it more, became more honest, let people in more, reaching out became a significant aspect in my recovery."

"I did not want to ask my husband for help or even tell him I had an eating disorder because I thought could not possibly understand and he would reject me, leave me. I kept my eating disorder hidden from him for years thinking our marriage would be over if I told him. In therapy I had to face the fact that living a daily lie was adding to my feeling of shame and unworthiness and contributing to my inability to get better. If I wanted to change I needed to tell my husband and ask for his support in many areas that could make a difference. However, I also had to accept that he might not be able to handle it and leave me. Of all the many decisions I had to make in order to get better this was one of the hardest. In the end I decided to tell him. I was finally able to accept that if he left me it would not be any worse than the situation I was in. We were strangers anyway and did not have a real relationship. So . . . with the help of my therapist, I told him. It was painful and hard and we had a rough time for a while, but we are still together. We made it and I made it but we needed a lot of help along the way."

"When I reached out to my mom and told her how I was feeling or that I was too fat, or wanted to get rid of calories, she would break down and cry

or get angry and start screaming, so I just stopped. I shut down and decided she was not ever going to be able to help me. My dad had remarried and was not in the picture and I really did not know who else I could turn to for help. So I tried to get better on my own. When I started therapy I did not want my mom to be a part of it. After about 6 or so sessions Carolyn convinced me to bring my mom in even though I was 23 and did not have to get her involved, plus I did not see the use of it. It is hard to describe all the things that happened but being in therapy together helped my mom and I understand each other and how to get along with each other and get out of our old dynamic. My mom came to understand more about eating disorders as an illness and not just me making bad choices. She learned what supported me and what sabotaged me. I also had to learn to accept her feelings and be ok if she cried or was upset. I learned how and when to ask for help or support and not set my mom up for failure or ask for things she could not possibly give. I am a good example that letting other people in and letting them help may seem impossible but with the right guidance it can work and can change everything."

USING TEXT MESSAGING FOR SUPPORT

Texting can be a great tool for reaching out. In the *8 Keys* book, we report research showing that texting actually assists people in changing behavior. You can text someone to help prevent yourself from engaging in an eating disorder behavior, get reinforcement for taking a risk, or get acknowledgment for doing something difficult. Texting is a way of reaching out that is immediate and simple. It might be hard at first to get yourself to text when you need help, but our experience shows you are more likely to do this than to call.

Texting provides connection, helps with accountability, can serve as a distraction, and may elicit a helpful idea or response from the other person. The person receiving your text doesn't even have to respond for it to work. Sometimes just sending the text is enough to get you through a hard time. If the person you text is busy, even a quick response can be the very thing that helps you over a hurdle. Chances are you already use texting to communicate, so you just need to work out how to use it as a method of support. Texting is a recovery tool you can use with peers, loved ones, and professionals.

HOW WE USE TEXTING WITH CLIENTS

Eating disorder clients need a significant amount of help to interrupt or stop their behaviors. As therapists, we are often the first people whom clients will feel comfortable reaching out to. We use texting with clients as a way of providing ongoing support between sessions. By letting clients start by texting us, we can get them familiar and comfortable with it and then have them transfer their texting to others.

We do not spend endless hours texting our clients, and we don't text with all our clients all the time. Usually we make specific texting goals with specific clients. Although there might be issues with texting (cell service, misinterpretation of the text, timing such that it's difficult to respond, boundary issues, and so on) the ability to engage with clients in the moment when they are actually struggling has helped facilitate progress to such an extent we can't imagine not doing it. Of course we aren't available to respond at all times, but sometimes just the act of sending the text is enough to help the client. Think about it, if you send a text for support, it means your Healthy Self has come forward and reached out. Once your Healthy Self is present it's easier to make healthier decisions. So even if you don't get a response, texting can help anyway.

Quote from a client

> *"One time early in treatment I had eaten lunch, but needed to have an afternoon snack. I sat in front of my trail mix and started questioning whether I needed it. I thought about throwing it away, but remembered how much I'd been urged to ask for help if I didn't want to do something, wasn't certain, or needed feedback. I knew if I reached out, I would feel more compelled to do what I didn't want to do. Eat the snack. I realized that was the perfect indicator I needed to reach out. I had to do the harder thing. I picked up my phone with shaking hands and texted my therapist, describing the situation. Most of the time she would get right back to me, but not this time. I was holding my phone waiting for a response. However, just the act of texting her made me feel my Healthy Self more present, and my Eating Disorder Self take a backseat. The thought crossed my mind that I didn't want to live a life where the decision to eat trail mix gave me anxiety and kept me from a life worth living. I put down my phone and picked up my food."*
>
> —AA

Although we use texting and email communication regularly with our clients, we respect that not all therapists or other health care providers are comfortable texting clients or with other outside communication between sessions. If you are seeking a therapist, dietitian, or other professional, you might want to consider asking about his or her policy regarding texting and other contact between sessions. Some professionals charge a fee for communication outside of sessions, or may incorporate this into their session fee. If you already have a therapist (or other professional) whom you like and want to continue seeing, but who does not have a "between session contact policy" or is not comfortable with texting, you will need to find other people to reach out to.

APPS FOR CONNECTION AND RECOVERY

There are eating disorder recovery apps that are similar to how we use texting but go beyond that, offering several features. Some apps include communications to your therapists creating a certain kind of "interaction" between sessions. If using an app seems interesting to you, we suggest you search the app store for your particular phone, and read recommendations and ratings online in order to find out the most recent information to help you decide which one works best for you. Below is a brief summary of popular eating disorder apps.

Recovery Record

This app allows the user to log meals and snacks, as well as thoughts and feelings. The information is compiled into feedback charts that can point out patterns and be shared with a therapist, support person, or other app users. This app offers numerous features and is HIPAA–compliant, meaning that your personal health information is protected according to law. Your clinician would pay a small monthly fee depending on the number of clients or patients linked to the app, and then would be able to monitor your progress, make customized forms, print reports, chart your weight, and see results of certain assessments.

Rise Up and Recover

Designed by someone who recovered from an eating disorder, this app is a much simpler version of Recovery Record. It allows users to log behaviors and set reminders, and provides a menu of coping skills to turn to rather than eating disorder behaviors. You can use this app to help with with accountability, including your treatment team, who can access it for free.

Rooted Recovery

Rooted Recovery's mission is to reduce the barriers to eating disorder recovery by providing greater access to specialized community-based care. Rooted Recovery provides a range of therapy and support services, one of which is the free mobile app (relaunching in 2016) that coaches individuals through their triggers while reinforcing healthy coping skills. The app includes trend reports for individuals and clinicians so that they can glean greater insight into the recovery and treatment process. The app also provides individuals with access to higher levels of support services and means to build connections within their home communities. Rooted Recovery's app and services were designed by eating disorder clinicians, patients, and advocates.

USING A RECOVERED PERSON AS A MENTOR

We believe the experience of going though our own recovery and now being recovered is a useful tool and significant factor in our success with our clients. Clients have repeatedly reported that having exposure to someone who has recovered was extremely helpful to their recovery. The recovered person does not need to be a professional. There are many recovered people who want to "give back" and are willing to help others. The key is finding someone who is truly recovered and knows how to share personal information about the recovery process that is helpful and not harmful. A recovered person acting as a support person or mentor should share only how he or she got better, and dealt with adversity, stayed motivated, and took on challenges, rather than details of how sick he or she was, or giving advice they aren't trained to give. The goal is for a mentor to inspire hope and give you useful ideas, so if you feel triggered or uncomfortable with your experience, find someone else.

FINDING A RECOVERED PERSON

You might wonder how to find a recovered person who can provide inspiration and support. An easy first step is to read books written by people who are recovered. Though it's not the same as having a real person to talk to, reading books written by people who have recovered can be very motivating and inspiring. Be careful not to read books about people who are still struggling. And be cautious, because many of these books give excessive, gruesome details about how sick the person was, which can be triggering and the opposite of helpful. The best stories are from those who are truly recovered and share how they got there and what might help you get there too. One book we often recommend is *Goodbye Ed, Hello Me* by Jenni Schaefer.

You might know someone who is recovered, a recovered person might speak at a local group event. There are also online organizations like Mentor Connect, started by Shannon Cutts, where you can find a recovered mentor. Recovered herself, Shannon knew people often need more support than they have the resources for, so she set up Mentor Connect, where anyone can sign up and be assigned a mentor.

Another place to find a mentor is in 12-step groups. In this setting, the term "sponsor" is used rather than mentor, but they serve a similar purpose. In fact the phrase, "been there, done that" is 12-step language that refers to how recovering addicts' personal experiences can be used to help others on the path to recovery. In 12-step groups you will hear people use the term "recovering" or "recovery" instead of "recovered." (Though in *The Big Book of AA* Bill W does use the term "recovered," it is not a term you hear in 12-step settings because the belief is that the addiction does not go away. Using the term "recovered" might cause an alcoholic or drug addict to believe he or she could drink, or use, in moderation.) In any case, although we believe you can be fully recovered from an eating disorder, we also have met many people who have stopped their eating disorder behaviors and gotten well with the help of the 12-step approach. You can find help and a sponsor at 12-step meetings, but make sure the person is far along and strong in his or her own recovery and is open to your individual ideas and goals about yours.

Whatever you do, be careful to find support people who do not find it necessary to share unnecessary details about how sick they were, for example, how much weight they lost or how much they purged. This kind of sharing is unhelpful and might trigger you or stir up competition in your Eating Disorder Self. It is important to note that even people still suffering from their own eating disorder can be helpful, but it is not the same thing as having help from someone truly free from the disorder and fully "recovered." Once you have found a mentor, it might be difficult to know how best he or she can help you, so we suggest several questions you might want to ask.

Questions for a mentor:

1. What are some ways you dealt with your body changing?
2. How did you sit with your feelings waiting for the urges to pass?
3. Were there any sayings or useful phrases that helped you?
4. What did you do when you felt like giving up?
5. How did you tell the truth about your behaviors if you felt guilty or scared to do so?
6. What were some turning points you can remember along the way?
7. How did you wean off the scale?
8. What helped you get away from all the numbers—weight, calories, miles run?
9. Did you ever think that recovery was just not going to happen for you?
10. How did you help keep yourself accountable?

ASSIGNMENT: QUESTIONS FOR YOUR MENTOR

What would you like to know from someone who has "been there, done that"? Make a list of questions you would like to ask someone who has gotten over their eating disorder. This will help prepare you for things to discuss when you find a person you think might be helpful for you. We will get you started and you can also choose from the list above.

1. *What tips do you have for dealing with your body image?*
2. *Were there any particularly good books that helped you?*
3. _____
4. _____
5. _____
6. _____
7. _____
8. _____
9. _____
10. _____

Personal Reflection: CAROLYN

Reaching out was not only a critical tool in getting over my eating disorder; it is critical for me today. When trying to get better from anorexia, I learned I was a terrible judge of my own body and need for food. It took me a while to see that my own judgment was way off and that I was so hard on myself and so scared of change that I had to rely on others I trusted to tell me whether or not I was eating or exercising too much or too little. Back then my drive for self-control and self-discipline led me to always err on the side of eating too little and exercising too much. I still have the same temperament that these days steers me in the direction of pushing myself too hard with work, not knowing when enough is enough and I need to rest, which gets me out of balance. I have learned to use others to give me a reality check. I rely on others to help me know when I am overworking, need to go on vacation, or let go of tasks. I often reach out to friends for advice, but even if I don't they know that I welcome and need their feedback (even if sometimes I resist it) to help me turn off my cell phone, and give responsibility to others. They are happy to steer me in the right direction, and it's especially helpful when they plan leisure activities and do something fun or relaxing with me.

Personal Reflection: GWEN

It took me quite some time to realize that others could be emotional resources for me. I only relied on myself from a very early age and kept almost all my thoughts and feelings inside. You might be imagining a shy or quiet person by that description, but I wasn't. I was talkative and funny and seemingly open. If you asked others, they would say I expressed all my thoughts and feelings and was open about things others were afraid to talk about. What they didn't know was that I decided which thoughts and feelings were the likable ones or the ones I wanted people to think about me, and I kept all the other ones inside. Asking for help was not even on my radar. It never even occurred to me, so you can imagine how hard it was for me to work on this Key. With Carolyn and the staff at Monte Nido, I learned that expressing my feelings and talking to others could help me take a different view of things or change how I felt. I started to get better at telling people what was actually going on with me and began to see others as resources.

Most of the people in my outside life didn't even know I had an eating disorder, so that was the first hurdle to overcome after leaving treatment. Sometimes the hardest things for us to do are the very things we need most, and this was certainly the case for me. I was so scared of the judgment of others I made my husband tell our friends and family so I didn't have to witness their reactions. Instead of judgment, I received cards, calls, and messages of support and encouragement, and many offers to talk or help in any way possible. At first I didn't take anyone up on their offers, but after awhile I realized I needed to ask for help if I wanted to stay well, and it turned out to be exactly what I needed—I was too lonely doing it alone. I remember exactly how I started. I called my friend Julie and told her how afraid I was to see everyone now that they knew I had an eating disorder, and I asked her to help me figure out what to say when people asked me how I was doing. She was so helpful. She told me I could say, "the truth, but not the whole truth," which was exactly what I needed to learn how to do. With her help, I realized I could be honest and not say more than I was comfortable sharing. This was my start, and from there I began to reach out to my friends for help on hard days, and as a result of this new openness, my relationships became more authentic and I felt more connected to my friends than ever before . . . and *that* is what I needed to get and stay well.

REACHING IN TO YOURSELF

Aside from other people, *you* are an important emotional resource—the most important one you have—so along with reaching out to others, you also need to be able to reach in and rely on yourself.

Even though you might not be able to do it now, eventually you will have to be there for you. People can't be there all the time, sometimes others will not have the advice you need, or you will overburden people if you *always* need them. The 8 *Keys* book and this workbook are both designed to strengthen your Healthy Self so that rather than relying only on others, you will eventually be able to guide and rely on yourself. Chances are you already can wisely advise, gently challenge, or successfully comfort someone else, so you can gradually learn to do it for yourself. If you are like most of our clients, you will get glimpses of reaching in to your healthy self along the way, and then at some point realize that you are there for you whenever you need.

SOME FINAL THOUGHTS

Reaching out to others is moving toward people and away from your behaviors. You might find this hard to believe, but start reaching out and you will start getting better, even if at first it does not stop your behaviors. You will not know all the ways that reaching out can benefit you until you do it. You will learn more about yourself and what will be helpful. You will become less afraid of asking for help, less automatic in your reactions, and also better at knowing what you need. Reaching out for help is not the sole answer to recovery, but it does provide a way to turn to relationships to get your needs met and put the eating disorder out of a job. Reaching out brings authenticity to your relationships with others.

In the last Key we take you even further beyond your connection with others, to the connection with your core essence and everything else. An authentic, meaningful, and purposeful life is not "out there" waiting for you to recover; it is already here for you now. It is not someplace waiting for you to get there. It is here already, available to you at all times in the deep acceptance of who you are. Actually, Key 8 will help you discover yourself beyond your body and your mind, not to who you are, but what you are, a spiritual being. True comprehension of this not only helps with understanding why you might have developed an eating disorder, but how to accept it, transform it, and let it go.

KEY 8
FINDING MEANING AND PURPOSE

> *"In order to be who you are, you have to be willing to let go of who you think you are."*
> —MICHAEL SINGER

> *"Who we are is naturally loving, accepting, deeply relaxed, and always at peace, never attached to any form, and who we are has never been seeking anything. It is naturally non-judgmental, choiceless, and always free from identification. It is the ocean, always at rest even amidst the storm of life, forever deeply allowing every wave without judgment, resistance, or attachment. The end of the search of a lifetime is not a future goal, but who we already are."*
> —JEFF FOSTER, FROM *DEEP ACCEPTANCE*

This Key goes beyond food, beyond risk factors, beyond feeling your feelings and challenging your thoughts. It is about healing on a deeper level, and is an aspect of true healing that is often left out of conventional treatment plans. This Key is about the essence of your being, your spiritual nature, and how developing that connection can help you become fully recovered and stay that way. *Spirituality* and *soul* are words that have so many interpretations they are surrounded by misunderstanding and confusion. When referring to spirituality, we aren't talking about religion. Religion can be a bridge to spirituality, but people often get stuck on the bridge. Spirituality is simply about transcending the limited view of one's self; recognizing you are more than an individual ego or the voice inside your head. During your life you have seen different thoughts, emotions, and the world pass before you. Being spiritual means understanding that you are the witnessing presence or consciousness that is aware of those thoughts, emotions, and events. Your true home is in the center of this consciousness. From that center you are aware of things but more importantly you have meta-awareness, meaning you are aware of being aware. This is what being in the seat of your soul means. We hope to give you an easy and practical way of understanding, accepting, and enhancing your inherent spiritual nature, thus providing deeper meaning, purpose and re-enchantment to your everyday life.

Regardless of days spent or progress made, when clients discharge from Monte Nido Treatment Center, they are given a graduation ceremony. All staff and clients sit together in circle to honor the graduate's progress in the healing journey, however big or small. Every graduate writes and reads out loud an "Eater's Agreement," which is a personal vow about their recovery and going forward in life. What clients write in their "Eater's Agreement" provides a glimpse into what we want to share in this Key, an aspect of healing that goes beyond making peace with food and "evidenced-based" protocols to matters of spirituality and soul. Consider this recent example:

My Eater's Agreement:

*". . . There are numerous unknowns as I venture out into my new life, but I am not afraid. I say to fear 'BRING IT' because **with my new awareness and sense of self, fear doesn't stand a chance**. I am prepared for the challenges I will face and I am confident in the overall outcome.*

***I refuse to conform any longer to the expectations society has deemed as ideal** because as of this very day the only ideal I must **conform to is that which resonates with my soul, and my soul no longer resonates with the pursuit of perfection**.*

*Today, **my pursuit is for authenticity**, and in this authenticity **I will celebrate the beautiful imperfections of others and myself**. The renowned psychiatrist Carl Jung once said, '**He who looks outside, dreams; he who looks inside, awakes.**' By looking within the shadows of my soul, I will discover my unclaimed talents and treasures and claim them for myself. These delightful finds, my precious gems, **the essence of my being, will unlock me from my self-induced imprisonment**.*

***I will take in each morsel with mindfulness, not merely morsels of food, but each morsel of every day**. I will feed my soul's desire to have a taste of*

LIFE. *My soul has been starved of memories and relationships (with myself and others), and that is precisely what I will fill the hunger of my heart with from this point forward.*

I will satisfy my soul by being alive in every sense of the word *and filling up on life's every opportunity, whether that means trying new things, being outlandish, going with the flow, or being REAL.* ***I agree to listen to my needs and honor them instead of turning to substitute fillers that will never suffice.*** *Sometimes I will need laughter, and other times tears. Sometimes I will need space, and other times connection. Sometimes I will need movement and other times rest.* ***Whatever the occasion calls for, I will respect my needs****, and the most pertinent is my need for affection and intimacy. Without fostering that my soul will perish—* ***our souls were all made for connection, and we are all inherently connected.***

To Myself and All Others Who Suffer:

If you must count something, count your blessings *instead of calories eaten and calories burned.*

If you must binge, binge on every experience life offers. ***Devour the sensations of the present moment*** *and fill yourself with delicious dreams and magical moments.*

If you must purge, purge with tears, with laughter, with love . . . ***allow all the emotions to flow through you and be released into the energy of the universe.***

If you must restrict, ***restrict the negative self-talk and detrimental influences so that they don't impact the quality of your life or suffocate your soul.***

Namaste."

Personal Reflection: CAROLYN

I have sat in hundreds of graduation ceremonies and read well over 1,500 Eater's Agreements and am personally blown away every time. This young woman's vow to herself, like most of them, acknowledges a kind of healing and way to live that brings a deeper meaning and purpose to recovery and to life. Please look at what she wrote again, focusing on the parts highlighted in bold, which all relate to things we will cover in this Key.

FROM SUPERFICIAL TO SPIRITUAL

If you are like most who suffer from an eating disorder, you are disconnected from, and most likely even at war with, your body. Your mind is in a state of constant chatter, judgment, and comparison. You are critical of yourself and others, out of balance, caught in habitual behavior patterns, and living in the past or future. You are unaware of your true essence beyond your body and your mind, because the environment we live in provides little mentoring to help you understand and develop who and what you truly are beyond these things. An eating disorder is the epitome of disconnect between body, mind, and spirit. Reconnecting will not only help you heal, but bring deeper meaning and purpose to your life. This might seem like a far-out or impossible task, or you might be wondering what the heck we are even talking about, but with guidance, what might seem odd, difficult, or impossible can become a natural part of the way you live.

Like most people, you want comfort, security, love, and happiness, but as long as you are striving to achieve any of these things through the pursuit of thinness or the comfort of food, your behaviors may have meaning and purpose temporarily, but they will keep you in a state of striving, misery, and unhappiness. You have fallen into the illusion that your worth is tied to the external, what you own, what you accomplish, and particularly how you look. Furthermore, you may not fully realize that it is your own thoughts and behaviors keeping you from the happiness you seek, and there is a way to overcome that.

Even if you partake in religious or spiritual teachings, these can hardly compare with the amount of energy poured into you through thousands of hours of media and advertising, all conditioning us into believing that humans exist to look good, work, earn money, and get stuff. Image consciousness has replaced spiritual consciousness, and consumerism has become the dominant world faith. It is no wonder you feel disconnected, empty, and search for connection, meaning, and fulfillment in places where they cannot be found.

Like us, you were trained to look for happiness as if it is a state outside yourself that you can somehow reach. Unfortunately, happiness is never finally "reached," it is a feeling that comes and goes. However, you can learn to experience more happiness if you understand the You that is the witnessing presence, and strive to live your life from this deeper state of awareness. Doing so will not only increase your happiness but bring you far more peace and contentment.

The concepts of spirituality and soul usually bring up old connotations and meanings that do not apply here, so please bear with us as we explain what we mean by these terms. Being spiritual does not mean you have to follow any religious dogmas or believe in concepts or beings that you can't prove exist. The root of the word "spirit" is *spiritus*, Latin for "breath," which basically means life force. Current scientific knowledge of the universe reveals that the life force inside of us is the same as that connected to everything else. The atoms that everything is made of—you, me, the stars, the trees, the ocean, clouds, dogs, elephants, ants, your carpet, this book—are all made up of the same basic life force. Whatever you call it, energy field, spirit, awareness, chi, quantum field, God, or consciousness, its existence is an awesome reality that most of us don't take time to fully appreciate. Ancient wisdom and modern science both point the way to an understanding of our selves and our world that extends far beyond our limited sense of self and separateness. You may have heard about such concepts, but most of us can barely, if at all, understand them. Your spirituality is about your understanding of and actions toward transcending a limited sense of self by recognizing this life force as your intrinsic essence and your connection to all other beings and the world around you.

Whether you have strong religious beliefs, or you are turned off by religion because you cannot accept what can't be proven, or you believe scientific evidence contradicts religious beliefs, what we will share with you about leading a more spiritual, soulful life will not be incompatible with any of these stances.

Quantum physics shatters our ways of thinking about the nature of reality and reinforces ancient eastern spiritual traditions like those found in Buddhism. Both teach about the energy field as the source of oneness connecting all things. Both help us transcend our narrow concept of self, opening up a whole new world of potential. Thus the spirituality we speak of is grounded in ancient practices, as well as a scientific understanding of the universe.

Scientific knowledge, however awesome it may be, is likely not enough to help you live a more spiritual life. Our scientific explanation for the things in our universe is cognitive and abstract. We don't feel it. It is as if scientific knowledge excludes a spiritual or transcendental understanding, but this is not at all true. To comprehend the spiritual nature of the universe, including yourself, you have to experience it, embody it. Mindfulness practices like yoga and meditation were designed for just such an embodied experience. In fact, Buddhism is a set of principles designed to help human beings quiet the ceaseless chattering mind of our ego, and sit in the "seat of awareness, consciousness or soul" realizing our true nature and connection to the bigger whole. We hope to give you exercises and assignments that will help you do just that.

Gwen: If you are like me, your head is already spinning and telling you to stop reading this stuff and go back to the Keys dealing with more concrete things. Try to ignore those thoughts for now. There is no harm in reading on—who knows, you might be surprised. I can promise that we won't advocate giving up your religion or adopting some new one. We will only describe things you can check out for yourself and decide if they are true or fit for you.

The Four Fold Way: Simple Spiritual Principles

In the *8 Keys* book we describe four concepts—Show Up, Pay Attention, Tell the Truth Without Judgment, and Don't Be Attached to the Results—which are spiritual principles or guidelines for living a more spiritual life that Angeles Arrien describes in her book *The Four-Fold Way*. They have their roots in Buddhism and other eastern philosophies and can be found in many spiritual traditions and mindfulness practices designed to help us free our minds from needless suffering. We practice these concepts in our own lives and teach them to our clients, with profound results.

The rest of the sections in this Key contain various assignments. Rather than writing this in numerous places, please be aware that there will be many opportunities for you to find exercises and practices that would be good to add to your weekly Goals Sheet. Keep that in mind as you go through this Key.

SHOW UP

> *"When you are recovered, you will not compromise your health or betray your soul. But unless you have a connection to your soul, why would this even matter?"*
> —CAROLYN AND GWEN,
> 8 KEYS TO RECOVERY FROM AN EATING DISORDER

How do you show up in life? Does your mind (ego) run the show, telling you what to think, how you measure up, or leading you to believe you are your thoughts, your emotions, even your feelings? Or have you learned that there is something else beyond all these things; the "being" that is underneath them all? Can you let your mind take a backseat and show up from that place of open awareness, or what we call "soul self"? Learning to recognize the difference between ego and soul, and how to show up from your soul self, has a profound aspect on healing, not just from an eating disorder, but also from an unfulfilled life. For a more thorough understanding of this subject matter, please see the references provided in the bibliography for this Key.

EGO AND SOUL ASSIGNMENT: WHO ARE YOU?

Make a list of a few things that describe who you are.

1. _____
2. _____
3. _____
4. _____
5. _____

THE EGO MIND

Chances are you described yourself using characteristics about your gender, how you look, your profession, your achievements, your hobbies, or perhaps even your thoughts and emotions. These are all aspects of your ego, your thinking mind, and your identity. The word "ego" comes from Latin, meaning "I." Your ego is the part of you that relates to "I," "me," and "mine." It is the part that defines you as separate from others.

Your ego is not bad; it is necessary to maintain a personal identity, negotiate the world, think effectively, plan, prepare, and provide. Obviously it is important. However, problems arise when you think your ego is all that you are. Unchecked, your ego will fall endlessly into comparisons, judgment, and disconnection. "I am fat," "She is skinny," "I am not good enough," "I feel hurt." When you criticize others or feel criticized, your ego is at work. When you are in resistance to "what is," your ego is at work. If you have an eating disorder, your ego has taken over and is running your life.

You need your ego to have a cohesive identity, to read this book, and to navigate living on the planet. But when you cannot quiet your mind, accept *what is*, and be in the moment, you have confused yourself with your ego and lost connection with your soul self.

ASSIGNMENT: RESISTANCE TO THE PRESENT MOMENT

Finish the following sentences:

I wish _____

_____

If only _____

_____

Things will be okay when _____

_____

I can't accept _____

_____

I am suffering because _____

_____

When people finally understand me, I _____

_____

I will be okay when _____

_____

Look over what you wrote. These thoughts are all generated by your ego resisting the present moment. Accepting what is does not mean you can't do things to change a situation in the future, but what it does mean is that in this moment you accept what is. For example, let's say you wrote, "I wish I had a different body shape." This is a statement of non-acceptance. Consider the alternative statement of accepting what is, "My body shape is unique to me and I know I cannot change that without hurting myself." Another example would be if you wrote, "I will be okay when I lose weight." An alternative statement of accepting the present moment could be, "I accept where I am right now, and if my healthy eating causes me to lose weight then it was meant to be."

Look at the sentences you completed and see if you can now come up with a few sentences expressing acceptance of what is right here and now.

1. *"I feel pain, reminding me there is a lesson here."*
2. *"I accept my body right now but that does not mean it cannot change."*
3. _____
4. _____
5. _____
6. _____
7. _____

It probably feels unsettling to write sentences expressing acceptance of the present moment. It might feel wrong, not true, or a bunch of nonsense. We will spend more time on acceptance versus resistance later on in this Key. We hope by the end, you will understand what we are getting at, and how important it is, and it will not feel foreign or weird. Practicing acceptance means tapping into your soul self.

SOUL SELF

> *"A leap in spiritual growth happens when you realize,*
> *You don't have a soul; you are a soul."*

We have used the term "healthy self" with clients, and in this book, to help distinguish the difference between your eating disorder and the healthy voice you also have inside. The term *soul self* is our attempt to describe your inner being, beyond your ego and even beyond your healthy self. It is a state of awareness or consciousness that is both independently yours and yet connected to the source of consciousness, the part that witnesses the coming and going of thoughts, feelings, identities, and experiences without judgment, knowing none of them are you because you are the witnessing presence of it all.

> *"There is nothing more important to true growth than realizing you are not the voice of the mind—you are the one who hears it. If you don't understand this, you will try to figure out which of the many things the voice says is really you. People go through so many changes in the nature of 'trying to find myself.' They want to discover which of these voices, which of these aspects of their personality, is who they really are. The answer is simple: none of them."*
>
> —MICHAEL SINGER

The term *soul self* is the closest we could get to describe your conscious awareness, but it is not the exact same thing. Your soul self is the way you manifest your connection to this deeper source of awareness or consciousness in the world. Your ego is the way you manifest your identity, wants, and desires.

When you are connected to your soul self, you can witness all the concerns of your ego passing before you, like waves coming and going in the ocean. You can witness them and let them return to the sea. From this place, you are more interested in your awareness of your thoughts than in the thoughts themselves. From this place, you don't have to act on the thoughts or the feelings; you can acknowledge them, but you do not have to react. (Tip: Remember the lessons from Key 4.) In this state there is no place for an eating disorder to gain footing. There is no need to binge, starve, vomit, or reach a number on a scale. These things have no meaning or significance for your soul self and are matters that your ego takes up.

Quotes from clients on discovering their soul selves

> *"Taking the time to connect with my soul self made me realize that it was only my ego that was concerned with numbers and scales and fat grams. Sitting quietly for a few minutes day after day, I was slowly able to sense a different part of me that felt no pull toward those things. I realized I was not my thoughts, I was the one who could watch them come and go, just like a bouncing ball or characters in a movie. I was surprised that sitting with my eyes closed, and paying attention to my breath for a few minutes every day, connected me to a deeper part of me, my soul. Once I had that connection lots of other things I used to get caught up in began to take on less and less meaning and importance and eventually my whole view of things and thus my behaviors toward them changed.*
> —J.F.

> *"I used to think I had no soul. I was not a religious person and could not imagine what else having a soul meant but to accept religion and believe in something no one could prove was true. However, when I stepped back enough times and mindfully separated myself from my thoughts, my soul simply came through. I can now recognize my thoughts and my emotions as stories from my ego. I can watch them come up and let them go and not get pulled into or react to them."*
> —LR

ASSIGNMENT: CONNECTING TO YOUR SOUL SELF

In order to help you connect with your soul self, there are a variety of simple tasks you can do. Try one of the following suggestions in the morning or evening, or before starting a difficult conversation, when you feel hurt, or just pick any time that works for you.

Soul self exercises

1. *Take at least a 30-minute silent walk in nature.*
2. *Go off so you can be alone somewhere and listen to beautiful music.*
3. *Think of a difficult situation you're in and how someone you consider very spiritual (e.g., Jesus, Buddha, or the Dalai Lama) would respond if in the same situation.*
4. *Sit quietly, close your eyes, and focus on your breathing for at least 5 minutes.*
5. *Go watch the sunset or moonrise in complete silence.*

After you have done at least one of the above exercises, write below what it was like for you, what you may have noticed or felt.

Soul self exercise: _____

_____

My experience: _____

_____

We suggest you experiment with these exercises and see how they feel and what, if anything, might be different from your normal state. Your journal might be the best place to explore your thoughts and feelings after each exercise.

ASSIGNMENT: WHAT'S COMING UP?

Take a minute to write down a few questions or concerns that have come up for you so far while working through this Key.

1. _____
2. _____

3. _____
4. _____
5. _____

See if your concerns and questions get answered as you proceed in the workbook, but if not, the resources we give might also help. And don't forget that it helps to share your experience with others. You can always write to us on our "8 Keys to Recovery from an Eating Disorder" Facebook page.

PAY ATTENTION

Are you aware of *how* you pay attention? Are you easily distracted? Can you quiet your mind? Can you sit and notice feelings without reacting to them? Are you aware of *what* you tend to pay attention to? Do you pay more attention to the size of your thighs or the size of your heart, the number on the scale, or the number of kind acts you initiated today, how many calories you have eaten, or how many people smiled at you? What you choose to pay attention to affects everything. "Energy follows thought." Think about that statement for a minute. It is a simple phrase but a very important concept to grasp. Whatever you are thinking about, whatever you are paying attention to, is where your precious energy goes, directing and affecting your whole life. Most people have no idea they have the ability to control where their mind goes.

ASSIGNMENT: ASSESSING YOUR ATTENTION

Quiz yourself on your ability to pay attention by answering the following questions either Yes or No (meaning most of the time).

_____ *Can you ignore the things you can't control and not let them cause you stress?*

_____ *Do you take the time you need to make people feel heard and understood?*

_____ *Do the things you pay the most attention to bring you happiness and joy?*

_____ *Would you say you don't waste time on things from the past?*

_____ *Are you able to live in the moment and not worry about the future?*

_____ *Does your focus stay on task (meaning your attention does not wander off)?*

_____ *Can you stop worrying and refocus your attention?*
_____ *Do you spend quiet time in nature?*
_____ *Do you find it easy to quiet your mind and relax?*
_____ *Are you able to pay attention to your emotions without getting caught up in them?*

Give yourself 1 point for every Yes response. A score under 10, or any No answers to the above quiz, indicates that you could benefit from learning more about how to pay attention in order to reduce suffering and bring more peace and happiness into your life.

How to Pay Attention

The first aspect to discuss is *how* to pay attention. It is difficult to separate *how you pay attention* from *what you pay attention to* because they are intimately connected. To help us organize the material we want to share, it is helpful to think of these two different aspects of attention. *How to pay attention* is about mindfulness.

MINDFULNESS

Mindfulness is the practice of paying attention with openness, acceptance, and nonjudgment.

Take a moment to consider what your life would be like if you could really do that: *pay attention to every experience with openness, acceptance, and nonjudgment.* This includes your own emotions, other people's "faults" or transgressions, everything. Practicing mindfulness is an ancient, well-known key to spiritual growth and freedom from suffering. Mindfulness is the path of bringing forth your soul self.

Many who read our original 8 *Keys* book admitted to us that the mindfulness practices were the hardest ones for them to do in the entire book. We know. This was true for us as well. However, we cannot say enough about how important and effective these practices are.

They will help you move beyond your relentless, chattering ego mind and closer to your essence or soul self. We strongly encourage you to try out some of the assignments in this workbook, or in some other way find a mindfulness practice that makes sense to you.

Research shows that mindfulness practices can actually change your brain in ways that help you develop skills, tune into your inner world, and regulate your emotions so that you can respond rather than react to situations and avoid getting overwhelmed, going into panic mode, or automatic pilot.

It is useful to look at the various aspects of mindfulness to enhance your understanding of what mindfulness practices have to offer. Researchers have broken down mindfulness into five dimensions. Going over these dimensions will help you understand the many areas in which practicing mindfulness can help you.

ASSIGNMENT: THE DIMENSIONS OF MINDFULNESS

Look at the various dimensions of mindfulness and the examples from clients stating their need for improvement in that particular dimension. Next, in the spaces provided, come up with a statement that reflects some aspect of mindfulness you need to work on.

Observing, noticing, attending to sensations, perceptions, thoughts, feelings (ability to be/stay present, witnessing your thoughts, feeling your feelings)

Concerns or statements that indicate help is needed in this dimension:

"I don't really know what I'm feeling most of the time."

"I get lost in my thoughts and my feelings."

_____
_____
_____

Drescribing/labeling with words (interoceptive awareness, ability to identify and describe what you feel)

Concerns or statements that indicate help is needed in this dimension:

"I don't know if I am feeling hungry or angry."

"I can't find the words to describe my feelings."

Nonreactivity to inner experience (emotional regulation, ability to tolerate your emotions, and respond rather than react)

Concerns or statements that indicate help is needed in this dimension:

"In times of difficulty I want to get rid of the feelings and I go to the food."

"My emotions are overwhelming and I shut down, restricting food helps me do that."

Acting with awareness (non-automatic pilot/concentration/nondistraction)

Concerns or statements that indicate help is needed in this dimension:

"My eating disorder behaviors are habitual and occur without much awareness"

"I was just on auto pilot. I don't even remember doing that."

Nonjudging of experience (acceptance of situation, self, and others, acceptance vs. resistance, elimination of negative self-talk)

Concerns or statements that indicate help is needed in this dimension:

"I am a glutton and I hate myself for eating all of that."

"I can't be happy until I lose weight."

You might have found that you could use help in all the dimensions of mindfulness, or you might have narrowed it down to one or two categories. Either way, there are a variety of mindfulness practices that can help you.

TRADITIONAL MINDFULNESS PRACTICES

There are many forms of mindfulness, but meditation is probably the oldest and the most studied. It is also the most misunderstood. As you will see, meditation is a lot simpler than what most people think. That does not mean it is easy to do, at least not at first.

Meditation helps by allowing you to step back from your ego mind into your soul self. All mindfulness practices are geared to help you work internally rather than trying to control external circumstances, which of course you cannot do. As Sam Harris writes in his book *Waking Up*, "This is not to say that external circumstances do not matter. But it is your mind, rather than circumstances themselves, that determines the quality of your life. Your mind is the basis of everything you experience and of every contribution you make to the lives of others. Given this fact, it makes sense to train it."

Although we will first describe meditation, it is important to state up front that there are many other things you can do besides meditate, including yoga, tai chi, silent nature walks, chanting, or simply counting your breath. All these practices have the intention of helping you pay attention with awareness, openness, and nonjudgment. When going through this Key, hold onto the fact that the mindfulness practices described here can help you build a foundation for doing the hard work of recovery, as well as dealing with the struggles inherent in simply living your life.

MEDITATION

Meditation is often thought of as being esoteric, taking a lot of time or skill, and practiced only by religious or highly spiritual people, like monks. Meditation is simply a way of paying attention, and it is increasingly being practiced by all kinds of people looking to improve their lives in numerous ways. Meditation is learning to pay attention to the essential nature of your being, what we have been calling soul self or conscious awareness. In meditation you are practicing meta-awareness (aware of being aware). Once you become conscious of consciousness, you become aware of who and what you are. As Michael Singer puts it in *The Untethered Soul*,

> "It's like you have been on the couch watching TV, but you were so totally immersed in the show that you forgot where you were. Someone shook you

and now you're back to the awareness that you are sitting on the couch watching TV. Nothing changed. You simply stopped projecting your sense of self onto that particular object of consciousness. You woke up. That is spirituality. That is the nature of self. That is who you are."

Research has shown meditation to help with many things: calm the nervous system, lower blood pressure, alleviate depression and anxiety, and even assist immune function, among other benefits. There are now countless studies and books on this topic whose surface we barely scratch, so please refer to the resources in the Bibliography for more information. However, it is worth pointing out a couple of important things.

People with anorexia and bulimia are shown to have a higher-than-normal tendency toward anxiety. Many are diagnosed with an anxiety disorder in their lifetime. One study showed that the area of the brain responsible for our emotions, the amygdala, is overactive in anorexia nervosa, similar to people with anxiety disorders. The area of your brain that puts your amygdala in check or balance and regulates your emotional reactions is called the prefrontal cortex. Your prefrontal cortex is responsible for a variety of functions.

Prefrontal cortex functions:
1. Body regulation — sympathetic/parasympathetic (gas/brakes).
2. Attuned communication — feeling felt.
3. Emotional balance — level-headedness, clear and focused.
4. Response flexibility — react vs. respond.
5. Fear modulation — alert calm.
6. Empathy — see from another's point of view.
7. Insight — mental time travel, past to present and future.
8. Moral awareness — think and behave for social good.
9. Intuition — gut feelings, wisdom of body.

The prefrontal cortex functions on this list are also associated with mindfulness practices. It appears that meditating seems to strengthen the fibers in the prefrontal cortex and helps train this part of the brain to override the amygdala, or emotional brain. This is very important for people with eating disorders, who need help regulating and responding to emotions. So you can tell yourself that the practices we call meditation are really just how one goes about training the brain, or more specifically, strengthening the prefrontal cortex to keep the amygdala under control.

There are many variations of meditation practice such as Vipassana, Insight Meditation, and Transcendental Meditation. The many forms of meditation all involve shifting from thinking to awareness, and learning to separate your thoughts from your inner essence or soul self. Although we give some guidance here, we encourage you to explore various options to see what works best for you. In *Waking Up*, Sam Harris describes the importance of meditation and the profound impact it can have on our lives, regardless of any religious affiliation. The following is his meditation guide for beginners we ask you to try.

ASSIGNMENT: HOW TO MEDITATE

Try these simple directions and see what happens.

1. *Sit comfortably, with your spine erect, either in a chair or cross-legged on a cushion.*
2. *Close your eyes, take a few deep breaths, and feel the points of contact between your body and the chair or the floor. Notice the sensations associated with sitting—feelings of pressure, warmth, tingling, vibration, etc.*
3. *Gradually become aware of the process of breathing. Pay attention to wherever you feel the breath most distinctly—either at your nostrils or in the rising and falling of your abdomen.*
4. *Allow your attention to rest in the mere sensation of breathing. (You don't have to control your breath. Just let it come and go naturally.)*
5. *Every time your mind wanders in thought, gently return it to the breath.*
6. *As you focus on the process of breathing, you will also perceive sounds, bodily sensations, or emotions. Simply observe these phenomena as they appear in consciousness and then return to the breath.*
7. *The moment you notice that you have been lost in thought, observe the present thought itself as an object of consciousness. Then return your attention to the breath—or to any sounds or sensations arising in the next moment.*

8. *Continue in this way until you can merely witness all objects of consciousness—sights, sounds, sensations, emotions, even thoughts themselves—as they arise, change, and pass away.*

ASSIGNMENT: MY MEDITATION PRACTICE

Find a time that works best for you: _____

Number of minutes (Tip: Start with as few as five.) _____

Place (choose a space where you are unlikely to get interrupted). _____
_____

After you have tried to do your initial meditating write about your experience and any challenges you had with the practice and what you think might make it easier, or any plans that might help you to hang in there.

My experience: _____

My challenges: _____

My plans: _____

Always remember there is no right or wrong way to meditate, and it gets easier over time, much easier. It may take time to feel yourself becoming calm or notice any benefits. Once you do experience any of those things, it becomes much easier to continue doing it. Try to practice at the same time or on some regular basis if possible. Once it becomes fairly easy you can increase the minutes or the days, but go slowly. Doing too much too soon easily leads to frustration, and you may want to give up.

    We are both proof that you don't have to believe in meditation for it to work. If you are at all like us, closing your eyes to meditate might seem silly, uncomfortable, or just not worth it. Hopefully you will try it, or at least another mindfulness practice anyway. You can practice right now. Accept whatever feelings exist, notice how you feel in your body reading through this Key or trying to do the assignments, let go of any fear, judgment, or negative feelings. Just let them pass. Sit quietly for a few minutes until you feel calm and neutral. Now that you are in a receptive place, read about a few other mindfulness practices you can try.

FOCUSING ON YOUR BREATH

Paying attention to your breath is a good and easy place to start because it is a simple, yet profound practice and is used in all other practices such as yoga and meditation. Your breath is always with you, it is automatic and rhythmic, so you can close your eyes and easily focus your attention on it. Unless you already meditate, you are probably not used to slowing down, turning your focus inward, and paying attention to things such as your breath. Over time, you will find this practice develops your ability to feel calm and centered, and not just while doing it, but at other times in your life. The simple practice of paying attention to your breath can help you become acquainted with your witnessing presence, or soul self.

ASSIGNMENT: COUNTING YOUR BREATH

This is a very easy but effective mindfulness practice. You simply find a place to sit, close your eyes, and begin to count each breath. Each inhale and exhale can count as one, or you can count your inhale as one and exhale as two. Doing this helps train your mind to block out other distractions and focus on one thing. When you become distracted, which you will, simply return to your focus on your breath and begin counting again. Set a timer and do this for just 5 minutes, and you will see not only how easy it is, but how calm you can get just by doing this. You can begin to lengthen the time to 10 minutes and longer if you wish. If you do this every day you will notice a difference in your ability to calm your brain and nervous system and the ability to notice and shift your mind back from distractions just by focusing on your breath.

Now try it for yourself.

My experience with counting my breath: _____

_____

_____

ASSIGNMENT: ANTI-ANXIETY BREATHING

The anti-anxiety breath is one of the exercises we use most frequently with clients. This simple breathing technique can calm an overactive nervous system rather quickly and has become a very handy tool. Some people have found that this breathing technique helped them reduce or eliminate the need for anti-anxiety medication.

Sit in a quiet, comfortable place where you can spend a few undisturbed minutes. Close your eyes, settle yourself into a comfortable sitting position, and pay attention to your breathing. Notice that you are paying attention to your life force. Count how long it takes you to inhale, and then try to extend your exhale two counts longer. For example, if you count to six while inhaling, you would count to eight while exhaling. Simply doing that for a few minutes has allowed highly anxious clients to be able to sit still in groups, get settled before starting a conversation or entering a new situation, and even quell a panic attack. We both practice anti-anxiety breathing when we are late in traffic, before a speaking engagement, and in many other situations where high anxiety is present.

My experience: _____

_____

_____

YOGA

In the *8 Keys* book we discussed yoga as an important mindfulness practice, and both of us have found yoga helpful in our own lives and in the lives of many of our clients.

Personal Reflection: CAROLYN

In 1996 when I opened Monte Nido, my first residential treatment center for eating disorders, I included yoga as part of the program but had no idea how integral yoga would become for all Monte Nido programs and for other eating disorder professionals and sufferers around the world. Yoga helped me recover, but I did not know how profoundly it would contribute to the recovery of so many others. Monte Nido's clients soon made it clear:

> "Yoga provided me with a healthy way to quiet my mind and actually listen to my body and my spirit."

> "Through yoga I acquired a gentleness and reverence for my body, that instilled in me the desire to care for it better."

> "Yoga brought me back to a connection I had as a child when my mind and body were not at war but rather worked together and felt as one."

The clients' reactions to yoga were beyond my expectations, and I am not alone in these findings. During my career, I have run into countless eating disorder professionals and sufferers who have had positive experiences with yoga. The term yoga comes from *yuj*, a Sanskrit word meaning "to yoke" or unite. Yoga poses and philosophical teachings are designed to help unite mind, body, and spirit.

Research has been surfacing in recent years showing that yoga can lead to less self-objectification, greater body satisfaction, and even fewer eating disorder symptoms. The constant positive feedback in my own life, my clients' lives, and those of other professionals inspired me to put together and edit the book, *Yoga and Eating Disorders: Ancient Healing or a Modern Illness*. The following is an excerpt:

> "Their minds and bodies at war, people with eating disorders are disconnected from their higher selves. They are in a state of constant comparison, judgmental of themselves, out of balance, caught in habitual behavior patterns, and living in the past or future. If pondered for even a moment, it makes sense that yoga, an ancient philosophy and practice designed to unify mind, body, and spirit, could help someone whose relationship with all three is so tragically disrupted."

Of course there are many kinds of yoga and yoga studios, so you could find yourself in a class geared to burning calories or looking like the best yogi, but with the right intention in mind you can find a yoga class or begin a practice at home that works for you. In the end you will know if you find a teacher, studio, or practice that feels right for you and aids you in your ability to go inside and connect with a deeper part of your self.

Other ancient mind and body movement practices like chi quong or tai chi are also methods to accomplish internal awareness of your soul self and the connection between body, mind, and spirit. You might find one of these practices more suitable for you than yoga. We do suggest you try these practices out and see how they fit for you. Please give it some time. You might fall in love after one class, but you might have to go to a few before it catches on. Just like meditation, you will discover a profound difference between doing yoga or tai chi once in a while and practicing on a regular basis.

Personal Reflection: GWEN

My relationship with yoga is a work-in-progress. It's improving. I always feel good when I leave, and by good I mean relaxed and energetic, pain free, and satisfied with myself. I did not initially take to yoga, and I find it hard to do. When Carolyn had us all doing "down dog" on the front lawn of Monte Nido 20 years ago, I was not among those who reacted enthusiastically. I am genetically inflexible and have never been able to touch my toes. I am consistently unable to balance on one foot due to an old injury and am surprisingly weaker than I look. Yoga is very difficult for me. What I came to realize is that, seemingly against all odds, yoga has a way of providing things we need that we might not even realize. Yes, yoga helped me with flexibility, quieting my mind, and connecting mind and body, but it helped me also with a difficult aspect of my temperament. Since I'm a longtime overachiever, it is very hard for me to do things I am never going to be good at. When I found myself watching the clock in class, I would practice shifting my attention back into whatever pose I was holding. I would breathe and practice tolerating my discomfort, or take child's pose instead of rolling up my mat and heading out early. I will go regularly for a few months then not go at all for a while, but eventually, I always come back. I can feel its benefits and the way it facilitates connection between my mind, body, and spirit.

BEGINNER'S MIND

Beginner's mind is a great mindfulness exercise for learning how to pay attention. Beginner's mind means seeing or experiencing something, like the taste of an apple, as if you were tasting it for the first time. This means doing the best you can to repress your knowledge or assumptions or expectations. Beginner's mind brings awareness to living fully in the moment. It shows you how differently you pay attention when you drop your preconceived ideas. Beginner's mind is a way to practice not taking things for granted just because you know what they are and experience them all the time. Children are good examples of beginner's mind, but it's easy for them, they are beginners. Dogs are also great examples; every time they see you, it's like the very first time all over again.

Taking the time to stop and pay attention to the awesome reality of a blooming rose, seeing the sacredness in what we have come to regard as ordinary, will increase your appreciation of nature and the world around you.

ASSIGNMENT: SEEING WITH BEGINNER'S MIND

Pick a natural object that you are familiar with and try to put aside all your knowledge of it for the time being. Touch it or hold it in your hand, smell it, look at its color and shape, taste it if appropriate. Describe the object without using its name, and try to explain this object as if you had never seen it and had just discovered it and its function or qualities. See how different it is to perceive this object without your mind's rational conditioning associated with it.

Describe the object without using its name: _____
_____
_____

Now let someone read what you wrote and see if they can guess what you were looking at.

What did you learn? _____
_____
_____

VISUALIZATION, A WAY OF PAYING ATTENTION

Visualization is another way of paying attention and is a significant resource for training your mind. When you visualize something you are focusing energy in that direction.

What you are about to learn is that visualization helps you access your inner wisdom and creates pathways in your brain that help make your intentions a reality. Research in neuroplasticity has shown that visualization is actually a form of practice that activates the same area of the brain as if you were actually doing whatever you are visualizing.

It is fairly well known that athletes and musicians use visualization to enhance their performance. However, you may not realize how incredible this is or how well it actually works. In his book *The Brain That Changes Itself,* Norman Doidges describes research showing that visualizing playing the piano is an astonishing way to practice. To briefly summarize: Two groups of nonplayers were taught to play something on the piano. Both groups were then told to practice the piece they were taught for five days. The first group was allowed to practice in the usual way, physically touching the keys. The second group had to practice by sitting at the piano, but rather than using their hands, they had to visualize playing. In three days, the "visualizing" players were as accurate as the physical players. In five days, the visualizers were still good but the actual physical players had improved more. But, it only took the visualizers one single two-hour physical practice session to catch up and perform as well as the group who had been physically practicing all along. This is only one of a number of astonishing examples that visualization is a form of practice, which can help you improve at a task. It is important to note that it was not visualization alone that worked, but a combination of visualization and practice. Doidges points out in his book that Russian athletes, who were the first publicly known Olympic athletes using visualization to enhance athletic performance, discovered the best combination was 50 percent physical practice and 50 percent visualization.

Visualization can help *you* recover by helping you prepare for and overcome challenging events, such as eating foods that seem scary like pasta, or resisting the urge to binge or purge. With visualization, you essentially imagine yourself in the situation and see yourself successfully handling it, step by step, in a healthy way. Don't forget, though, visualization alone will not be enough to enhance your "performance" so you will actually have to physically eat the pasta, sometimes in addition to visualizing yourself eating it, for real changes to take place in your ability to eat it comfortably. However, if pasta is very scary for you, you can start by just doing visualizations of yourself being able to eat it, even before ever actually doing it. Visualizing ahead of time has helped clients get through numerous challenging events and situations.

A client describes her experience:

"I had a really successful first experience using visualization before eating a very scary food for me . . . a muffin. I realized I was spending the majority of my day visualizing how things will be catastrophic, or how specific foods might make me feel uncomfortable or "fat." Using visualization to entertain a positive outcome helped me see a different possibility. The step-by-step practice I learned included being very specific. In this first experience, I visualized how I'd choose the muffin I wanted. Then I saw myself deliberately tasting the muffin before eating other foods on my plate. I visualized myself eating it calmly while chatting with friends. Visualization offered me a safe way to practice eating scary foods that reduced my anxiety substantially around many things related to my eating. I have made this a continued part of my recovery and am now using it to envision comfort with my changing body."

—J.B.

ASSIGNMENT: USING VISUALIZATION TO SUPPORT AND ENHANCE MY RECOVERY

Below are various visualizations we have successfully used with clients. You can try one of our examples, but in the space provided write down one you would like to try. Be sure to have the uninterrupted time and space to be able to fully visualize the whole experience—what you are wearing, your surroundings, the smell and taste of the food, etc. This is not an exercise to rush through. It can be helpful to have someone else, like your therapist or dietitian, guiding you through the experience, but it is not necessary.

Visualize yourself:

    Eating a food you have eliminated from your diet and tasting and enjoying it .

Eating pizza with a friend, having a nice conversation and not purging later.
Eating with your family at the dinner table.
Buying new clothes and trying them on without looking at the sizes.
Going to a restaurant and ordering freely what you want, without concern for calories and then eating it and going home and being ok.

Personal visualization idea _____
_____

What happened when I practiced visualizing _____
_____

We suggest you add visualization to your weekly Goals Sheet.

WHAT ARE YOU PAYING ATTENTION TO?

We have just looked at how you pay attention, and now we turn to *what* you pay attention to. In our first book, we talk about "soul lessons" and "soul moments," which are terms we use to describe various exercises, activities, and assignments we give clients to help them direct their attention toward matters of spirituality and soul. Soul lessons involve learning to pay attention to your own sacred core essence and the sacredness of life. Soul moments are reminders of your connection to something greater than yourself and help you remain grateful for things that might be ordinary in some sense, but full of awe and wonder when you take the time to really pay attention to and appreciate them.

BODY AND SOUL

Over identification with, and emphasis on, the body is one of the most basic forms of an unchecked ego. Healing negative body image is an important aspect of eating disorder recovery. We do not use traditional body image assignments, such as body tracings or the majority of exercises we have found in use at treatment programs. Our experience has shown that focusing directly on your body image is not helpful and in fact can make things worse. Traditional body image exercises keep the focus on your body. Think of this analogy. If we said, "Don't think about a white horse," we are pretty sure you would immediately picture . . . a white horse. This is our experience of using traditional body image exercises. Instead, we have found that it is wiser to turn your focus to what is more important, or what truly matters.

One of the criteria for having an eating disorder is that your self-evaluation is unduly influenced by body weight and shape. Rather than "working" by directly focusing on your body image, we prefer to help transfer your self-evaluation to matters of the heart and soul. Therefore our philosophy of healing is, "Instead of cursing the darkness, bring in the light." (This quote has been attributed to so many people we cannot say for sure who the original source is.)

Bringing in the light means bringing in care of the soul. Care of the soul does not mean not caring about your body or detaching from your body, it means attaching a soulful meaning to it. By caring for your soul, you are healing your body image. When your life is filled with soul moments, mindfulness, and seeing the ordinary as sacred, you focus less on yourself and your body image and more on your relationships and the world around you. Through this, you can learn to see your body as your precious "earth suit" that allows you to experience life. Care of the soul leads to loving and respecting your body and accepting what you can and can't change about it *without compromising your health or betraying your soul.*

BODY AND SOUL EXERCISES

In addition to encouraging yoga and meditation to clients and weaving the concept of ego vs. soul throughout the treatment process, we also include practices we call "body and soul" exercises. Over the years we have accumulated quite a few body and soul exercises for use in groups or with individual clients. We invite you to explore these body and soul exercises on your own or with a friend, or take them to therapy.

ASSIGNMENTS: BODY AND SOUL

1. *Write a general description of how you define body and how you define soul. You can periodically revisit and revise your definition. We suggest you look at the resources suggested in this workbook, try a few assignments here, and then write your definitions.*

2. *Get a box of Angel Cards. (Tip: you can order them online.) Each day or each week, draw an angel card from the deck and use the information on the card as a guide to help you pay attention to certain aspects of yourself.*

3. Write a meal blessing that you can read to yourself before meals, reminding yourself how the food becomes your body. (See Key 5 for details and an example.)
4. Write about a few ways in which your ego has led you astray recently, and then write how your soul self sees the situation.
5. Listen to the song The Healing Room. Take some time and listen to it a few times, and then write what it means to you. (We would love to hear if anyone ever wants to share their responses.)
6. Find a poet you like. If you don't know any, we suggest Mary Oliver, Pablo Neruda, or Maya Angelou. Get opinions from others; there are countless poets out there, but chances are a good friend will turn you on to one who you really like. Read a poem at night to put the day to rest with beauty, or read one every morning to start your day.
7. What does religion vs. spirituality mean to you? This is also a good question to visit and revisit.
8. Listen to the song "Me" by Paula Cole and write about how you might relate to it, or if you don't then why not. (And let Carolyn know if you don't relate to it because she cannot imagine that happening.)
9. How do you know when your soul self is in charge?
10. Name two things that your ego is attached to in relationship to your body.
11. Write a letter from your soul self to you when you were a young child.
12. List five ways your ego mind reacts to things and five alternative ways to "respond" from your soul self.
13. Come up with a quote that is a reminder of soul or reenchantment for you and make a sign to put up somewhere you will see daily, or put the saying in your wallet or purse. Send the saying to a few close friends.
14. Grow some flowers, vegetables, or herbs. Growing a life form is a lost art, taken for granted. It brings reconnection with the miracle of life.
15. Bring "soul" to a dining experience by using linens, putting flowers on the table, lighting candles, or reading a blessing.
16. Listen to a Deva Premal and Miten CD. Much of their music is mantras turned into songs. It might be a stretch for some readers, but many are touched by their music.

PAYING ATTENTION TO NATURE TO REENCHANT YOUR LIFE

Our attention is constantly being pulled in all directions, to our iPhones and iPads, computers, traffic signs, televisions, and radios, Google Maps, and department stores, and we have forgotten to pay attention to the natural world around us, which offers so much richness in terms of inspiration and awe.

HOW AWARE ARE YOU OF THE NATURAL WORLD AROUND YOU?

See how many of the following questions or statements you can answer without any help.

1. Can you describe the five trees closest to your home?
2. What time does the sun set today or rise tomorrow?
3. Do you know exactly what the Winter Solstice is?
4. Do you know how big the sun is compared to the earth?
5. Why are there beautiful colors during a sunset?
6. Describe what an atom really looks like?
7. What kinds of birds live in your area?
8. How can you tell if the moon is waxing or waning?
9. Describe the last time you took five minutes to gaze at the full moon.
10. Describe how the ocean tides and a menstrual cycle are tied to the moon.

If you had a hard time with the above assignment, don't feel bad—most people do. Most of us visit nature in the form of a vacation, going to the beach on the weekend, or perhaps a daily run in the park. However, paying attention to nature as part of a daily appreciation is a way you can begin to direct your energy. Next time you go outside, look around and see what nature is around you. Where do you live in terms of the natural world, where is the nearest, largest tree, are flowers blooming anywhere, is there snow on a nearby mountain, how close is a body of water or a hillside, have trees started to lose their leaves, do you hear creatures at night?

NATURE, THE COSMOS, AND SPIRITUALITY

Knowing what we now know about the cosmos, our natural world, and our integral part in it shows us the interdependence of everything and the mystery and awe of the universe we live in.

Primitive people spent time in nature, observing the seasons, the life-giving sun coming up every morning, the importance of the stars, and the connection of all things. They noticed, paid attention to, depended on, and were in awe of all these things. They had no science to understand their awe of the universe, but had a spiritual relationship with things, for example, worshipping the sun or praying for rain.

In todays "evidence-based" culture, scientific explanations of our environment and the universe have led to a situation where logical explanations have taken the awe out of our experience of it. However, science does not have to be at odds with spirituality. It is the combination of the awesome scientific knowledge we have of our universe, and an embodied experience of it, that leads to a spiritual experience or understanding. Knowing what is actually happening during a sunset is one thing, but knowing this combined with taking the time to go out and appreciate the experience of it brings a deeper sense of appreciation and awe.

SOUL MOMENTS

Soul moments are moments that move you, or touch you deeply and provide an experience of awe or reverence that is hard to describe in words but is felt in a meaningful way. Some examples of soul moments are:

- Witnessing the birth of an animal or human.
- Staring into someone's eyes for more than 30 seconds.
- Singing or chanting music with moving or uplifting messages.
- Sitting quietly in a forest, or watching a magnificent waterfall.
- Gazing at the moon or planets, especially through a telescope.
- Watching the snow falling in the mountains.
- Lighting candles and praying with others.

Keeping track of soul moments will help you turn your attention to the awe of life, and is important to set as a goal, because there are so many other things that demand your attention on a daily basis. Remember it is what you pay attention to shapes where your energy goes and the quality of your life.

ASSIGNMENT: MY SOUL MOMENTS

Take a week to seek out and pay attention to soul moments. Write them down and add a few sentences of why it was a soul moment and your experience of it.

Soul moment: _____
_____
_____

Experience: _____
_____
_____

Soul moment: _____
_____
_____

Experience: _____
_____
_____

Soul moment: _____
_____
_____

Experience: _____
_____
_____

We have come to the end of the principle on "paying attention." Everything, in one way or another, has been about mindfulness, a different way of paying attention to your self and the world around you. When you can develop a mindful presence, you can distinguish the difference between this presence and your fearful thoughts or response patterns. When you are in touch with this presence, you can more readily separate it from your Eating Disorder Self. You can see you are not your "Eating Disorder Self" and in fact are far more powerful than that. This presence will put your Eating Disorder Self out of a job.

ASSIGNMENT: MINDFULNESS AGREEMENT

Similar to an Eater's Agreement, we sometimes have our clients write a mindfulness agreement. This can serve as a reminder for what they want to be paying attention to. Read this one from one of our clients, and perhaps at some point you might find it useful to write one for yourself.

Mindfulness Agreement:

In my Eating Disorder Self, I could have never imagined that I would have the ability to be mindful. I was so wrapped up in my food, exercise, and rigid daily life that there was no room for all that encompasses mindfulness: openness, acceptance, nonjudgment, and being present.

I now realize I always have a choice—a choice of how I will respond to my circumstances in any moment, if I can stay present enough to be aware of them.

From this day forward, I choose to make the effort to be mindful in all aspects of my life.

I will no longer spend my days on autopilot. I agree from this day forward to be accepting of the present, be open, aware, and willing to stay in the now.

I know I may get caught up in the everyday life of my everyday life, and when this happens I promise myself that I will be awake enough to recognize this, stop, and find my true self again, take a breath, and start to feel again. Feel my breath enter then leave my body in the way it wants to in that moment, and then take deeper ones to bring me back.

I will be mindful of the things around me that really matter, love, air, water, breath, where I am in the world at that moment, and feel my feet on the ground again.

I will be open to feel what I'm feeling without judgment or criticism, reassure myself and keep going, or stop if I need to. It's all what my mind makes of it. I choose to no longer search for ways to be miserable. I deserve to be happy, and my soul desires happiness.

TELL THE TRUTH WITHOUT JUDGMENT

The skills learned by practicing the first two principles, "showing up" and "paying attention" will help you with the third, "truth without judgment." It is an important concept we follow in our own lives and teach to our clients. Telling the truth without judgment is easy to do when you are happy with things. It is difficult to do when someone hurts or upsets you or you are angry.

Telling the truth without judgment means being honest without being negative, critical, or blaming. Learning how to do this will make your message much more likely to be received. In order to tell the truth without judgment, you need to calm and neutralize any anger or negativity you have before you attempt to communicate. It's not just the words you use that communicate but your nonverbal messages as well. It is crucial to do what it takes to get your body calm and back to neutral. You might simply need to take some time to calm down, you might do breathing exercises, or you could meditate. The key is not to let your hurting ego run the show, because telling the truth without judgment means you speak from your "soul self," the calm inner wise core we have been talking about.

ASSIGNMENT: MAKING JUDGMENTAL STATEMENTS NONJUDGMENTAL

Look at the phrases or sentences below and rewrite them, taking out the negativity while maintaining the core message. This is much easier to do when you are not in a difficult situation or angry and upset. However, this practice will help familiarize you with what truth without judgment looks like.

Example:
   You are a liar.
Change to:
   You have a hard time telling the truth.

Example:
   You are lazy and can't be counted on.
Change to:
   I'm worried you will not follow through when I'm counting on you.

Tip: One way to do this is to think about why you are upset, or how it makes you feel when this person does something that hurts or upsets you, instead of just describing the behavior or name calling. Instead of, "You're always late because you don't care about anyone but yourself," try, "When you are late, it makes me feel like you don't care about me and that hurts."

Now try writing some truth without judgment statements

"You are selfish and don't care about anyone."
Change to: _____
_____

"You spent the whole evening getting drunk and acting like a fool."
Change to: _____
_____

"I hate how she shows off."
Change to: _____
_____

Write down a few judgmental, blaming, or negative comments you have made in the past and then change them to truth without judgment statements. (Tip: Keep in mind that in real conversation your tone and body language count for a lot.)

"My original statement."_____
Change to: _____
_____

"My original statement."_____
Change to: _____
_____

"My original statement."_____
Change to: _____
_____

KEY 8: FINDING MEANING AND PURPOSE

ASSIGNMENT: PRACTICING TRUTH WITHOUT JUDGMENT

Think of a person with whom you are upset or have unfinished business with, and write down what you would say to him or her, uncensored, without holding anything back.

_____
_____
_____

Now write your truth about the situation, telling the person what you need to communicate, but without any negative comments or judgment.

_____
_____
_____

Next time you are upset with someone, practice telling the truth without judgment and write about your experience below. Were you able to do it? How did the other person respond? Is there anything you would do differently next time?

_____
_____
_____

Telling the truth without judgment does not ensure that others will not get mad or be hurt. You can only do your part. However, just like a tuning fork that sends out a certain vibration, we have found that when you stay connected to your soul self you can help bring out the soul self in others. Practicing truth without judgment will help improve the quality of your interactions and relationships. We have yet to find anyone who says otherwise. The following examples illustrate how these concepts have helped clients.

> "When I first learned truth without judgment I found it so simple to understand, yet difficult to do. The main reason is that when I'm angry and feeling the most judgmental it is hard to quiet my screaming upset ego and stop it from dumping all the negativity in my head onto the person I'm mad at. What really got me hooked on truth without judgment is that when I could do it, I discovered how great it worked. What I was communicating

came across, but the other person was way less defensive and I got into far fewer arguments. I feel better inside when I have to approach people now with a difficult subject, because anger usually stays out of it when I can stick to truth without judgment through the whole conversation. This gets harder when the other person gets angry and negative, but it's not impossible. I'm not exaggerating that this one concept has changed my relationships and my life."

—PN

"*Truth without judgment is one of the most important things I learned in treatment. I used to blame everyone around me for my feelings. I wanted people to change. If anyone hurt me, I felt justified telling them off, being critical and negative. The problem is this was not really working, and I was miserable most of the time. The concept of ego and soul was helpful, but I did not think of myself as a spiritual person and did not grasp how to live from my "soul self "until I learned truth without judgment. It is not esoteric; it is simple. All I had to do was practice staying calm and not use any blaming, negative, or judgmental words. I'm not saying it was easy at first, it was hard, but once I got it, I could not believe how it made me, and the people around me, feel. I remember when I realized that although I had not thought of myself as a spiritual person, practicing truth without judgment is a spiritual tool that changed my life, so I guess I can say I am kind of spiritual after all."*

—CS

Showing up, paying attention, and telling the truth without judgment may seem difficult, but the reality is that following these principles gets easier as you practice and see the benefits. There will be times when your ego is the only part of you showing up, your words fly out of your mouth full of judgment, or you have neglected paying attention in some important way. Once you realize what is happening, you can just get yourself back on track. Doing what you can to live by these guidelines will bring positive results, and the feedback and reinforcement you get will help you to continue following these principles until over time they become your natural way.

NOT BEING ATTACHED TO THE RESULTS

We have already discussed the concept of acceptance. There are only two ways to deal with something: acceptance or resistance. There is no other way. The fundamental wisdom of this fourth principle, "not being attached to the results," means realizing you can choose to resist what is, or accept what is. Acceptance is the key to less suffering and a more soul-led life.

Most people have a hard time with this principle. You might think it means not caring about what happens, or that you should never try to change anything. Caring about what happens is important, but accepting what happens is critical if you want to remain free from needless suffering. This means letting go of what has already happened in the past, and accepting what is true in the present moment. It does not mean you can't do anything to change a situation that is ongoing. For example, if you have a broken foot you have to accept it, not be in resistance to the fact that it is broken. Resistance might manifest as anger, blame, swearing, or being in denial. Acceptance does not mean you say, "Oh well, I accept my foot is broken now and there's nothing I can do." Acceptance means you accept that it is broken and that negative resistant behaviors are counterproductive, but you can focus on the best way to treat the break, so you can heal quickly. (In Key 5, we discussed accepting your weight in this same way.)

Not being attached means accepting the things you cannot change, or that are not worth the energy, money, or effort to change. Nonattachment is learning how to live a life of acceptance, as opposed to resistance.

Accepting the present moment means accepting every thought, sensation, feeling, and perception that comes—all of it, even stuff you find unacceptable. We know this is a difficult concept, and not easy to do, but once you get the hang of it, you will be surprised at how much easier it is than suffering with resistance to everything that is already happening anyway. Suffering is often seen as something that just happens to you and you have no control over the coming or going of it in your life. Feeling like a victim, you try to escape or avoid it, but it still seems to find you. You have forgotten your true nature and become a "separate self" who is at war with the present. Suffering is really a signal. It is your guide telling you to come back to the present, to acceptance, to wholeness. When you stop resisting your experience in the moment, you are able to respond to life as it is now, rather than as you want it to be.

Eckhart Tolle, in *The Power of Now*, writes, "*Accept the present moment as if you had chosen it.*" Again, (because we know from experience how difficult this will seem at first), acceptance does not mean giving up any attempts to change a situation or prevent bad things from happening. It means admitting and accepting the truth of the moment, however much you would like it to be different. See the following example of how one client learned to use this concept.

> "After months of fighting, my girlfriend broke up with me and I was in a lot of pain. At first I started getting angry at her, wanting to battle it out, talk her into staying, even berating her. Then I realized I was attached to having things my way, and to the way we used to be, instead of accepting the obvious: We no longer get along. Yes it was very hard to accept, but it was the truth. Then I remembered something I learned in therapy and I asked, myself, 'What if I accept this as if I had chosen it?' It is such a simple but profound question to ask that allows you to really look at your lessons . . . I realized that in a way, of course, I had chosen it. All my actions up to that point, all our fighting, all the things I said, all ended up with the break-up. It hit me that I can be in pain over something but accept it, learn my lessons from it and move on."

ASSIGNMENT: ACCEPTANCE VS. RESISTANCE

1. List something that you are having a hard time accepting.

2. Write your feelings about why you are resisting rather than accepting what is.

3. How long are you willing to stay in resistance, nonacceptance, or attached to the outcome you desired?

4. What do you think would help you get to acceptance?

(Tip: Read the rest of this Key and then come back to this assignment and see if you can write from a place of "not being attached to the results." Include why you decided to "let go" rather than resist, and how you helped yourself come to and accept this view.)

The principle of nonattachment can be applied to every area of your life. You do what you can to change things that can be changed, but then you let go. This principle is discussed in the "Serenity Prayer," used at Alcoholic Anonymous.

LET GO OR BE DRAGGED

Personal Reflection: GWEN

One of my favorite sayings is, "Let go or be dragged." I have no idea who said it, but I love it so much I have it on a magnet and say it to myself and to others whenever it fits, which is often. Recently I was having a party at my house, and I wanted everything to be ready and perfect before any guests arrived. As the time neared, I realized I forgot about the outside heaters, feeding my animals, cleaning off the patio furniture, and several other things. I could feel myself tense up, my anxiety started soaring, and I started *barking* at my son, who was helping me. I was running around trying to do everything before anyone showed up. I suddenly realized how crazy I was acting and how horrible I felt. "Let go or be dragged" popped into my head and immediately stopped my self-inflicted suffering. Who cares if I was lighting the heaters or feeding my animals when people were there? People actually love watching my potbelly pig, Wilma, eat her dinner. There was no reason I had to do everything before guests arrived. I had become attached to that plan and was making myself, and everyone around me, miserable. I had to let go and accept the present situation or be dragged down in discontent and disappointment.

NONATTACHMENT AND YOUR BODY

One of the most profound uses of not being attached is perhaps one of the hardest areas to apply it: the relationship you have with your body.

If you are having a difficult time with your body, it means you are attached to it being a different way. Your body is not really the problem; it is your resistance to your body and the emotional reaction created by that resistance that causes pain. Although you will get sick of hearing us say it, you are more in control of your happiness and unhappiness in this area than you want to believe. Hopefully this entire 8th Key has given you a glimpse into the reality that true happiness is rarely (if ever) achieved by simply changing something external. We repeatedly see clients lose weight, get liposuction, breast surgeries, and tummy tucks and still hate their bodies, because the real problem is an inside job, not an outside job. Your inner states of consciousness are far more influential than your outer circumstances. The way you experience life is created by the state of mind with which you meet it.

ASSIGNMENT: BODY ACCEPTANCE

1. *How would you feel about and treat your body if you truly practiced acceptance versus resistance?*

   _____
   _____

2. *What your life would be like if you woke up one morning and were in total acceptance your body's natural size and shape?*

   _____
   _____

3. *Write about a day in your life living with acceptance rather than resistance to your body.*

   _____
   _____

THE GOOD NEWS AND THE BAD NEWS ABOUT BODY IMAGE

We understand that accepting your body might sound like an impossible task right now, but as you learn, practice, and get healthier, it does get a lot easier. The good news about body image is that you don't have to resolve all your body image issues to recover. In fact, it is very likely that you will continue to encounter some body image issues throughout life. Welcome to living in this culture! You will continue to be exposed to toxic messages about body and weight, and as a sensitive being, it would be hard for you not ever to be affected by it. People *without* eating disorders have body image issues. The difference between them and you is that when they talk about having body image issues, they don't starve or harm themselves to solve or manage these feelings, nor do they measure their self-worth only by this one aspect of themselves. Learning to accept and respect your body could be one of your biggest challenges and may require ongoing work and attention from you. Being recovered and maintaining a healthy weight will lessen your body image distress and distortion, because it is easier to cope with anything when you have mood stability, emotional regulation, and resiliency. Having a negative body image doesn't feel good, but just like any other difficult feeling you can get through it without having to act on it.

ASSIGNMENTS: NONATTACHMENT

1. *Write down other examples of things you have become attached to.*

   _____
   _____
   _____
   _____

2. *Write down things you can do or say that might help you let go of attachment to the things you listed above.*

   _____
   _____
   _____
   _____

3. *Make a list of the advantages and disadvantages of letting go and not being attached. Carefully go over the list and see if you can now get rid of what at first seemed like disadvantages of letting go.*

   _____
   _____
   _____
   _____

Practicing all the principles for living: showing up, paying attention, telling the truth without judgment, and not being attached to the results, can be life-altering, and the essence of what we would call being a spiritual person. Being guided by these spiritual principles will not only help you get over your eating disorder, it will also lead you to a more free and soulful life.

ASSIGNMENTS TO HELP YOU REMEMBER AND PRACTICE THE FOUR PRINCIPLES

Create an altar. Drop any old or negative connotations you have for this word, and see what we mean by it. You need only to find a special place in your home where you can put special objects that will serve to remind you on a daily basis of each one of the four principles. Try to find a place that is out of the public way but in an area you would frequent often so you get several reminders. (Tip: Directions for making an altar are described in the 8 Keys *book but are also easy to look up.)*

Write out the four principles on a small piece of paper and carry it in your wallet so you can look at it as a reminder.

Blow up a beautiful photograph that might represent the principles, label it with the principles and find a special place to hang the picture where you see it every day.

Write in your journal about how you are practicing the principles in your life and how doing so is making a difference.

Teach the principles to other people and see how it helps them.

OUR FINAL THOUGHTS

Taking the time to practice mindfulness skills, participate in soul lessons, see things with a beginner's mind, and bring reverence and sacredness to yourself and those around you will help you create a more spiritual and soulful life. You cannot control everything that happens to you, but you can control how you react to what happens. Living in acceptance helps you decrease needless suffering and let go of unnecessary attachments you may have. This does not mean you have to just sit by and accept everything that happens without ever trying to make changes. It means you first have to pay attention, accept things for what they are, and then determine what you can do. You can live your life in resistance to things or learn when to accept and move on. Letting go of your eating disorder will help you live a more meaningful life and, on the other hand, living a more meaningful life will help you let go of your eating disorder. Both are true and up to you.

After reading through the Keys to recovery, and taking some steps on your own, hopefully you have a better idea of what it might be like for you when, like us, you can look back and see your eating disorder as a thing of the past. When that time comes, you will be recovered. You will no longer have an Eating Disorder Self, but instead will be living your life as a fully whole, integrated person. You will understand your issues, but no longer use eating disorder behaviors to cope. You will feel your feelings and know how to challenge your thoughts. You will eat freely but consciously. You will have no need for scales or diets. You will continue to be aware of and work on any problematic behaviors that need to change. You will get your needs met from your relationships rather than your eating disorder, and live a soul-led life that brings you meaning and purpose.

WRITING ASSIGNMENT: A DAY IN MY LIFE WHEN I AM RECOVERED

We have come to our last assignment in this workbook. By doing this last assignment, you will have the opportunity to write your own final thoughts and create a personal ending of this book for you. In Key 1, we asked you to write about a day in your life when you are recovered. Take some time to visualize once again a day in the future when you are free from your eating disorder. Where are you, and who are you with? Get very specific in your imagery. What are you wearing? What is going on in your life at this time? Are you working or going to school? Are you in a relationship? Imagine yourself sitting down to have a meal. Are you with someone or by yourself? Where are you having this meal? What are you eating? How does it feel to be free of negative or fearful thoughts about the food and your body? What kinds of friends do you have? What brings meaning to your life? Spend some time with this visualization, and then write it down. Remember, visualization is practice. Having a clear image of what your life will be like and writing it down is an example of setting an intention for where you are headed. Carry a copy of this assignment with you, and hang a copy of it somewhere where you can see it every day. You can even send us a copy if you like.

> *"Steering hope away from false gods, shepherding the focus back toward the heart, learning to see one's private pain in a larger context, coming to link body with spirit: This, of course, is the essence of revolutionary work."*
>
> —CAROLINE KNAPP, APPETITES

Our best to you on this journey.

Mitakuye Oyasin. (Look it up!)

Carolyn and Gwen

References and Resources

Resources for Each Key

Key 1:

Prochaska, J. & DiClemente, C. (1983) Stages and processes of self-change in smoking: toward an integrative model of change. *Journal of Consulting and Clinical Psychology, 51*(3), 390–395.

Prochaska, J. O., DiClemente, C. C., & Norcross, J. C. (1992). In search of how people change: Applications to addictive behavior. *American Psychologist, 47,* 1102–1114.

U.S. Department of Health and Human Services. *The health benefits of smoking cessation: A report of the surgeon general.* U.S. Department of Health and Human Services, Public Health Service, Centers for Disease Control, Center for Chronic Disease Prevention and Health Promotion, Office on Smoking and Health. DHHS Publication No. (CDC) 90–8416, 1990.

Ryan, M. J. (2003). *The power of patience: How to slow the rush and enjoy more happiness, success, and peace of mind every day.* New York: Broadway Books.

Costin, C. & Grabb, G. S. (2012). *8 keys to recovery from an eating disorder: Effective strategies from therapeutic practice and personal experience.* New York: W. W. Norton & Company, Inc.

Project Heal (http://theprojectheal.org/) is a nonprofit organization committed to providing grant funding for people with eating disorders who cannot afford treatment, promoting healthy body image and self-esteem, and serving as a testament that full recovery from an eating disorder is possible.

Manna Fund (http://www.mannafund.org/) is a nonprofit organization dedicated to providing hope and financial assistance to individuals who need treatment for eating disorders. Manna Fund provides funds for residential and inpatient eating disorder treatment for individuals lacking insurance coverage or for those with inadequate insurance coverage. Manna Fund grants scholarships to recipients by providing direct payment to partnering eating disorder treatment facilities.

Mentor Connect. (http://www.mentorconnect-ed.org) offers an on line community where those in recovery from eating disorders can connect with mentors and peers for support.

Key 2: *None*

Key 3:

Stice, E., Maxfield, J., & Wells, T. (2003). Adverse Effects of Social Pressure to be Thin on Young Women: An Experimental Investigation of the Effects of "Fat Talk." *International Journal Of Eating Disorders*, 34(1), 108-117.

Gross, J., & Rosen, J.C. (1988). Bulimia in adolescents: Prevalence and psychosocial correlates. *International Journal of Eating Disorders*, 7, 51–61.

Kronenfeld, L. W., Reba-Harrelson, L., Von Holle, A., Reyes, M. L., & Bulik, C. M. (2010). Ethnic and racial differences in body size perception and satisfaction. *Body Image*, 7(2), 131–136. doi:http://dx.doi.org/10.1016/j.bodyim.2009.11.002

Bulik, Cynthia. M. (2010). Specialist supportive clinical management for anorexia nervosa. In Carlos Grilo & James E. Mitchell (Eds.), *The treatment of eating disorders: A clinical handbook* (pp. 108–128). New York: Guilford.

Wade, T. D., Bulik, C. M., Neale, M., & Kendler, K. S. (2000). Anorexia and major depression: Shared genetic and environmental risk factors. *The American Journal of Psychiatry*, 157(3), 469–471.

Strober, M. & Peris, T. (2011). The role of family environment in etiology: A neuroscience perspective. In Daniel Le Grange & James Locke (Eds.), *Handbook of assessment and treatment for children and adolescents with eating disorders.* New York: Guilford.

Pope, H., Phillips, K. A., & Olivardia, R. (2000). *The Adonis complex: The secret crisis of male body obsession.* New York: Free Press.

Andersen, A. E., Cohn, L., & Holbrook, T. (2000). *Making weight: Men's conflicts with food, weight, shape, & appearance.* Carlsbad, CA: Gürze Books.

Key 4:

Singer, M. A. (2007). *The untethered soul: The journey beyond yourself.* Oakland, CA: New Harbinger Publications.

Burns, David D. (1980). *Feeling good: The new mood therapy.* New York: Morrow.

Harris, S. (2014). *Waking up: A guide to spirituality without religion.* New York: Simon & Schuster.

Siegel, Daniel J. (2010). *Mindsight: The new science of personal transformation.* New York: Bantam.

Costin, C., & Kelly, J. (Eds.). (2016). *Yoga and Eating Disorders: Ancient healing for modern illness.* New York: Routledge.

Neff, K. (2011). *Self-compassion: Stop beating yourself up and leave insecurity behind.* New York: William Morrow.

Germer, C. K. (2009). *The mindful path to self-compassion: Freeing yourself from destructive thoughts and emotions.* New York: Guilford Press.

Key 5: None

Key 6: None

Key 7:

Strober, M. & Peris, T. (2011). The role of family environment in etiology: A neuroscience perspective. In Daniel Le Grange & James Locke (Eds.), *Handbook of assessment and treatment for children and adolescents with eating disorders.* New York: Guilford.

Key 8:

Singer, M. A. (2007). *The untethered soul: The journey beyond yourself.* Oakland, CA: New Harbinger Publications.

Foster, J. (2012). *The deepest acceptance: Radical awakening in ordinary life.* Boulder, CO: Sounds True.

Doidge, N. (2015). *The brain's way of healing: Remarkable discoveries and recoveries from the frontiers of neuroplasticity.* New York: Penguin Books.

Doidge, N. (2007). *The brain that changes itself: Stories of personal triumph from the frontiers of brain science.* New York: Viking.

Smalley, S. L., & Winston, D. (2010). *Fully present: The science, art, and practice of mindfulness.* Cambridge, MA.: Da Capo Lifelong.

Costin, C., & Kelly, J. (Eds.). (2016). *Yoga and eating disorders: Ancient healing for modern illness.* New York: Routledge.

Swimme, B. (1996). *The hidden heart of the cosmos: Humanity and the new story.* Maryknoll, NY: Orbis Books.

References

Andersen, A. E., Cohn, L., & Holbrook, T. (2000). *Making weight: Men's conflicts with food, weight, shape, & appearance.* Carlsbad, CA: Gürze Books.

Bulik, Cynthia. M. (2010). Specialist supportive clinical management for anorexia nervosa. In Carlos Grilo & James E. Mitchell (Eds.), *The treatment of eating disorders: A clinical handbook* (pp. 108–128). New York: Guilford.

Burns, David D. (1980). *Feeling good: The new mood therapy.* New York: Morrow.

Costin, C., & Kelly, J. (Eds.). (2016). *Yoga and eating disorders: Ancient healing for modern illness.* New York: Routledge.

Costin, C., & Grabb, G. S. (2012). *8 keys to recovery from an eating disorder: Effective strategies from therapeutic practice and personal experience.* New York: W. W. Norton & Company, Inc.

Doidge, N. (2015). *The brain's way of healing: Remarkable discoveries and recoveries from the frontiers of neuroplasticity.* New York: Penguin Books.

Doidge, N. (2007). *The brain that changes itself: Stories of personal triumph from the frontiers of brain science.* New York: Viking.

Foster, J. (2012). *The deepest acceptance: Radical awakening in ordinary life.* Boulder, CO: Sounds True.

Germer, C. K. (2009). *The mindful path to self-compassion: Freeing yourself from destructive thoughts and emotions.* New York: Guilford Press.

Gross, J., & Rosen , J.C. (1988). Bulimia in adolescents: Prevalence and psychosocial correlates. *International Journal of Eating Disorders, 7,* 51–61.

Harris, S. (2014). *Waking up: A guide to spirituality without religion.* New York: Simon & Schuster.

Kronenfeld, L. W., Reba-Harrelson, L., Von Holle, A., Reyes, M. L., & Bulik, C. M. (2010). Ethnic and racial differences in body size perception and satisfaction. *Body Image, 7*(2), 131–136. doi:http://dx.doi.org/10.1016/j.bodyim.2009.11.002

Neff, K. (2011). *Self-compassion: Stop beating yourself up and leave insecurity behind.* New York: William Morrow.

Pope, H., Phillips, K. A., & Olivardia, R. (2000). *The Adonis complex: The secret crisis of male body obsession*. New York: Free Press.

Prochaska, J. and DiClemente, C. (1983) Stages and processes of self-change in smoking: toward an integrative model of change. *Journal of Consulting and Clinical Psychology, 51*(3), 390–395.

Prochaska, J. O., DiClemente, C. C., & Norcross, J. C. (1992). In search of how people change: Applications to addictive behavior. *American Psychologist, 47*, 1102–1114.

Ryan, M. J. (2003). *The power of patience: How to slow the rush and enjoy more happiness, success, and peace of mind every day.* New York: Broadway Books.

Siegel, Daniel J. (2010). *Mindsight: The new science of personal transformation*. New York: Bantam.

Singer, M. A. (2007). *The untethered soul: The journey beyond yourself.* Oakland, CA: New Harbinger Publications.

Smalley, S. L., & Winston, D. (2010). *Fully present: The science, art, and practice of mindfulness.* Cambridge, MA.: Da Capo Lifelong.

Stice, E., Maxfield, J., & Wells, T. (2003). Adverse effects of social pressure to be thin on young women: An experimental investigation of the effects of "fat talk."*International Journal Of Eating Disorders, 34*(1), 108–117.

Strober, M. & Peris, T. (2011). The role of family environment in etiology: A neuroscience perspective. In Daniel Le Grange & James Locke (Eds.), *Handbook of assessment and treatment for children and adolescents with eating disorders*. New York: Guilford.

Swimme, B. (1996). *The hidden heart of the cosmos: Humanity and the new story.* Maryknoll, NY: Orbis Books.

U.S. Department of Health and Human Services. *The health benefits of smoking cessation: A report of the surgeon general.* U.S. Department of Health and Human Services, Public Health Service, Centers for Disease Control, Center for Chronic Disease Prevention and Health Promotion, Office on Smoking and Health. DHHS Publication No. (CDC) 90–8416, 1990.

Wade, T. D., Bulik, C. M., Neale, M., & Kendler, K. S. (2000). Anorexia and major depression: Shared genetic and environmental risk factors. *The American Journal of Psychiatry, 157*(3), 469–471.

Index

Abercrombie & Fitch, 67
abusive relationship syndrome, 6–7
acceptance
   of body, 249
   resistance *vs.*, 247–48
action(s)
   change-related, 11, 15–16
   in triggering behaviors, 86
"A Day in My Life When I Am Recovered," 28–29, 252
addiction
   eating disorder similarities to, 62
   eating disorder *vs.*, 62
addiction to food
   eating disorders not about, 62
advanced meal sessions, 147–48
altar
   creation of, 251
ambivalence
   motivation effects of, 5–6
ambivalent thoughts
   noticing, 33
Andersen, A., 65
anger
   author's personal reflections on handling, 116
   feeling and transforming, 110–11
anti-anxiety breathing, 229
anxious/energetic
   keeping in check, 74–75
app(s)
   for connection and recovery, 201–2
appearance
   obsession with, 63–69
Appetites, 253
Arrien, A., 214
attention
   assessing your, 220–21
   paying, 220–29 (*see also* pay attention)
attitude
   as body image issue, 68
avoidant/careful
   keeping in check, 75

beginner's mind, 232
behavior(s)
   as body image issue, 69
   changing, 159–86 (*see also specific types and changing your behaviors*)
   counting, 171–72
   eating disorder (*see* eating disorder behavior(s))
   exercise, 170–71
   recovery-sabotaging (*see* recovery-sabotaging behaviors)
   triggered by your thoughts and feelings, 85
behavior change
   described, 9
biological makeup
   eating disorders related to, 70–80
BMI. *see* body mass index (BMI)
body
   nonattachment and, 248–49
body acceptance, 249
"body and soul" exercises, 236–37
body image
   eating disorders fueled by, 63–69
   good and bad news about, 249–50
   healing negative, 235–36
   improving, 65–66
   issues related to, 67–69 (*see also* body image issues)
   signs of hope related to, 66–67
body image issues
   attitude, 68
   behaviors, 69
   perception, 67–68
body mass index (BMI)
   French Parliament on, 66
body weight
   learning to accept natural, 153–54 (*see also* weight)
breath
   during meditation, 228–29
breathing
   anti-anxiety, 229
Bulik, C., 70

bulimia
   CBT for, 81, 89
Burns, D., 92

Carpenter, K., 56
CBT. *see* cognitive behavioral therapy (CBT)
challenging my eating disorder self/strengthening my healthy self goals, 2
change
   behavior-related (*see* changing your behaviors)
   difficulty with, 160
   motivation and, 9–17
   preparation for, 11, 14–15
   reasons for, 160
   resistance as normal, 162–63
   self-compassion and, 185
   stages of, 10–17 (*see also* stages of change)
   in your food rules, 130
changing your behaviors, 159–86. *see also specific behaviors, e.g.,* recovery-sabotaging behaviors
   communicate with at least 3 people before engaging in behavior, 176–77
   compassion and, 185
   difficulty with, 160
   helpful quotes of mantras, 184
   journal or write letter to yourself or someone else before behavior, 177
   letting go, 185–86
   notice difference, 175–76
   reasons for, 160
   recovery-sabotaging behaviors, 161–62
   resistance to, 162–70 (*see also specific types and* resistance to change)
   reward or consequence for, 181
   set timer to delay behavior, 177
   suggestions for, 174–84
   take small steps, 175
   track behavior, 174
   transitional objects in, 177–81 (*see also* transitional object(s))
   write eating disorder self/healthy self dialogue before engaging in behavior, 176
chaos
   with food, 125–27
chatter
   freeing yourself from your, 97
chronic procrastination, 10–11
cognitive behavioral therapy (CBT)
   for bulimia, 81, 89
   described, 89
cognitive distortions, 92–108
   dialogue with, 95–96
   freeing yourself from voice inside your head, 96–104
   responding to, 94

your personal, 92–93
Cohn, L., 65–66
comfort(s)
   types of, 113
comments from others
   about eating disorders, 46–50
comparing yourself to others
   as recovery-sabotaging behavior, 173–74
compassion
   change and, 185
   self-, 113–15, 185 (*see also* self-compassion)
compassion mantra, 115
compulsive exercise
   changing, 171
   getting feedback from others about, 171
   as recovery-sabotaging behavior, 170–71
   signs of, 170
connection
   food as source of, 152
connection to others. *see also* reaching out to others
   need for, 187–88
conscious eater
   from meal plan to, 143–44
Conscious Eating, 130–36
   described, 130
   in practice, 136–53
Conscious Eating assessment, 132–36
Conscious Eating guidelines, 131–32
   one-day assignment, 137–39
consequence(s)
   for changing behavior, 181–84
contemplation, 10–11, 13–14
controlling/directing
   keeping in check, 75
coping
   eating disorder behavior and, 85
   thoughts and feelings related to, 84–85
cosmos
   nature and spirituality and, 239
Costin, C., xi–xvii, 31–32, 51–52, 72, 76, 99, 102, 116–19, 121, 151–52, 180–81, 184, 205, 211, 214, 229–31, 253
counting behaviors
   as recovery-sabotaging behavior, 171–72
creativity
   food as source of, 151
critical voice, 94
cultural focus on thinness
   effects of, 63–64
cultural influences
   limiting, 65–66
Cutts, S., 203

Dalai Lama, 118
Deep Acceptance, 209
dialogue

with cognitive distortions, 95–96
with eating disorder self and healthy self, 52–55
difficult feelings
    exploring, 105–8
    identifying, 104
discharging energy, 97–98
distortion(s)
    cognitive, 92–108 (*see also* cognitive distortions)
    distraction(s)
    from feelings, 112–13
    types of, 113
Doidges, N., 233

Eater's Agreement, 210–11
    author's personal reflection on, 211
    example of, 210–11
eating
    conscious (*see* Conscious Eating)
eating disorder(s)
    addiction similarities to, 62
    addiction *vs.*, 62
    biological makeup and, 70–80
    comments from others about, 46–50
    Conscious Eating, 130–36
    coping with thoughts and feelings through, 84–85
    cost *vs.* benefit of, 41–42
    eating disorder self *vs.*, 32
    exploring your, 79–80
    factors contributing to, 61–81 (*see also* specific factors)
    fueled by obsession with appearance and weight, 63–69
    genetics in, 70–80
    getting over, 188–89
    "it's not about the food," 61–81
    reaching out to others rather than to, 187–207 (*see also* reaching out to others)
    responding to comments from others about, 46–50
    risk factors for developing, 69–80
    what it does for me, 39–40
eating disorder behavior(s)
    coping and, 85
    feelings when interrupting, 104
    journaling before engaging in, 50–52
    noticing my thoughts before engaging in, 52
    overt (*see* overt eating disorder behavior(s))
    reaching out to others to target specific, 197–99
eating disorder recovery. *see* recovery
eating disorder self
    dialogue with, 52–55
    dialogue with healthy self, 33–34
    eating disorder *vs.*, 32

healthy self in healing, 31–59 (*see also* healthy self)
integration with healthy self, 35–38 (*see also* integration)
learning from and taking responsibility for, 38–39
recognizing, 32–59
resistance to, 32–33
saying goodbye to, 56–58
thought/feeling/urge/action chain and, 86–87
write letter back from, 58
writing goodbye letter to, 57–58
eating disorder thoughts
    talking back to, 45–46
eating disorder voice, 32, 94, 190
eating patterns
    food journal in noticing, 139–40
ego and soul assignment, 215
ego mind, 215–17
Einstein, A., 184
energy
    discharging, 97–98
exercise(s)
    "body and soul," 236–37
    compulsive, 170–71 (*see also* compulsive exercise)
exercise behavior
    changing, 171

feeling(s). *see also* thought/feeling/urge/action chain
    acknowledge, 108–15
    actions, 86
    author's personal reflections on handling, 115–21
    case examples, 102–3
    dealing with, 102–8
    difficult (*see* difficult feelings)
    distraction from, 112–13
    eating disorder in coping with, 84–85
    feel your, 83–121
    getting them out of your body, 109–10
    handling, 115–21
    identifying with your, 108–9
    identify your, 101–2
    observing, 112–13
    over-identifying with your, 109
    purpose of, 99
    responding to, 99, 103–4
    transforming your, 109–12
    in triggering behaviors, 85
    types of, 103–8
    understanding your, 99–108
    urges, 85–86
    vulnerability to, 101
    when I interrupt eating disorder behavior, 104

feeling bad
    betting better and, 188–89
Feeling Good, 92
feeling worse while getting better, 112
finance(s)
    motivation effects of, 8
food
    addiction to, 62
    eating disorders are more than about, 61–81
    as miraculous wonder, 151
    relationship with, 123–58 (*see also* relationship with food)
    rigidity and chaos with, 125–27
    soul, 150–53
    as source of connection, 152
    as source of creativity, 151
    as source of pleasure, 150
    as source of soulfulness, 152
food behavior goals, 2
    examples of, 140–41
    making, 140–41
    writing, 141
food journal, 138–39
    components of, 138
    example of, 4, 138–39
    noticing your eating patterns from, 139–40
    personal, 139
food rituals
    as recovery-sabotaging behavior, 172–73
food rules, 127–36
    challenging, 129–30
    listing and exploring, 128–29
    reasons for, 127
Foster, J., 209
four principles
    remember and practice, 251
French Parliament
    on BMI for models, 66

genetics
    eating disorders related to, 70–80
Germer, C., 114
getting better
    feeling bad at first, 188–89
    reasons for, 7–8
    reasons for not, 9
goal(s). *see also specific types, e.g.,* food behavior goals
    food behavior, 140–41
    suggestions for setting, xv–xvi
    types of, 2
    weekly (*see* weekly goals)
Goals Sheet, xv, xvi
Goodbye Ed, Hello Me, 203
goodbye letter to your eating disorder self
    writing, 57–58
go-to people, 196

Grabb, G.S., xi–xvii, 55–56, 102–3, 116–20, 145–47, 149, 151, 157, 184, 205–6, 214, 231, 248, 253

Harris, S., 99
healthy self, 31–59
    dialogue with, 52–55
    dialogue with eating disorder self, 33–34
    eating disorder self integration with, 35–38
    finding, 43–44
    in healing eating disorder self, 35
    recognizing, 32–59
    strengthening, 44
    thought/feeling/urge/action chain and, 87–88
healthy self come back, 58–59
healthy self concept
    resistance to eating disorder self *vs.*, 32–33
healthy self statements
    creating, 45
healthy voice, 32
Holbrook, T., 65–66
hope, 20–22
    defined, 20
    signs of, 66–67
hopefulness
    degree of, 20
Horace, 123
hunger scale, 137–38
hurt
    author's personal reflections on handling, 118–19

impulsive/spontaneous
    keeping in check, 74
integration
    of eating disorder self and healthy self, 35–38
    stages of, 36–38
interview questions
    for someone who is recovered, 24–26
"it's not about the food," 61–81

journal(s)
    food, 4
journaling, 251
    before engaging in eating disorder behavior, 50–52
judgment
    truth without, 242, 244–45
judgmental statements
    making them nonjudgmental, 242–43

Knapp, C., 253

let go or be dragged
    author's personal reflection on, 248
letter from eating disorder self

writing, 58
letting go
   in changing your behaviors, 185–86
life
   relationship to (*see* relationship to life)
Loving Kindness to Yourself, 185

maintenance
   change-related, 11–12, 16–17
Maitri, 185
Making Weight, 65
Mandela, N., 26
Manna Fund, 8
mantra(s)
   in changing your behaviors, 184
   compassion, 115
   personal, 185
Meal Blessings, 152
meal challenges
   triggering, 148–50
meal plan(s), 141–44
   to becoming conscious eater, 143–44
   example of, 143
   making, 142–44
   need for, 142
meal sessions
   advanced, 147–48
   author's personal reflection on, 145–47
   therapeutic, 144–50
meaning
   finding, 209–53
meditation
   benefits of, 225
   focusing on breath in, 228–29
   in paying attention, 224–39
   prefrontal cortex functions in, 225–26
   procedure for, 226–28
mentor(s)
   questions for, 204
   recovered person as, 202
Mentor Connect, 203
Mey, J., 17
mind
   beginner's, 232
   ego, 215–17
mindfulness
   beginner's mind in, 232
   benefits of, 221–22
   described, 221
   dimensions of, 222–23
   in paying attention, 221–24, 229–35
   traditional practices, 224
   yoga in, 229–31
Mindfulness Agreement, 241
Mindsight, 99
miraculous wonder
   food as, 151

Monte Nido Treatment Center, xiii, 157, 210, 229–31
motivation, 5–17
   ambivalence effects on, 5–6
   assignment for, 12–17
   change and, 9–17
   defined, 5
   financial situations limiting, 8
   lack of, 5–6
   looking at your, 6
   readiness and, 9–17
motivation goals, 2

natural body weight
   learning to accept, 153–54 (*see also* weight)
natural world around you
   awareness of, 238–39
nature
   cosmos and spirituality and, 239
   paying attention to, 238–39
Neff, K., 114
nonattachment, 250–51
   your body and, 248–49
nonjudgmental statements
   from judgmental to, 242–43
not reaching out to others
   countering reasons for, 194–96
   reasons for, 193

Obama, B., Pres., 20
observation
   self-, 113
obsession with appearance and weight
   eating disorders fueled by, 63–69
obsessive/thorough
   keeping in check, 74
over-exercising
   as recovery-sabotaging behavior, 170–71
overt eating disorder behavior(s)
   changing, 161
   resistance to changing, 163
   types of, 161

patience, 17–20
   defined, 17
   exploring, 19–20
   insights about, 19
pay attention, 220–29
   described, 224
   focus in, 235
   how to, 221–29
   meditation in, 224–39
   mindfulness in, 221–24, 229–35
   to nature to reenchant your life, 238–39
   visualization in, 233–35
people
   relationship to (*see* relationship to people)

perception
  as body image issue, 67–68
personal accounts
  importance of, xiii–xiv
personal mantras, 185
Phillips, K., 65
pieces of my puzzle, 76–79. see also Real Issues
pleasure
  food as source of, 150
Pope, H.G., Jr., 65
pre-contemplation, 10, 13
prefrontal cortex
  functions of, 225–26
preparation for change, 11, 14–15
present moment
  resistance to, 216–17
procrastination
  chronic, 10–11
professional help
  self-help vs., xii–xiii
Project Heal, 8
purpose
  finding, 209–53

quote(s)
  in changing your behaviors, 184

reaching in to yourself, 206
reaching out to others, 187–207
  apps for, 201–2
  authors' personal reflections on, 205–6
  choosing whom and how, 196
  getting better feels bad at first, 188–89
  go-to people, 196
  guidelines for when, 190–91
  need for, 187–88
  to put eating disorder out of your life, 189–90
  questions related to, 189
  reasons for not, 193 (see also not reaching out to others)
  resistance to, 192–93
  to target specific eating disorder urges and behaviors, 197–99
  texting, 199–201
readiness
  motivation and, 9–17
Real Issues, 76–79
  exploring, 78–79
  writing examples of, 76–78
reasons you cannot get better, 9
reasons you want to get better, 7–8
recovered. see also recovered people; recovery
  "A Day in My Life When I Am Recovered," 28–29, 252
  getting there–being, 22–29
recovered people, 23–24

client's quotes, 26–27
connecting with, 23–24, 202–4
interviewing, 24–26
as mentors, 202
questions for, 204
recovery
  apps for, 201–2
  phases of, 22–23
  visualization in supporting and enhancing, 234–35
Recovery Record, 201
recovery-sabotaging behaviors, 161–62
  checklist of, 162
  comparing (your body) to others, 173–74
  compulsive exercise, 170–71
  counting calories, fat grams, carbohydrates, etc., 171–72
  food rituals, 172–73
  resistance to changing, 163–64
  types of, 170–74
recovery sabotaging goals, 2
relationship(s)
  supportive, 187–207 (see also reaching out to others)
relationship goals, 2
relationship to life
  relationship with food vs., 73
relationship to people
  relationship with food vs., 73
relationship with food, 123
  advanced meal sessions, 147–48
  changing your, 130
  Conscious Eating, 130–36 (see also Conscious Eating)
  food behavior goals, 140–41
  food journals, 4, 138–40 (see also food journal)
  food rules, 127–36 (see also food rules)
  hunger scale, 137–38
  meal plans, 141–44 (see also meal plan(s))
  questions related to, 124–25
  relationship to people or life vs., 73
  rigidity and chaos, 125–27
  soul food, 150–53
  therapeutic meal sessions, 144–50
  triggering meal challenges, 148–50
resistance
  acceptance vs., 247–48
  to change (see resistance to change)
  to present moment, 216–17
  to reaching out to others, 192–93
resistance to change
  as normal behavior, 162–63
  of overt eating disorder behaviors, 163
  reasons for, 165–70
  of recovery-sabotaging behaviors, 163–64
resistance to eating disorder self

healthy self concept *vs.*, 32–33
responsibility
   for eating disorder self, 38–39
result(s)
   not being attached to, 246–47
reward(s)
   for changing behavior, 181–84
rigidity
   with food, 125–27
Rise Up and Recover, 201–2
risk factors
   for developing eating disorders, 69–80
   to pieces of your puzzle, 76–79
ritual(s)
   food, 172–73
Roosevelt, T., Pres., 173
Rooted Recovery, 202
rule(s)
   food-related, 127–36 (*see also* food rules)

Saadi, 17
sadness
   author's personal reflections on handling, 117–18
Saint-Exupéry, A., 184
scale
   getting rid of, 156
Schaefer, J., 203
scurvy, 151
self
   eating disorder (*see* eating disorder self)
   healthy, 31–59 (*see also* healthy self)
   soul, 217–20 (*see also* soul self)
self-care goals, 2
self-compassion, 113–15
   assessment of, 114
   change related to, 185
Self-Compassion, 114
self-help
   professional help *vs.*, xii–xiii
self-observation, 113
self-talk
   in specific situations, 90–91
   what I say to others *vs.*, 91–92
shame
   author's personal reflections on handling, 119–21
Siegel, D., 99
Singer, M.A., 83, 99, 209, 217, 224–25
Smith, R., 185
soothing things, 113
soul
   care of, 235–36
soul and ego assignment, 215
soul food, 150–53
   author's personal reflections on, 151–52
soulfulness
   food as source of, 152
soul lessons, 235
soul moments, 235, 239–41
   defined, 239
   examples of, 239
   writing, 240
soul self, 217–20
   clients' quote on discovering, 218
   connecting to, 219
   described, 217–18
   exercises, 219–20
spiritual
   from superficial to, 212–14
spirituality
   cosmos and nature and, 239
   defined, 209–10
   described, 209–10
spirituality/soul goals, 2
spiritual principles, 214–21
stages of change, 10–17
   action related to, 11, 15–16
   assignment for, 12–17
   contemplation, 10–11, 13–14
   current, 12–17
   maintenance, 11–12, 16–17
   pre-contemplation, 10, 13
   preparation for change, 11, 14–15
   termination in, 12
statement(s)
   healthy self, 45
   from judgmental to nonjudgmental, 242–43
Strober, M., 70, 188
superficial
   to spiritual, 212–14
supportive relationships
   reaching out to, 187–207 (*see also* reaching out to others)
support systems
   texting, 199–201

talk
   self- (*see* self-talk)
termination
   change-related, 12
texting
   with clients, 200–1
   for support, 199–201
The Adonis Complex, 65
The Brain That Changes Itself, 233
The Four-Fold Way, 214–21
The Mindful Path to Self-Compassion, 114
The Power of Now, 247
therapeutic meal sessions, 144–50
The Untethered Soul, 83, 99, 224–25
thinness
   cultural focus on, 63–64

thought(s). *see also* thought/feeling/urge/action chain
   actions, 86
   ambivalent, 33
   author's personal reflections on handling, 115–21
   become observer of, 98–99
   challenging your, 94–108
   distorted, 92–108 (*see also* cognitive distortions)
   eating disorder, 45–46
   eating disorder in coping with, 84–85
   handling, 115–21
   noticing, 52
   in triggering behaviors, 89–92
   urges, 85–86
thought/feeling/urge/action chain, 85–92
   actions in, 86
   eating disorder *vs.* healthy self and, 86–89
   thoughts in, 89–92
   urges in, 85–86
   write your, 88–89
Tolle, E., 247
trait(s)
   accepting, 73–76
   channeling, 73–76
   keeping in check, 73–76
   liability *vs.* asset, 70–80
   types of, 71–80 (*see also specific traits*, e.g., impulsive/spontaneous)
transforming your feelings, 109–12
   anger, 110–11
transitional object(s)
   author's personal reflection on, 180–81
   in changing behaviors, 177–81
   clients' experiences with, 178
   described, 177
   finding or creating, 179
   using, 179–80
Transtheoretical Model, 9
triggering meal challenges, 148–50
   author's personal reflections on, 149–50
truth without judgment
   practicing, 244–45
   telling, 242
Tzu, L., 184

underlying issues goals, 2
urge(s)
   reaching out to others to target specific, 197–99
   in triggering behaviors, 85–86

visualization
   client's experiences with, 234
   in paying attention, 233–35
   in supporting and enhancing recovery, 234–35
vitamin C deficiency, 151
voice
   critical, 94
   eating disorder, 32, 94, 190
   healthy, 32
voice inside your head
   freeing yourself from, 96–104
vulnerability
   to feelings, 101

Waking Up, 99
weekly goals
   example of, 2
   goal worksheet, 3
   importance of, xv
   types of, 2
weighing yourself
   letting go of, 157–58
weight
   getting rid of scale, 156
   learning to accept natural, 153–54
   let go of weighing yourself, 157–58
   obsession with, 63–69
weight range
   physical indicators of healthy, 154–55
   psychological and social indicators of healthy, 155–56
Weinberg, G., 20
what I say to others
   vs. to myself, 91–92
Wilde, O., 184
Winfrey, O., 184

yoga, 229–31
   authors' personal reflections on, 229–31
Yoga and Eating Disorders: Ancient Healing for a Modern Illness, 99, 230
Your Dieting Daughter, 76
Yutang, L., 21

About the Authors

CAROLYN COSTIN, MA, MED, LMFT, CEDS, FAED recovered from anorexia in her twenties, became a therapist, and saw her first eating disorder client in 1979. In 1996, after successfully directing other programs, Carolyn created Monte Nido, the first residential eating disorder treatment program in a home setting, and became the first to use professional staff recovered from eating disorders. As Chief Clinical Officer, Carolyn grew Monte Nido into Monte Nido & Affiliates with 12 residential and day treatment facilities in California, Massachusetts, New York, and Oregon.

Carolyn's clinical insight, personalized approach, and extensive experience underlie Monte Nido's treatment success. Carolyn is a tireless advocate, consultant, and media expert on eating and exercise disorders, frequently training clinicians and speaking locally, nationally, and internationally.

Carolyn is a Fellow of the Academy of Eating Disorders, editor for *Eating Disorders, The Journal of Treatment and Prevention*, and trustee of the International Association of Eating Disorder Professionals.

Carolyn's books (*The Eating Disorder Sourcebook, 100 Questions and Answers About Eating Disorders, 8 Keys to Recovery From an Eating Disorder, Your Dieting Daughter, Yoga and Eating Disorders,* and *8 Keys to Recovery Workbook*) explain eating disorders to sufferers, their loved ones, and the public and help professionals to treat these complex illnesses in an effective way.

GWEN SCHUBERT GRABB, MFT, is a highly trained psychotherapist specializing in all facets of eating disorder prevention and treatment. She currently works in private practice in the Los Angeles area where she treats individuals and families, runs recovery groups, and provides consultation for professionals. Gwen serves on the board of the *South Bay Eating Disorder Coalition* and on the advisory board for *Arete Magazine*. She is a member of the International Association of Eating Disorder Professionals, National Eating Disorder Association, and the American Psychotherapy Association.

In 1996, Gwen was one of the first to be treated at Monte Nido under the care of Carolyn Costin. After her own successful battle with an eating disorder, Grabb became a passionate advocate for others struggling to recover from this difficult and complicated illness. She worked for many years at a multi-level eating disorder treatment facility before opening up her own private practice. Along with her books *8 Keys to Recovery from an Eating Disorder* and *8 Keys to Recovery from an Eating Disorder Workbook,* Gwen has written and created over 100 group therapy guides, which are used by therapists in treatment centers across the country.

ALSO AVAILABLE FROM THE 8 KEYS TO MENTAL HEALTH SERIES

8 Keys to Raising the Quirky Child:
How to Help a Kid Who Doesn't (Quite) Fit In
Mark Bowers

8 Keys to Eliminating Passive-Aggressiveness
Andrea Brandt

8 Keys to Recovery from an Eating Disorder:
Effective Strategies from Therapeutic Practice and Personal Experience
Carolyn Costin, Gwen Schubert Grabb

8 Keys to Parenting Children with ADHD
Cindy Goldrich

8 Keys to Building Your Best Relationships
Daniel A. Hughes

8 Keys to Old School Parenting for Modern-Day Families
Michael Mascolo

8 Keys to Practicing Mindfulness:
Practical Strategies for Emotional Health and Well-Being
Manuela Mischke Reeds

8 Keys to Safe Trauma Recovery:
Take-Charge Strategies to Empower Your Healing
Babette Rothschild

8 Keys to Brain–Body Balance
Robert Scaer

8 Keys to Stress Management
Elizabeth Anne Scott

8 Keys to End Bullying:
Strategies for Parents & Schools
Signe Whitson